D1251901

UNFINISHED REVOLUTIONS

Unfinished Revolutions

Yemen, Libya, and Tunisia
after the Arab Spring

IBRAHIM FRAIHAT

Yale

UNIVERSITY PRESS

NEW HAVEN AND LONDON

Published with assistance from the Louis Stern Memorial Fund.

Copyright © 2016 by Ibrahim Fraihat.

All rights reserved.
This book may not be reproduced, in whole or in part, including illustrations, in any form (beyond that copying permitted by Sections 107 and 108 of the U.S. Copyright Law and except by reviewers for the public press), without written permission from the publishers.

Yale University Press books may be purchased in quantity for educational, business, or promotional use. For information, please e-mail sales.press@yale.edu (U.S. office) or sales@yaleup.co.uk (U.K. office).

Set in Electra LH type by Newgen North America.
Printed in the United States of America.

ISBN: 978-0-300-21563-2 (hardback : alk. paper)

Library of Congress Control Number: 2015946973

A catalogue record for this book is available from the British Library.

This paper meets the requirements of ANSI/NISO Z39.48–1992 (Permanence of Paper).

10 9 8 7 6 5 4 3 2 1

For those who spoke out against oppression
but died before they saw justice prevail

CONTENTS

Part II. Approaches of Reconciliation

Part III. Agents of Reconciliation

ACKNOWLEDGMENTS

When I told my wife I was going to Sanaa after the fall of former president Ali Abdullah Saleh, she became very concerned, even though it was certainly not my first visit to the country. Months later, her concerns only intensified when she learned that I was also going to Libya after Muammar Qaddafi's removal from power. "Why do you go to conflict zones in the middle of all this instability? It's not safe." I wasn't choosing to do this now, I replied—it was a choice I made fifteen years ago when I began my Ph.D. program in conflict resolution at George Mason University. It was a conscious decision to dedicate the rest of my career to understanding the phenomenon of conflict and how societies can work to bring these conflicts to an end.

Given my academic background, I immediately realized that the real challenge for Arab Spring societies would begin the day they toppled their autocratic rulers. They faced the massive task of rebuilding Arab societies that have been wracked by colonialism and dictatorships for the past century. Changing leaders can take days but changing institutions and rebuilding states can take years, if not decades. There is no better testament to this than the American invasions of Iraq and Afghanistan, which toppled regimes in a few days but failed to rebuild states over the next fourteen years.

Whether they follow civil wars, dictatorships, or foreign occupation, transitions to a new state of civil peace are often chaotic, cumbersome, lengthy, and even violent. Arab societies are no exception. The idea of this book comes from the understanding that, in fact, there has been no such successful transition in the recent history of the Arab world, which only heightens the risk of societies sliding into chaos or even greater violence, as has happened in Yemen and Libya. Transition in Iraq following the American invasion twelve years ago has failed, and the transitions in Egypt, Libya, Yemen, and even Tunisia continue to struggle. The serious lack of expertise in how these transitions unfold and how to respond to them in an Arab regional context made research that responds to this gap necessary.

The search for "ground truth" has rigorously guided this three-year research project, incorporating over two hundred interviews with national figures in Libya, Yemen, and Tunisia. I spoke with senior government officials, heads of political parties, representatives of civil society organizations, revolutionary and militia leaders, former regime loyalists, tribal leaders, members of displaced communities, scholars, journalists, and officers in a number of international organizations. This approach aims to ensure that the research addresses the real challenges facing Arab societies in transition by examining the views of the concerned actors themselves: how they see these transitions, what is at stake for them, and what it would take to deal with their concerns. It allowed those most affected by the transition to speak for themselves and express what solutions they want to see rather than proposing ready-made formulas extracted from the literature.

There has never been a dull moment in three years of conducting this research. I have had to reschedule research trips at the last minute time and again, once after one of the conflict parties closed the Sanaa airport. I found myself walking in remote areas in Yemen with a dozen armed men taking me to interview their tribal leader. Conversations with internally displaced communities in the Nafousa Mountains and other remote areas of Libya were difficult and disheartening. Candid conversations with Libyan revolutionary leaders in their military bases were particularly enlightening. When I traveled to Tunisia, my wife was relieved that I was finally going to a relatively stable and safe area. But she was soon concerned again following news that violent clashes had erupted in the Tadamun neighborhood in Tunis after authorities banned the annual Salafi conference that was planned in the city of Kairouan.

Writing on the political developments in the Middle East region has meant trying to hit a moving target. By the time you finish an article on any particular subject it is probably obsolete. This book has avoided focusing on fast-moving events such as elections or specific crises. Instead, it targets strategic themes that are likely to shape the future of these transitions for years or even decades to come. Disarmament of ex-combatants, displacement, national dialogue, institutional reform, and truth seeking remain a core set of issues. Even countries that underwent similar transitions decades ago are still debating the best approaches to dealing with their pasts and to properly addressing the traumas of victims and their relatives.

These themes are relevant not only to the future of Yemen, Libya, and Tunisia but also to other countries in the region that will eventually face transitions of their own. Syria, for example, will never be able to undergo a successful transition without addressing the millions of currently displaced and the enormous number of would-be ex-combatants. It will have to also deal with members of the former regime, accountability, reparations, investigating the truth of the past, and so on. This book affords these countries the chance to learn about challenges, mistakes, and lessons learned by their regional neighbors in Libya, Tunisia, and Yemen. There is no need to re-invent the wheel.

This research project results from the input of countless people across the Arab world, more than I can mention here. I am indebted to all of them for their support, as the project would never have been completed without their patience, along with their belief in supporting successful, smooth, and non-violent transitions in Arab societies. Some two hundred people gave me the time to discuss their views of the transition and how it could best be achieved. I am deeply grateful for the invaluable contributions from my assistants in Libya, Yemen, and Tunisia: Sufyan Omeish, Abdulhakim Helal, and Hend Hassassi, respectively. They worked incredibly hard in difficult circumstances to achieve what seemed at times an impossible mission, given the logistical difficulties posed by countries in the midst of revolutions. Their thoughts and feedback on the interview process were extremely helpful.

I am immensely thankful to Bill Hess, my research assistant at Brookings, who worked tirelessly to ensure the highest quality and standards for his contributions. With incredible patience and attention to detail, he gave me great suggestions for improving the manuscript while tackling the many challenges we encountered. Bill was always the first person to read over my drafts, and he always responded with helpful feedback and clarifying edits.

I am also appreciative of the great assistance provided by Courtney Freer and Rabea Binhalim with the literature review and for discussing with me their observations and thoughts on the debates in the field.

I am grateful to the Brookings Institution and the Brookings Doha Center for providing a supportive work environment and enabling a research platform for high-quality products. Specifically, many thanks go to the staff of the Brookings Doha Center for their unlimited encouragement and support in completing this project.

I am deeply indebted to my professors at George Mason University's School of Conflict Analysis and Resolution (S-CAR)—Terrence Lyons, Dennis Sandole, Kevin Avruch, Richard Rubenstein, Chris Mitchell, and Tamra d'Estree—for their incredible support when I was a Ph.D. student and even after my graduation. My work on the ground would not have been possible without the education and training I received at S-CAR. I am emphatically thankful to Birzeit University in Palestine for defying the Israeli military orders to close by offering us a parallel education system in my freshman year. Attending classes in hotels, professors' houses, and other public facilities were formative times in my life. The feeling of being caught "illegally" receiving an education was always an incredible motivation for me to pursue further degrees and research projects like this book.

A central aspect of this research is the challenge it poses to existing conflict resolution theories and how they are formed. Therefore, the opportunity to teach a course on post-conflict reconstruction at Georgetown University in Qatar afforded me the chance to test many established notions of conflict resolution and understand how they work in practice. With my students, I was able to work through narratives put forward in scholarly literature and compare them with the findings of my fieldwork. I am grateful to the faculty of Georgetown and Dean Gerd Nonnenman for giving me an academic home away from home in Doha and to my students for challenging me to be clear and concise in my explanations.

ACKNOWLEDGMENTS

I am immensely grateful for the extraordinary support, guidance, and follow-up of Jaya Chatterjee, the Yale University Press editor that first embraced my proposal and shepherded this project through the review and approval stages. Over a yearlong publication process, Jaya was always responsive, precise, and professional; her comments on the structure of the book were particularly helpful. Having the opportunity to work with Jaya has been one of the true rewards of this research project. My sincere thanks also goes to Margaret Otzel and Margaret Hogan for their thorough and excellent work in editing the book and preparing it for publication.

I am very thankful to my brothers, Mohamed, Rabah, Ayoub, and Khader, and to my dear friend Jamal al-Sayyed, who always had faith in me and encouraged me to engage in groundbreaking initiatives.

Finally, the greatest portion of my love and appreciation goes to my family, who paid more than their fair share in seeing this research completed. My wife, Abeer, and children, Lana, Leena, Dina, and Tayem, were patient, understanding, and supportive of my work, even when they saw me providing news analysis on television more often than in real life. I admit the price they paid is high, especially at times when I was in the remote areas of other countries when they needed me. I am looking forward to making it up to them now that this research project is complete.

ABBREVIATIONS

AQAP	al-Qaeda in the Arabian Peninsula
CIP	Commission for Integrity and Patriotism (Libya)
CPR	Congress for the Republic (Tunisia)
CSOs	civil society organizations
DDR	disarmament, demobilization, and reintegration
FRC	Fact-Finding and Reconciliation Commission (Libya)
GCC	Gulf Cooperation Council
GNC	General National Congress (Libya)
GPC	General People's Congress (Yemen)
HAICA	High Independent Authority for Audiovisual Communication (Tunisia)
HOR	House of Representatives (Libya)
ICC	International Criminal Court
IDPs	internally displaced persons
INRIC	National Authority for Reform of Information and Communications (Tunisia)
JMP	Joint Meeting Parties (Yemen)
LIFG	Libyan Islamic Fighting Group
LWPP	Libyan Women's Platform for Peace
NCA	National Constituent Assembly (Tunisia)
NDC	National Dialogue Conference (Yemen)
NGOs	non-governmental organizations

NTC	National Transitional Council (Libya)
PIL	Political Isolation Law (Libya)
PRCs	Protection of the Revolution Committees (Tunisia)
RCD	Constitutional Democratic Rally (Tunisia)
SJC	Supreme Judicial Council (Libya)
SLWB	Society of Libya without Borders
SSC	Supreme Security Committee (Libya)
SUNR	Society of Understanding and National Reconciliation (Libya)
UGTT	Tunisian General Labor Union
UN	United Nations
UNDP	United Nations Development Programme
UNHCR	United Nations High Commissioner for Refugees
UNSMIL	United Nations Support Mission in Libya
WSC	Wisemen and Shura Council (Libya)

The very first slogan the Syrian revolution raised was "One, one, one, the Syrian people are one." It meant to emphasize that the Syrian people, regardless of their religion, ethnicity, or political affiliation, were united with one voice. In Yemen, the parliamentary opposition, known as the Joint Meeting Parties (JMP), put aside political and ideological affiliations and maintained a robust alliance that included Islamists, Socialists, and Ba'athists during the revolution that toppled former president Ali Abdullah Saleh. Coupled with the quick removals of Tunisia's Zine El Abidine Ben Ali and Egypt's Hosni Mubarak, the popular nature of the Arab Spring revolutions led the populations involved to hope they could proceed in a similarly unified manner in transforming their societies into free and prosperous systems. What they did not foresee at the time, however, was that the removal of power structures in this fashion—even though they were dictatorial and repressive—would open a Pandora's Box. This is a lesson of Iraq, where the United States removed Saddam Hussein's regime by force in a quick campaign and then spent the following decade trying to piece the country back together, to no avail. The problem was no longer about the old rulers but the process of change itself.

The transition process that follows regime change is inherently complex and can revive old, sometimes forgotten issues. Furthermore, making rapid changes to societies that have largely stagnated due to decades without meaningful reforms often generates new concerns. Both sets of issues can be highly contentious, serving to divide societies that thought they could maintain a sense of unity after the removal of their dictators. Instead, national unity is replaced with polarization nearly as soon as the regime that used to severely restrict any sort of dissent or disagreement is no longer in place. When a Tunisian official was asked whether the country's transitional government would demand the extradition of Ben Ali, he seemed confident that the former president was the least of their concerns. "Keeping the Tunisians united behind one goal of transitioning peacefully to democracy is our major and only objective at the moment," he said.[1] Unfortunately, polarization has escalated to new levels, with various groups even justifying the use of violence, as the cases of Libya, Yemen, and Egypt have shown. In extreme situations, it is all transitioning countries can do to avoid sliding into civil war, with many succumbing.

Yet polarization in the wake of regime change is not inevitable. In this book I argue that for Arab societies to successfully transition from the upheaval of the Arab Spring to sustainable peace and stability, they must engage in inclusive and comprehensive national reconciliation. Through national reconciliation, these societies can avoid civil conflict and maintain or regain national unity. Embracing such a process helps to keep societies united and focused on overcoming the enormous challenges that political transitions cause.

Polarization in post-revolution states can stem from a variety of sources, including pre-regime issues, repression of the now-defunct regime, the sudden influx of political actors and increase in political activity, and the revolutions themselves. Pre-regime issues are those that existed in the past, even before the rulers that were overthrown during the Arab Spring came to power. The past regimes either ignored or manipulated these issues to serve their own agendas, but these concerns need to be addressed now that those regimes have fallen.

Polarization may also result from actions taken by the repressive Arab regimes. Each of the regimes that fell during the Arab Spring committed massive injustices against their populations and left various segments of their societies with deep grievances. Removal of those regimes opens the door for numerous social conflicts, especially between those who benefited from the former regimes and those who suffered under them.

Another source of division is the popular political participation that did not exist under the former dictatorships. In the previous era, policy decisions in these countries were made in a top-down fashion with an almost complete absence of public participation. These Arab populations were never part of a truly representative social contract. They did not even have a say in those rulers coming to power in the first place as some of them, like Ben Ali and Muammar Qaddafi, took office in coups, and others, such as Mubarak and Bashar Assad, were appointed successors. Now that some of these leaders have been dethroned by popular uprisings, the corresponding Arab publics have the opportunity—and challenge—of forging social contracts and electing representative governments and heads of state.

This situation lends itself to high levels of polarization for several reasons. Arab populations in the post-colonial era do not have any experience in forging social contracts as authoritarian rulers came to power immediately after their countries gained independence. Suddenly faced with fundamental questions of the nature of their states for the first time, these populations are struggling with the lack of a clear vision of the ultimate objectives of their uprisings. People are not certain whether they want Western-style democracy, something akin to Turkey's Islamic model, their own version of democracy, or perhaps not democracy at all. Additional potentially divisive issues will come up as debates on the nature of the social contract begin, including whether Sharia law should be a—or perhaps the only—source of legislation.

Finally, the uprisings themselves were tumultuous affairs that created new issues which contribute to high levels of polarization. This is particularly true in Libya, where the conflict that removed Qaddafi from power forced at least one million refugees and internally displaced persons (IDPs) from their homes, a number equal to one-sixth of Libya's population. In addition, the 2014 civil war has become probably the most serious impediment to a peaceful transition in Libya. In Tunisia, a number of groups that helped to lead the uprising then morphed into self-appointed "Protection of the Revolution Committees" (PRCs). The existence of PRCs has become a major source of controversy within Tunisian society, as some parties want them to continue playing a major role while others think they should have been disbanded as soon as Ben Ali's regime fell.

These issues and others have led to highly polarized societies in the Arab Spring countries, making successful transitions closer to utopia than reality as long as such deep divisions persist. Polarization in Yemen reached unprecedented levels after the revolution. A South-North split exists along territorial lines with southerners insisting on secession from the North, or at a minimum a federal system followed by a referendum that they hope would lead to independence. There are also schisms along religious and socioeconomic dimensions. In 2014, the same Shi'ite Houthis that fought six wars against Saleh between 2004 and 2010 in Yemen's northern Saada province clashed with Muslim Brotherhood–affiliated Islamists and a Salafi movement before successfully overrunning Sanaa. Most importantly, the Houthis, who many Yemenis view as Iranian proxies, seized power in a coup in September 2014, and in January 2015 began to push south, provoking Saudi Arabia's massive aerial bombardment against them. These developments have significantly exacerbated sectarian tensions and allowed Sunni extremism to thrive. Additionally, the youth organizations that largely led the Yemeni uprising have added a new element to the political polarization between the old regime and their traditional rival, the JMP.

In Libya, polarization has never been more intense. The uprising not only dismantled the former regime but also shattered Libyan society. It divided Libyans across many categories and severely weakened social cohesion. The first division the uprising created was between the regime loyalists and the revolutionaries who led the revolt against Qaddafi. Secret prisons and torture against former regime elements, as frequently reported by international rights organizations, have become one of the most salient characteristics of post-uprising Libya. Qaddafi loyalists have made several attempts to regroup, especially in Sabha, Libya's south-central region, in addition to engaging in a more organized resistance in exile. But the subsequent fracturing of the revolutionaries themselves has actually been more damaging. The revolutionaries that prevailed against Qaddafi have split into dozens of independent militias spread all over the country with each seeking to dominate its own territory. The militias quickly came into conflict with each other, and the fighting reached unprecedented levels in May 2014, when retired General Khalifa Haftar formed a coalition and launched a military campaign called Operation Dignity to eliminate Islamists from Libya's political landscape. Libya's revolutionaries formed a counter alliance called Libya Dawn—or Fajr Libya—to defeat Haftar and his allies. This encounter eventually led to structurally dividing Libya by creating two parliaments, the General National Congress (GNC) in the west of Libya, which supported Libya Dawn, and on the other side the House of Representatives (HOR), which supported Haftar or Operation Dignity. Two governments were also formed, one backing Operation Dignity and the other Libya Dawn. The uprising also caused divisions between cities and tribes that supported the revolution and those that were considered to have opposed it; some tribes are now supporting Haftar while others are supporting Islamist parties and militias. Furthermore, divisions appeared not only in the groupings of towns and tribes within Libya, but in the national discourse as well. For example, the Libyan revolution labeled entire towns and tribes as *azlam* (cronies) or *tahaleb* (algae, because green was Qaddafi's symbolic color), and the others as "victorious." Of course, azlam are associated with shame and disgrace while the "victorious" are considered honorable.

Even Tunisia, the country with the most successful transition thus far, has its own share of post-revolutionary divisions. In particular, an ultra-conservative versus liberal divergence between Salafi groups and some of the liberal, secular parties that were suppressed under Ben Ali has become pronounced. Some extremist groups have even resorted to violence against the state and other targets, including the dramatic March 2015 attack on Tunis's Bardo Museum, a suicide bombing against tourist sites in the city of Sousse, and frequent clashes with the Tunisian Army in the Sha'anbi Mountains.

Egypt has become divided into three groups: the Muslim Brotherhood, the General Abdel Fattah el-Sisi–led Salvation Front, and Foloul, the remnants of the Mubarak regime. It is striking to notice that the least relevant of these blocs is in fact the Foloul (though it is still strong), and that the most vicious polarization exists between the Brotherhood and the Sisi regime.

This is a clear example of an uprising causing polarization: the nature of Egypt's division has transformed from a diverse opposition pitted against the Mubarak regime to a three-front confrontation among the Brotherhood, Sisi regime, and Foloul. Also, another layer of polarization exists along religious lines as Egypt's Copts are occasionally leveraged to serve certain agendas.

This book focuses on Yemen, Libya, and Tunisia because they are the only three countries that, after ousting their autocrats during the Arab Spring uprisings, are still attempting to transition from authoritarian systems to more inclusive, representative governance. In Egypt, the military has halted and reversed this process, seizing power, imprisoning many of the Islamists that had been in power, and clamping down on the media and dissent. Syria has not undergone regime change, and there are still many possible outcomes of its ongoing conflict. Syria will certainly need national reconciliation once its conflict ends, but until it does, any assessment would be severely limited. Iraq is clearly also still in need of national reconciliation, and this analysis references its failures as cautionary examples, but its political transition was not part of the recent Arab Spring, and was instigated by a foreign intervention rather than a domestic uprising.

More importantly, examining these specific countries is useful because they are each taking different approaches to their transitions, especially when it comes to dealing with former regimes and the concepts of peace and justice. Taking a zero-sum approach, Libyans dismantled their former regime by force and decided to pursue justice excessively, to the point of revenge and retaliation. Victims have become victimizers in many cases, employing secret prisons, torture, and flawed trials much as Qaddafi did. Yemen chose to forgo the pursuit of justice by granting Saleh immunity in return for his leaving power without what would have surely been a bloody fight. The transition deal, however, has enabled former regime elements to maintain their influence in the new system, hindering Yemen's ability to press forward with badly needed reforms. Even worse, Saleh's immunity paved the way for a counter-revolution, as it allowed him to ally with the Houthis in taking over the country. Tunisia has taken a completely different approach, striving to implement the rule of law. Through an inclusive, civil society–led process, it established a pragmatic transitional justice law to guide its adjudication of the former regime's abuses. These three different approaches have serious implications for the trajectories of the transitions, which currently appear to range from the successful consolidation of democracy in Tunisia to renewed civil conflict in Libya. Clearly, there are lessons to be learned that should contribute to theory development.

Overcoming Polarization through National Reconciliation

The Arab Spring uprisings have caused polarization in some situations and exacerbated it in others. These deeply divided and shattered Arab Spring societies are unlikely to make successful transitions to new systems of governance or any other forms of stability as long as this state of polarization prevails. Political fissures will prevent them from forging new social contracts, reforming state institutions, or rebuilding their ruined economies—all core demands of the uprisings in the first place.

To transition to sustainable peace and stability, then, Arab Spring societies must deal with their deep rifts by engaging in inclusive and genuine national reconciliation processes. With a broad and representative national reconciliation process, parties will have the opportunity to express both their interests and concerns with regard to the transition process in general and the specific issues that divide them. An inclusive and transparent national reconciliation process is the approach most likely to address the social and political grievances of the greatest number of parties, helping them to make a clean break with the past and move forward toward forging a new social contract. Early engagement of a wide range of actors will allow the parties to develop ownership of the transition processes and national reconciliation. Ownership will be essential for any sustainable reconciliation effort to take place.

National reconciliation, therefore, is the process of addressing the grievances of parties to a conflict with the aim of redefining their relationships and forging a new social contract. As J. Lewis Rasmussen puts it, a "social contract must be struck among the various groups within society; a state of reconciliation among these groups is necessary for maintaining such a social contract, itself necessary for a sustainable peace." Similarly, John Paul

Lederach understands reconciliation as "a process of change and redefinition of relationships." It follows that national reconciliation is not a fixed concept; it adapts based on culture and other contextual factors. It overlaps, and is sometimes confused, with other transitional processes such as transitional justice and national dialogues.[2]

Indeed, one of the challenges of national reconciliation is that the above definitions can be vague and confusing for ordinary citizens. Without a standard, practical definition for reconciliation, individuals' positions on whether to embrace a reconciliation effort are often based on their (usually biased) impressions of the process. Some Libyans, for example, reject the idea of reconciliation because they think it means ignoring the past and not seeking accountability for past crimes. They ask, "How can we reconcile after all we suffered during and before the war? We can't. We have to talk about justice before we address reconciliation."[3] That is why, in the case of Arab Spring societies transitioning from dictatorships to civil peace, an effective national reconciliation process must include a national dialogue among primary stakeholders, seeking the truth of what really happened in the past, providing reparations for victims' past injuries, holding the former regime accountable for its actions, and reforming state institutions.

Successful reconciliation processes will help Arab Spring populations to move past their grudges and grievances, preventing them from defining their countries' futures. Reconciliation cannot fully erase the damage rendered in the past, but it can prevent such harms from being the driving factors in parties' relations and futures. If the parties do not come together to address their pasts and collaboratively move forward to build new futures for their societies, the Arab Spring uprisings will ultimately replace dictatorships with new forms of exclusionary systems.

Four years after the uprisings, that is exactly how the situation is turning out in Libya. Revolutionaries have dominated the state and excluded the entire prior system through strong-arming parliament into enacting the Political Isolation Law (PIL), which prevented anyone who worked with the former regime from holding a government position for ten years. Meanwhile, some of the revolutionaries have committed similar atrocities to those of the former regime, especially torturing opponents in secret prisons. These actions heighten polarization, which in Libya even extends to the celebration of the primary political national holiday. Libyans that supported the revolution now commemorate its start date, February 17, but the excluded former regime loyalists still observe September 1, the anniversary of Qaddafi's 1969 coup.

A comprehensive national reconciliation process would attempt to bring resolution to these and many other varied issues. Even those who abused power in the former regime should have a place in the new Libya after their cases have been adjudicated through the application of a sound transitional justice law, apology-forgiveness mechanism, simple restitution process, or some other agreed-upon method. The Arab Spring countries have a wide array of daunting challenges in front of them, but first and foremost they need to develop singular national narratives to which their populations can relate. An inclusive national reconciliation process is the best hope for achieving this aim.

Launching a wide and representative *national dialogue* among all primary stakeholders in the Arab Spring societies represents the actual starting point for an inclusive national reconciliation process. National dialogue is essential for a transitional reconciliation for three primary reasons. First, unlike the Bolshevik Revolution, for example, the Arab uprisings were born leaderless and without a specific ideology to guide their trajectories after successfully forcing autocrats from power. In particular, the youth who played instrumental roles in mobilizing these revolutions are still not certain what forms of governance they ultimately desire. Therefore, national dialogues are necessary as opportunities for Arab societies to construct their theoretical frameworks for what they want their post-revolution futures to look like. The one thing Arab Spring populations know that they want is peace, and national dialogues could help them achieve this. Second, debating issues of transition within a national dialogue framework provides legitimacy to outcomes reached through this process. This is especially important in the case of the Arab uprisings as these countries are attempting to shift national decision-making from a top-down dictatorial approach to more of a participatory, bottom-up approach. It is no longer the ruler determining the nature and enforcement of the constitution for the people, but the people who debate and adopt it. Finally, a national dialogue represents the perfect conflict resolution mechanism for Arab societies in transition to learn how to solve their national problems through dialogue rather than force.

Another essential component in conducting national reconciliation in the Arab Spring societies is to have a sound and responsible *truth-seeking process* that dives into the past to determine what really happened under the former dictatorships. In the past few decades, Arab societies have suffered tremendous traumas under ruthless leaders, and acknowledging and facing those atrocities is essential for collective societal healing. Providing people with closure to their ordeals can help them move forward toward reconciliation. Closely related to healing, truth seeking contributes to establishing public records and the construction of a common history. Moreover, truth seeking contributes to reconciliation by promoting justice. It exposes the perpetrators of atrocities committed in the past few decades and helps hold them accountable for their crimes. Another significant reason why Arab Spring societies need to embrace truth seeking is to learn from their mistakes and guide institutional reforms that can prevent atrocities from happening again in the future.

Reparations are also needed to address rifts and build reconciliation in divided Arab Spring societies. Significant portions of these societies were harmed by former dictatorships' repression. This includes political prisoners; victims of torture; individuals who "disappeared"; opposition figures who were exiled, executed, or assassinated; and all those who suffered unjustly for merely being opposed to the regime or being in the wrong place at the wrong time. There are two types of reparations that can be administered to victims of state repression and their families: material and moral support. Material reparations are essential as they relate to the victims' livelihood and their ability to reintegrate in their own societies. Former prisoners are particularly important as they enjoy high levels of legitimacy in their own societies, mainly because they resisted regimes at times when the rest of their societies either accommodated the dictatorship or simply remained silent. Moral support to victims and their families is very much needed as it assures families that the struggles of their loved ones were not in vain. Many of the grievances that divide Arab societies today could be addressed by public showings of moral support, which have a powerful impact on people and can contribute to justice and civil peace.

Ending polarization and moving toward national unity, reconciliation, and civil peace also requires the delicate *handling of former regime elements* who were involved in corruption and human rights violations. On the one hand, new authorities want to ensure that these figures are held accountable for their crimes, but on the other, they should not allow the pursuit of justice to become vengeful and retaliatory, as this would risk creating new victims and new grudges that will lead to protracted instability in the future. This is especially important in an Arab context, as the region has historically struggled with achieving the right balance. In almost every case, such imbalances have functioned as sources of continued instability and deep divisions. In Iraq, the American policy of de-Ba'athification went too far and served as a major source of violence, instability, and sectarianism, all of which continue more than a decade later. Lebanon, conversely, did not go far enough in the 1989 Taif Agreement that ended its civil war, allowing all the major warlords to escape prosecution for their crimes. Arab Spring societies are at risk of repeating these mistakes and are strongly encouraged to learn about the dangers that each extreme entails.

While a national dialogue, truth-seeking efforts, reparations, and pursuing accountability will go a long way toward addressing the deep divisions that exist in transitioning Arab countries, they must not neglect *institutional reform*. Deep institutional reform can structurally adapt state institutions in a way that protects human rights and ensures violations will not reoccur. Suitable institutional reforms protect human rights by creating accountability and transparency rather than leaving individual leaders free to follow their own whims. Equally important, making these structural changes will deliver needed assurances to the polarized populations that the state and its institutions can be trusted going forward. This in turn should bring them a vital step closer to ending their divisions and embracing newly created systems and structures that are fair for everyone, even those who served under the former regime. Parties in a state of conflict usually develop a deep mistrust for the opposing institutions, individuals, and processes. Enacting serious reforms can address this mistrust.

Iraq demonstrates the danger of failing to achieve genuine national reconciliation. Today, thirteen years after the U.S. invasion and ouster of Saddam Hussein's regime, Iraq remains extremely polarized along sectarian lines. These fissures have caused significant strife within Iraq and throughout the region. By thoroughly undergoing the national reconciliation processes of national dialogue, truth seeking, reparations, accountability, and institutional reform, Arab Spring societies can avoid Iraq's fate. They will effectively deal with the causes of polarization that plague their countries and at the same time establish a solid foundation for sustainable peace and stability. They will address many potential causes of future violence and instability, and set their revitalized countries on a new path. Only then will the Arab Spring uprisings be successful in creating new, inclusive societies that bury the legacies of corrupt rulers and their cronies.

National Reconciliation in Context

Although national reconciliation is vital for a successful transition from the upheaval of the Arab Spring to sustainable peace and stability, as this book argues, the final outcome of the entire transition process is not solely determined by national reconciliation. Other factors also impact the fate of post-conflict transitions. Four layers of transition generally follow the removal of a dictatorship or the end of a civil war (fig. 1). Taken together, they determine the level of success a society will have in transitioning to peace and stability. The first layer is transitional justice, which is dealing with past human rights violations through truth seeking, reparations, and holding perpetrators accountable. This is a *past-oriented* approach that focuses mostly on helping victims come to terms with what happened to them and move forward. National reconciliation, the second layer, is broader. It includes and builds on the issues of transitional justice. It too involves dealing with the past but also addresses issues dividing a state at *present*. Therefore, in addition to truth seeking, reparations, and accountability, national reconciliation deals with

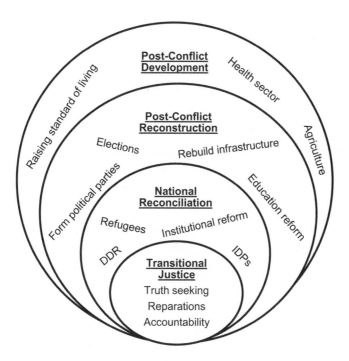

Fig. 1: National Reconciliation in Context

current issues like resettling refugees and IDPs; the disarmament, demobilization, and reintegration (DDR) of ex-combatants; national dialogue; and institutional reform, all of which are essential for a society to heal its wounds, reconcile, and move forward. Reforms are usually particularly important for security sectors, which, in all three countries, may have been responsible for torture, assassinations, disappearances, and executions. Stepping back further, post-conflict reconstruction, the third layer, is needed to rebuild a war-torn or underdeveloped country. Reconstruction includes additional processes like rebuilding infrastructure, reviving the economy, forming political parties, reforming the educational system, and more. Lastly, a society that hopes to emerge fully from dictatorship or civil war will have to undertake post-conflict development. This fourth layer focuses on raising standards of living and enacting further reforms, including in the health, industry, and agricultural sectors.

This book focuses on national reconciliation because when a transitioning state embraces this process, it will acquire valuable momentum needed to move forward and deal with the equally challenging issues of the reconstruction and development layers. National reconciliation targets polarization by engaging all key stakeholders in inclusive processes that enable them to, at a minimum, learn about and acknowledge other narratives, and ideally settle on a single national one. National dialogues prevent the dominance of exclusive narratives, helping parties to agree on many issues and acknowledge different interpretations of what happened in the past. Only after having found some common ground will the parties proceed comfortably toward handling the issues that caused the people to revolt, like the economy and especially jobs. Crossing the national reconciliation threshold will put the transitioning countries in a strong position to emerge successfully from the Arab Spring era.

Of course, transitions, including those of the Arab Spring, can succeed in implementing transitional justice and achieving national reconciliation but may fail in the next challenges of reconstruction and development. East Timor is a clear example of a country that successfully completed most of its post-conflict transition checklist but failed miserably to build a strong economy. As a result, many East Timorese currently live on less than a dollar per day. They surely did not have that economic hardship in mind when they decided to secede from Indonesia. The East Timorese succeeded in transitional justice, reconciliation, and to a certain extent reconstruction, all of which helped their country escape instability and renewed conflict and violence, but they have struggled to follow through with the final stage, development.

For all the promise of national reconciliation, it is not always sufficient for creating a stable, prosperous country, and it is more easily outlined than achieved. Nonetheless, it must be pursued in transitional contexts where divisions and deep-seated tensions exist in an attempt to prevent troubled states from remaining in, or descending into, devastating cycles of impoverishment and conflict. As there are surely many more conflicts and political transitions to come, both in the Arab world and beyond, methods of resolving them constructively must be further examined, discussed, and refined.

Furthermore, the relationships among the various phases of post-conflict transition are not linear. Transition processes do not typically engage fully with transitional justice before moving on to national reconciliation, to be followed by reconstruction and terminating with development. Instead, transitioning states often handle many issues that fall under different layers simultaneously. Furthermore, when states choose to tackle specific issues depends on national priorities, resources, and other pressing factors.

One final clarification regarding processes of transition should be made here, and that is on the question of "transition to what?" Considerable discussion in the literature refers to "democracy" as the destination of post-conflict transition processes. This is not necessarily the case for the post–Arab Spring transitions. As the discussion in this book shows, the Arab uprisings were spontaneous, leaderless, and lacked an ideological or theoretical framework that advised on their progress and final destination. Arab publics revolted against decades of repression carried out by dictatorships without considering what types of governance they wanted to have after the fall of these repressive regimes. Democracy is certainly one option, but not the only one. Even if democracy were the goal, would it be Western democracy, Turkish-Islamic democracy, an indigenous Arab version of democracy, or something else entirely? The discussion in this book does not assume any of these options, and instead refers to the goals of the transitions being peace, stability, and development, leaving the specific forms of governance to emerge as a result of future debate and negotiations among the people themselves.

Methodology

This book is primarily based on original field research conducted over the past four years in Yemen, Libya, and Tunisia. It is the result of hundreds of interviews with national figures including senior government officials, heads of political parties and civil society organizations, militia leaders, tribal leaders, members of displaced communities, scholars, journalists, former regime loyalists, and representatives of a number of international organizations. The selection of the interviewees followed a snowball sampling method in the three countries. Interviews were conducted in a semi-structured style, and each interview lasted between one and three hours. I also conducted secondary research, including a full literature review of the existing texts on conflict resolution in states undergoing political transitions. Although, as mentioned above, there is scant academic literature on the subject of political transitions and national reconciliation in Arab contexts, journalistic sources have been used to glean additional information about events on the ground in transitioning Middle East countries.

Outline of the Book

Part I devotes individual chapters to Libya, Yemen, and Tunisia in order to provide background information and discuss the divisive issues that are specific to each. In Libya, this is the need to disarm the country's numerous militias, the displacement of approximately one-sixth of its population, and the continuation of a destructive conflict. In Yemen, the unique issues include the desire of many southerners to secede and the armed Houthi movement in the North that continues to wreak havoc in multiple provinces. While Tunisia has had the most successful transition thus far, its fledgling government is dealing with challenges from groups that have appointed themselves as guardians of the revolution as well as a competition between Salafists and liberals over the direction of the country. Chapter 4 compares these issues and identifies the challenges that Libya, Yemen, Tunisia, and many other transitioning countries share.

Part II is the core of the book. Chapter 5 argues that an inclusive national dialogue is the starting point of a comprehensive national reconciliation process. Indeed, a national dialogue gives the transitioning societies a needed opportunity to develop visions and frameworks for their futures, gives legitimacy to the transition process, and encourages negotiation rather than violence as a solution to disputes. Ideally, a national dialogue will also set the course for the overall national reconciliation process, which should include some agreed-upon form of truth seeking, reparations, accountability, and institutional reform. Truth seeking, the focus of chapter 6, provides closure and healing for grieving victims and their families while also promoting justice. It gives transitioning countries an opportunity to learn from past mistakes.

Chapter 7 discusses reparations, which, whether material or symbolic, are another important part of the pursuit of justice and healing. Done correctly, reparations can bring previously marginalized and abused segments of society back into the mainstream where they can make positive contributions to the development of the country. The other side of the reparations coin is accountability and lustration, the subject of chapter 8. Determining how to adjudicate the crimes and personnel of the prior regime is the key question during most political transitions, and Libya, Tunisia, and Yemen are all grappling with that. Although prosecuting former leaders can be difficult, their victims often demand that they be held accountable for the abuses they ordered and committed. Some transitioning societies also deem it necessary to purge their bureaucracies in order to cleanse tainted government bodies and truly move forward. Even if these societies effectively address these personnel issues, however, they will not accomplish successful transitions unless they enact institutional reforms, as discussed in chapter 9. More transparency, inclusivity, and the establishment of the rule of law will build trust between the states and their societies, and make stability and even flourishing possible in the long run. The chapters of this section analyze and compare each country's progress, or lack thereof, in pursuing these essential national reconciliation processes.

Part III is devoted to actors that have played key roles in the countries' transitions thus far and can be expected to contribute to national reconciliation processes. Chapter 10 details how domestic civil society groups have been essential to Tunisia's progress, particularly in the development of a transitional justice law, hosting a national dialogue, and negotiating an end to a major political deadlock. In Libya, civil society organizations (CSOs) are developing rapidly and have proven valuable in defusing tribal conflicts and providing basic services. Chapter 11 focuses on the role of women. It describes how they were critical to launching the revolutions in Yemen and Tunisia. The chapter argues that women must continue to be involved in reshaping their countries, particularly in Yemen, where their increased role represents a sea change in terms of women's place in society, a promising development. One additional agent of reconciliation, tribes, is addressed in chapter 12. In Yemen and Libya, tribes are key stakeholders that have been manipulated and marginalized for decades. This chapter finds that with the security and power vacuums created by the fall of the regimes, tribes are well placed to contribute to the stability and development of their countries.

PART I

Issues of Reconciliation

ONE

Libya

A fter forty-two years of tyranny, the Libyan people rose up against Colonel Muammar Qaddafi on February 17, 2011. Eight months later, Qaddafi was dead—killed in the battle for his hometown, Sirte. Libyans celebrated the collapse of the Qaddafi regime, and their National Transitional Council (NTC) declared the country's liberation. They soon realized, however, that some of their greatest challenges were still ahead. Less than three years after revolutionaries removed Qaddafi from power, they themselves turned against each other, waging a brutal civil war that spread to large parts of Libya.

Qaddafi came to power in a bloodless coup against King Idris in 1969 and established the Great Socialist People's Libyan Arab Jamahiriya (state of the masses), premised on his own philosophy of governance—the "Third Universal Theory."[1] He used his philosophy of Jamahiriya to ensure that state institutions were built to serve his regime. The national army was marginalized, with Qaddafi instead empowering security apparatuses that were completely loyal to him, such as the powerful 32nd Reinforced Brigade of the Armed People. More broadly, he exercised absolute political power, banning political parties and imprisoning, exiling, and even executing opposition leaders without trials. For forty-two years, Qaddafi not only prevented the formation of political parties and civil society organizations but also invested very little in the development of his country. He left Libya with minimal development in almost every sector—including education, health, industry, and agriculture—and a corrupt and inefficient bureaucratic apparatus.

When demonstrations broke out in Benghazi and elsewhere, Qaddafi met them with defiance, famously threatening to "cleanse Libya house by

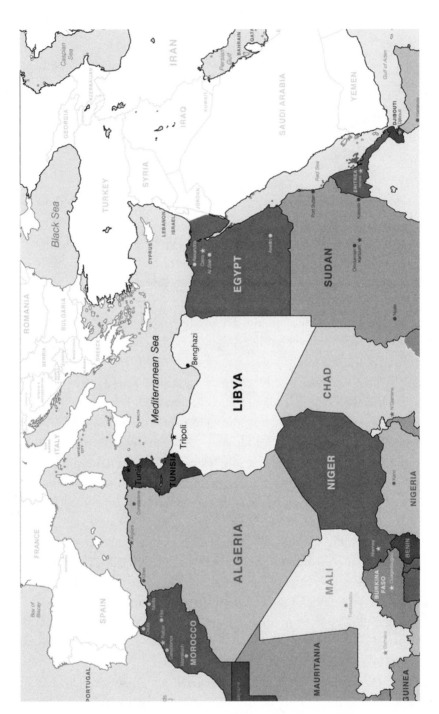

Fig. 2: Libya and Tunisia in a Regional Context

Credit: iStock.com (adapted)

house," and launching a punishing military campaign to put down the uprising. In less than a week, his Khamis Brigade had seized the city of Misrata and his forces were on the brink of launching a crushing assault on Benghazi, the cradle of the revolution. The United Nations (UN) Security Council's Chapter 7 authorization of military intervention with the imposition of a no-fly zone reversed the war's momentum, but not enough to spare Libya from additional months of grinding combat. Finally, on October 20, 2011, rebels captured and killed Qaddafi while he was attempting to flee his hometown. With his death and the dismantling of his regime, the Libyan state collapsed, leaving the country in chaos.

The regime's overthrow left a power vacuum that has been filled by, among others, transitional governments, revolutionaries, political parties, and non-governmental organizations (NGOs), which have competing agendas and no history of cooperating with one another. As a result, the country's transition has struggled through a series of fits and starts as first the NTC and then the popularly elected General National Congress (GNC) failed to effectively assert their authority and were routinely disrupted by armed rebels. The country's premiership has been a revolving door, and Libya has had dueling governments since August 2014.

Early in Libya's transition, the NTC did take several initial steps to promote national reconciliation, including the enactment of a "Laying a Foundation for National Reconciliation and Transitional Justice" law that, among other things, established a Fact-Finding and Reconciliation Commission. The NTC also launched the Ministry for the Affairs of the Families of the Martyrs and Missing in November 2011, which quickly set about obtaining international funding and assistance in tackling the country's large number of missing persons cases. Libya's first freely elected parliament in decades, the two-hundred-seat GNC, took power in August 2012. Some of its members participated in a December 2012 conference on truth seeking and reconciliation, organized by the UN and Libya's Fact Finding and Reconciliation Commission, which produced a number of important recommendations. Several of them were incorporated into Libya's new transitional justice law, passed in December 2013, but as of mid-April 2014, the law was still "no more than ink on paper" according to Human Rights Watch. As of

September 2015, Libya had started a constitution-drafting process but had yet to make any meaningful progress on a national dialogue, truth seeking, reparations, or institutional reform. Overall, both the NTC and GNC seemed to be more dedicated to protecting revolutionaries and punishing the former regime and its supporters than to pursuing national reconciliation.[2] After 2014 and the launching of Operation Dignity and Libya Dawn's fighting, the entire process was put on hold. Attention turned to this conflict and away from reconciliation efforts.

As a result, Libya continues to suffer from a myriad of old and new issues that challenge its unity and the government's ability to execute a transition from dictatorship to civil peace. Libya has never been divided the way it is today, more than four years after the outbreak of its revolution. The country's severe instability and then civil war have continued to generate new problems that need to be resolved before sustainable peace can be realized. The following three issues are only some examples of the many problems preventing genuine reconciliation in Libya, thereby threatening the transition process.

Culture of the Victor

The "culture of the victor" that has prevailed since the collapse of the Qaddafi regime has sharply divided Libyan society. National reconciliation cannot be achieved as long as the rigid and polarizing division between *azlam* (regime loyalists) and *thuwar* (anti-Qaddafi revolutionaries) prevails.

This culture of the victor has led to the classification of entire towns and tribes as either thuwar or azlam. The victorious thuwar have been treated with honor and dignity, while the azlam have been publicly identified with shame, defeat, and guilt. Broadly applying these labels has produced a Libyan society that is deeply and structurally divided. "Libyans are now labeled as either 'thuwar' or 'azlam,' and this is keeping the country divided," said former GNC member Salem al-Ahmar in an interview. He explained, "This is unfair. The 'thuwar' label is given to a small number of towns like Misrata, Zentan, and Souq al-Jumaa, as if the rest of the country didn't contribute to the revolution. 'Azlam,' on the other hand, has been generalized to include many who played no part in supporting Qaddafi. [The] Warfalla [tribe], for example, consists of almost one million people. It's unfairly and incorrectly being described by some as 'azlam,' when in fact only a few dozen [of its members] were truly allied with Qaddafi. The same thing applies to Bani Walid, where only a few people fought with Qaddafi; now the entire town, with over 80,000 people, is being treated as azlam. This must end if we want to build a new stable and prosperous Libya."[3]

Libya's culture of the victor also extends a selective reading of history that is itself polarizing. During Qaddafi's forty-two years in power, various parties struggled against his dictatorship. Although the February 17 Revolution marked his overthrow, the struggle against Qaddafi was cumulative; all contributions to resisting and destabilizing the Qaddafi regime are important and deserving of recognition, regardless of when exactly they took place. For example, the death of student leader al-Sadeq al-Shuwaihdi, executed in 1984 for organizing anti-Qaddafi protests, deserves the same attention as those killed by Qaddafi's military during the 2011 revolution.[4] Nevertheless, Libya's prevailing discourse revolves entirely around the glorification of the February 17 revolutionaries; others are hardly mentioned. "Bani Walid was one of the first to rebel against Qaddafi," said al-Ahmar. "Bani Walid conducted a failed coup against Qaddafi in 1993 and, of course, experienced harsh retaliation as a result. We paid a high price in 1993 when the rest of the country was just watching. This now seems to be forgotten."[5]

The prevalence of this culture of the victor has divided Libya in other ways, most notably through what Rania Swadek, a civil society specialist, described as revolutionaries' feelings of "entitlement" to special rights.[6] Victorious revolutionaries believe that they deserve their own military forces and secret prisons. For instance, in the case of Zentan, revolutionaries have demanded the right to hold Muammar Qaddafi's son Saif al-Islam in their own prison and try him in a local court. Many in the tribe view trying Saif al-Islam in a Zentan court as a badge of honor, but it has raised questions across the country about the rights of a single town to assume the mantle of the state. Some people have even gone so far as to refer to Zentan authorities as "the state of Zentan."

To give reconciliation an opportunity to succeed, this polarizing language must change. If anything, it is pushing the other party—allies of the former regime—to regroup and launch a counter-revolution. This language of exclusion must be replaced with inclusive terms, as the new Libya should have an equal place for everyone.

Disarmament

A key requirement for the success of any post-conflict process of national reconciliation is the restoration of state sovereignty, which entails the disarmament and demobilization of ex-combatants and their reintegration into society. Disarmament is not easy, but it is certainly crucial — reconciliation cannot be achieved in an environment controlled by militias. The failure of the UN's disarmament efforts in Cambodia in the early 1990s allowed the Khmer Rouge to boycott elections and the country's civil war to continue. Successful disarmament requires sufficient funds, detailed planning, and a strategy for reintegration; otherwise, as seen in El Salvador, crime will rise, security will deteriorate, and any peace process will be threatened.[7] This has been Libya's experience. Revolutionaries successfully toppled the former regime, but in the four years since, they have refused to disarm and become part of the country's new state structure. Visiting Tripoli two years after the removal of Qaddafi, it was immediately apparent that Libya was being ruled by two regimes operating in parallel: the official government, represented by the GNC and cabinet, and an array of revolutionary militias, which held the real military power. Later, divisions among and within the militias themselves started to emerge. As a result, dozens of militias throughout the country have claimed authority over their pieces of land. Ultimately, as of January 2015, the militias had hijacked Libya's transition, and the country was no longer merely divided into two states but into dozens of fiefdoms. Officially, Libya started to have two parliaments and two governments for the primary two factions, Operation Dignity and Libya Dawn. When the state itself is divided, a reconciliation process is a non-starter. To bring Libya back together and end its polarization, ex-combatants must begin a process that leads to disarming and joining the official state structure.[8]

Although Tripoli once hosted the Supreme Security Committee (SSC), which had significant power and included representatives from a wide variety of military groups, there was ultimately no clear and defined structure that organized Libya's revolutionaries. Dozens of military councils across the country operate independently, with no clear command structure governing them. Almost every major town in Libya has its own military council.

The revolutionaries' main objective, as they present it, is to "protect the February 17 Revolution" and its accomplishments. It is generally understood that what they need to protect against is a possible counter-revolution by regime loyalists. The revolutionaries also claim to want to ensure a successful transition from dictatorship to democracy, and there certainly is a sizable segment of the revolutionaries that has refused to disarm out of a genuine commitment to that goal. Others, however, are motivated by mistrust of the transition itself. The lack of a credible state-building process, often manifested as an absence of security, has discouraged revolutionaries from committing to the transition, which, in turn, further impairs state-building efforts—a vicious cycle. Many revolutionaries and individual Libyan civilians feel that they must take responsibility for their personal security. They view their own machine guns as their best "insurance policy," and therefore refuse to hand the weapons over to the state. As Dirk Salomons puts it, ex-combatants and their leaders "must have faith in a future where the advantages of peace outweigh those of war."[9] The new Libyan state's efforts to provide that future have, to this point, failed.

But some observers (and even revolutionaries) believe that the militias have been penetrated by opportunists who joined up after the revolution to pursue their own interests. In fact, the number of "revolutionaries" who joined the militias after Qaddafi had been defeated far exceeded the number that fought against the regime during the first eight months of Libya's uprising. "The total number of revolutionaries who fought Qaddafi across the entire country was less than 40,000," said a prominent militia leader. "We fought from day one of the revolution in Misrata, and we know our estimate is very accurate. We don't understand how the number has reached 200,000. We don't know where that 160,000 came from. Of course, there are many opportunists who want to take advantage of the revolution."[10] Many ex-combatants are reluctant to disarm and join the formal structure of the state simply because they would likely lose the privileges they enjoyed after the revolution. The SSC benefited from power and a budget that allowed it to provide incentives greater than anything the new state could offer. The maintenance of the status quo has therefore emerged as a, or *the*, primary interest of many Libyan revolutionaries.

Attempts to disarm these powerful militias and integrate their members into the country's security services have been largely unsuccessful. The numbers of revolutionaries who have disarmed and joined the police and military are dwarfed by the estimated 200,000 fighters across the country. In March 2013, for example, Interior Minister Ashour Shuwail announced that approximately 5,000 rebels had graduated from police training. Shuwail had said in January 2013 that 26,000 fighters under the SSC's umbrella had applied to the police force. According to Chief of Staff Yousef al-Manqoush, 5,000 rebels had officially joined the Libyan military as of February 2012. All of these numbers represent real progress, but, at best, they likely account for less than one-quarter of the fighters throughout Libya.[11]

Furthermore, the still-armed rebels have frustrated efforts to restore the rule of law and impose accountability after the revolution. Since his capture in November 2011, Saif al-Islam al-Qaddafi has been held by the Zentan Revolutionary Council, and as of September 2015 was still being tried in a Zentan court. The governing NTC, meanwhile, bowed to pressure from the militias and in April 2012 passed laws 35 and 38, granting immunity from prosecution to revolutionaries who may have committed war crimes or human rights violations, by granting amnesty for acts "made necessary" by the February 17 Revolution.[12]

Tensions between the Libyan state and various revolutionary councils spiked in early 2013 when the GNC debated the proposed PIL. On March 5, 2013, armed protesters barricaded a GNC meeting and demanded that its members pass the law. The GNC had already relocated from the main parliament complex in February after wounded veterans of the revolution occupied the building, demanding to be sent abroad for medical treatment. When lawmakers were finally able to leave the building, gunmen among the protesters shot up the car of GNC speaker Muhammad Magarief, who announced the next week that the GNC would suspend its work due to security concerns. Armed protesters demanding the law's passage continued to besiege state institutions, surrounding Libya's foreign ministry in April. Even worse, in October 2013, the Operations Cell of Libyan Revolutionaries, a militant group, kidnapped Prime Minister Ali Zeidan for several hours. He later claimed this group was hoping to "overthrow the government" and went so far as to accuse members of the GNC of involvement in the abduction.[13] Multiple failures to disarm the powerful militias led Khalifa Haftar to launch his Operation Dignity to impose security in Libya, but this turned out to be just another alliance of militias that significantly exacerbated the security situation and officially divided the country among the various militia alliances while marginalizing the role of the central state.

Solutions for the complex and fraught relationship between Libya's state and revolutionaries should take into consideration that many revolutionaries are sincere in their desire to safeguard the February 17 Revolution and refuse to disarm for that reason. Their refusal to disarm, though well intentioned, harms Libya's transition more than it helps to "protect the revolution and its accomplishments." For that reason there is no alternative to disarming and joining the official structure of the state. Perhaps Libya's revolutionaries were best described by Tunisian politician Said Ferjani, who stated, "Libya's revolutionaries are legitimate but lack legitimacy."[14] While many Libyans sympathize with the revolutionaries' goal of forming a new post-Qaddafi order, they have not necessarily rallied to provide support for the revolutionaries since Qaddafi's defeat. Furthermore, the tensions between the state and revolutionaries have arisen primarily due to disagreements about the methods used to stymie a counter-revolution, rather than a lack of consensus about the inherent correctness of that goal. As a Misrata militia leader explained, "We have no problem joining the state. We have no demands that would benefit us personally. If we were pursuing our self-interest, we could simply achieve that with no problem. We have the power, and we could secure our own gain if that were the goal, but it isn't. Our goal is to hold the leaders of Qaddafi's brigades responsible."[15]

Nonetheless, while both the state and the revolutionaries share the same objective of a successful transition, the intense distrust between them makes their differences over tactics more difficult to resolve. The revolutionaries' perception that the state is stocked with Qaddafi loyalists, and the state's perception that the revolutionaries are mainly self-interested, makes reintegration particularly difficult. Still, Libya must work toward a mutual understanding through a state-revolutionaries dialogue. This dialogue should focus on how to achieve the parties' shared goals: a successful transition and sustainable peace. The dynamic where revolutionaries make their case by besieging ministries and other state institutions must be replaced with an institutionalized forum to allow for the peaceful exchange of views and the exploration of points of mutual agreement. A trusted third party who could act as a facilitator would improve the dialogue's chances of success.

Civil War

The lack of such a dialogue and failure to disarm revolutionaries has allowed a much bigger problem to emerge and sabotage Libya's transition and national reconciliation process: civil war.

The prevalence of militias in Libya undermined the authority of the central government and worsened security to unprecedented levels, thereby causing conditions conducive to the emergence of new militias. Libyans found themselves caught in a vicious cycle where the presence of militias contributed to a security vacuum that encouraged the formation of additional militias. Instead of filling the security gaps created by Qaddafi's fall, revolutionaries have exploited and widened them. Driven by their internal agendas, revolutionaries started to fight each other, competing for power and resources. Much like what occurred in Liberia, fear and distrust has made the militias hesitant to negotiate, much less disarm, and economic incentives motivate them to conquer territory. Libya is a resource-rich country, and revolutionaries can benefit more from maintaining their own militias than by disarming and joining state institutions. No government job, including military posts, no matter the rank, can provide the income, power, prestige, and autonomy of being a militia commander. As Mieczyslaw P. Boduszynski and Kristin Fabbe put it, "Militias in Libya offer young men power, prestige and money exceeding anything that the official state can provide. Why would a vendor or a mechanic return to his prewar job if he can make more money and garner more respect as a militia member?"[16]

When I visited with a number of revolutionary militias in Tripoli in 2012, it was obvious that they functioned like a state within a state. When pressed on why they were not disarming and joining state institutions such as the army, they emphasized the need to maintain a strong position from which to protect the February 17 Revolution and prevent a counter-revolution. Again, many are sincere about this goal. The challenge becomes where to draw the line between those that are motivated by good intentions and those merely seeking personal benefits.

This competition escalated and became more clearly defined in 2014. In May, Khalifa Haftar, a former general who returned to Libya during the uprising to fight against Qaddafi and ultimately became a militia commander, launched what he called Operation Dignity, a campaign to eliminate all Islamist and pro-Islamist militias in Libya. Based in the eastern part of the country, Haftar's forces started to attack both February 17 revolutionaries who fought against Qaddafi and Ansar al-Sharia, a Salafi jihadi militia based in Benghazi. These groups and others formed an alliance called the Shura Council of Benghazi Revolutionaries to fight back. In western Libya, including Tripoli, Haftar allied with the powerful Zentan militia, which played a prominent role in the fight against the Qaddafi regime but is more tribal than ideological. Another anti-Haftar alliance, Libya Dawn (Fajr Libya), emerged in response, composed of the powerful Misrata militia, Islamist factions called the Libya Revolutionary Operations Room and Libya Shield Force, and tribal militias such as the Zawyan and Sibratan. Although Libya Dawn includes tribal and regional militias, it is often referred to as an Islamist force. The outcome of all these developments is that Libya is facing a brutal, two-front civil war in which Haftar, with the backing of Libya's internationally recognized government and elected House of Representatives (HOR) based in the eastern city of Tubruk, is perpetuating his Operation Dignity against the Shura Council of Benghazi Revolutionaries in the east and Libya Dawn in the west (fig. 3).

The emergence of Haftar and his claims to be Libya's savior are not surprising, as the lack of security, weakness of the central government, and prevalence of militias have left Libyans considerably frustrated. This has led some Libyans, including civil society activist Sufyan Omeish, to think that the country probably needs a "fair dictator" that would lead Libya out of its chaos and through its troubled transition.[17] As I wrote previously, "If General [Haftar] didn't exist, the Libyan people would have created him. His emergence shouldn't be surprising, given the country's disarray. If anything, it's surprising that he, or someone like him, didn't appear much sooner."[18] Unfortunately,

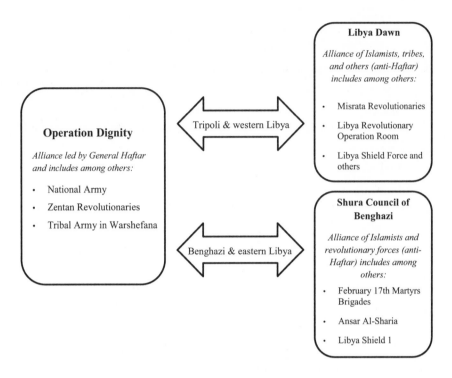

Libya Dawn

Alliance of Islamists, tribes, and others (anti-Haftar) includes among others:

- Misrata Revolutionaries
- Libya Revolutionary Operation Room
- Libya Shield Force and others

Operation Dignity

Alliance led by General Haftar and includes among others:

- National Army
- Zentan Revolutionaries
- Tribal Army in Warshefana

Tripoli & western Libya

Benghazi & eastern Libya

Shura Council of Benghazi

Alliance of Islamists and revolutionary forces (anti-Haftar) includes among others:

- February 17th Martyrs Brigades
- Ansar Al-Sharia
- Libya Shield 1

Fig. 3: Mapping Libya's 2014 Civil War

by using his power to attempt to eliminate his rivals rather than bring about an inclusive national dialogue, Haftar has actually increased Libya's security problems and set the stage for a protracted civil war.

The war has had serious implications for Libya's transition and national reconciliation process. First of all, it has exacerbated some of the impediments to reconciliation that pre-dated the conflict, specifically Libya's struggles with disarmament, discussed above, and its displacement crisis, discussed below. The war has also created a new division within Libyan society that has further polarized the country. General Haftar's campaign has defined the intra-revolutionaries' civil war as a struggle between Islamists and non-Islamists. This characterization has not only inflamed domestic tensions along those lines but also encouraged regional actors to intervene. Egypt and the United Arab Emirates have gone so far as to conduct air strikes in support of Haftar, while Libya Dawn is reportedly receiving support from Turkey and Qatar. This regional dimension only adds to the complexity of the transition process and makes Libya's crises particularly difficult to solve.

Libya's civil war has also put the country's major transition tasks on hold as they become less of a priority and as the state institutions that should handle them become paralyzed. For example, Libya's latest parliament, the popularly elected HOR, which assumed power from the GNC in August 2014, should be overseeing the writing of a constitution and the development of a transitional justice law. Due to security concerns, it ultimately relocated to the remote eastern city of Tobruk where its influence diminished, and in November 2014, Libya's Supreme Court declared the body to be unconstitutional in a controversial ruling rejected by the HOR. Meanwhile, a number of Islamist, former GNC members who failed to win seats in the HOR have, with the support of Libya Dawn, propped up the officially defunct GNC as a rival government in Tripoli. More quietly, the constitutional assembly that Libyans elected in early 2014 to draft a new constitution was still functioning as of September 2015, but was making little progress in the face of increased pressure from the rival governments. These developments have effectively paralyzed Libya's entire transition process.[19]

It is very unlikely that Libya's civil war will end in a definitive military victory for either side in the foreseeable future, as they are evenly balanced and both enjoy external support. This only increases the importance of Libya's pursuing a national dialogue sooner rather than later. Its civil war needs a negotiated agreement in which all parties take part. A military solution is not feasible, hard as it may be for the parties to accept in this early stage. Lebanon's civil war, for example, lasted for fifteen years without any faction being able to claim victory before finally negotiating the Taif Agreement. Libyan militias should avoid learning this lesson the hard way and embrace a diplomatic solution. Prolonging the civil war will only make Libya's national reconciliation efforts and transition to peace and stability that much more difficult.

Displaced Communities: IDPs and Refugees

Displacement is a major obstacle to rebuilding social cohesion in post-conflict Libya. In this instance, displacement should be understood to include both IDPs and refugees who fled their homes as a result of violence, whether during the 2011 uprising or during all of the fighting that has followed. There can be no national reconciliation in Libya while an integral part of Libyan society is living in camps inside and outside the country.

The UN High Commissioner for Refugees (UNHCR) estimated that over one million people, including approximately 660,000 Libyans, fled the country due to its violent 2011 uprising, and the Internal Displacement Monitoring Centre reported that the number of IDPs peaked at 550,000. These people gravitated to special camps or Libya's urban areas where they faced difficult conditions. Many of the refugees and IDPs were later able to return to their homes, but in 2014, Libya's civil war precipitated a new wave of displacement. In December 2014, UNHCR reported that more than 394,000 Libyans had been forced to leave their homes due to the fighting in eastern, southeastern, and western Libya. Most of those that remained in the country scattered across thirty-five overwhelmed towns and cities, with many sheltering in schools and other public places.[20] UNHCR has estimated that some 56,000 of these IDPs are people who were still displaced as a result of the 2011 uprising.[21] Libya's more than 400,000 IDPs are facing a number of serious challenges. Most obvious is the violence that likely caused them to flee in the first place. Libya's civil war, like the 2011 uprising before it, has subjected populated residential areas to significant fighting, the use of heavy weaponry, and indiscriminate shelling and bombardment. The resulting extensive destruction of many urban areas throughout Libya and the evictions that occurred after Qaddafi's fall have created a severe housing crisis, leaving many Libyan IDPs to live in schools, unfinished administrative buildings, metal hangars, and parks, often with minimal access to clean water and heat. Some IDPs have also lost their freedom of movement, with violence or armed groups preventing them from fleeing or accessing badly needed food and medical supplies. Another challenge is the severe lack of medical supplies and competent care, as compounded by looting, reduced imports due to the conflict, and the flight of foreign medical personnel. Moreover, specific groups of IDPs, including the Tawergha, Mashashya, Gualish, and Tuareg, remain vulnerable to retaliatory attacks, intimidation, and other abuses as they face protracted displacement.[22]

The decisive defeat of the former regime and the killing of Qaddafi left his loyalists in disarray. Fear of retaliation—especially given the absence of the rule of law and the collapse of state security institutions—led large numbers of former regime elements and their families to flee the country. When it comes to IDPs, one of the most serious problems in Libya has been the case of Tawergha. According to residents of neighboring Misrata, Tawergha fighters affiliated with the Qaddafi brigades were responsible for a systematic campaign of rape and murder when they besieged Misrata for two months during the revolution. After the fall of Qaddafi, Misrata militias took revenge, forcing all 42,000 residents of Tawergha from the town, leaving it completely deserted. The majority of Tawerghans relocated to three camps, but others have sought refuge in Libyan cities or have fled the country.

Still, Misrata residents demand retribution, even destroying the Tawerghans' town to prevent the return of its inhabitants. According to Fred Abrahams, a special adviser at Human Rights Watch, "Tawerghans have been hunted down, detained, tortured and killed. Satellite imagery analyzed by Human Rights Watch corroborates what we saw on the ground: the systematic destruction of the town's residential, commercial and industrial structures after the fighting had stopped in an apparent attempt to prevent returns."[23] Ali al-Tawerghi, a representative of the Tawergha IDP camp in Janzour near Tripoli, argues that Tawerghans are now themselves the victims of atrocities. "Before we uncover the truth of past violations," al-Tawerghi said, "we need to uncover the truth of present violations. There is no transitional justice. There is only one justice, and that is the justice of the victor."[24]

A resolution of the conflict between Misrata and Tawergha and reconciliation between the towns seems far off—and allegations of rape greatly complicate matters. Misratans seem willing to consider a negotiated resolution over the killings that took place during the siege of Misrata. They are not, however, willing to discuss rape. As Minister of Justice Salah al-Marghani explained, "Libyans' cultural heritage [their value system] can provide means of dealing with crimes such as murder or robbery, but not systematic rape. Accepting compensation for rape is a stigma. Even discussing rape is a source of embarrassment. Our legal system has regulations for how to deal with individual cases of rape, but not when a town is accused of rape by another town. Neither our legal nor our value systems can inform us what to do in this case."[25]

For the Misratans, the crimes committed are ultimately beyond repair. They refuse to negotiate or list specific demands. According to Haidar Hasan, a member of the Misrata military council in Tripoli, "There is nothing to talk about regarding Tawergha and their war crimes in Misrata. Time is a great healer, and we should not talk about the problem now. Let the Tawerghans go wherever they want, but [there can be] no return to Tawergha."[26] Nevertheless, it should be mentioned that the UN efforts to mediate between the two parties led in January 2015 to some understandings between the municipalities of the two towns, which allowed for a committee from Tawergha to visit their prisoners in Misrata prisons. The two parties also recognized the right of Tawerghans to return to their town, though implementation of this right is not a possibility in the near future.[27]

While the case of Tawergha may be the most dramatic instance of displacement in Libya, it is certainly not the only one. There are several other tribal conflicts that have contributed to displacement of certain communities in Libya, including struggles between tribes like the Mashaysha, al-Qawalish, Awainiyya, Western Rayayneh, Tuareg, and Tebu, to name a few.

Division between Qaddafi's loyalists and opponents has appeared as a common factor in almost all cases of displacement in Libya, but other factors have contributed to the Libyan conflicts, including land disputes, historical grievances, race, tribal rivalries, the 2014 militias civil war, and others. For example, the tribal conflict in the Nafousa Mountains between the Zentan (who joined the revolution) and the Mashaysha (who are accused of being regime loyalists) is also based on land disputes that date back to the colonial era. Even in the Tawergha-Misrata case, many Libyans believe race and class to be major factors that complicate the conflict and make it more difficult to resolve. Tawerghans are dark-skinned and are said to have origins elsewhere in Africa, while Misratans are lighter and descend from a mix of Arabs, Turks, and Circassians. Tawerghans are also believed to have been enslaved in the past by Misratans. More recently, Misrata has been a major market and source of jobs for Tawerghans, and until the 2011 revolution, many Tawerghans depended on Misrata for their jobs and livelihoods. The inflamed conflict between them, then, has had wide-ranging social, political, and economic consequences.

Although displacement—and the conflicts driving it—present an enormous challenge to national reconciliation in Libya, it is possible to work toward overcoming it. The following considerations should serve as a starting point for a long-term resolution of the displacement problem.

First, there should be no doubt that the pain that Misrata and many other communities suffered under Qaddafi is serious and must be addressed. Especially during the revolution, the former regime became more lethal than ever. If the government fails to provide a suitable alternative that addresses their grievances, it is natural for these groups to resort to extrajudicial retribution for the wrongs done to them.

Second, most IDPs and refugees were not directly, or even indirectly, involved in the apparatus of the Qaddafi regime. The majority of Libyan IDPs, in fact, are the families—children, parents, and spouses—of individuals who served in the former regime in some capacity. Indeed, during my visit to the Janzour camp near Tripoli, it was clear that most of the camp's residents were women, children, and the elderly. Most of those who were directly involved with the former regime had fled or were in the prisons of Misrata revolutionaries. The disproportionate suffering of those least culpable for regime offenses is tantamount to collective punishment.

Lastly, many others—especially among Libya's refugees—were Qaddafi sympathizers, but they were not involved in violations. They fled the country because of the collapse of security and their fear of retaliation against former regime allies. In extreme cases, some of them fled because they had appeared on Libyan television attending Qaddafi's last speech in Tripoli's Shuhada Square.

All three of these considerations necessitate the creation of a legal framework that deals fairly with all parties; a transitional justice law is particularly important here. Such a law would obviate aggrieved communities' urges to pursue vigilante justice. Moreover, its targeted application—encompassing all those genuinely culpable for offenses—would negate the need to indiscriminately threaten entire communities. An end to this collective punishment would allow many of the innocent in Libya's IDP camps to return to their homes.

Some regime sympathizers, meanwhile, could be willing to return to Libya to face charges, if they are first assured that the state, not individual militias, is in control of internal security, and that they will not be subjected to random acts of violence and revenge. The state has an indispensable role to play here and must come to monopolize the use of force. Indeed, agreements between Libya's tribes are not sufficient to make such guarantees, as there will always be hardliners who will act against agreements. "Even if the tribal sheikhs approve the agreement," said the head of a local reconciliation committee, "no one will be able to guarantee that the youth will abide by it and not attack the returnees."[28]

The need for state intervention goes beyond the establishment of the rule of law. The state's role includes putting in place an array of conditions needed to facilitate the return of displaced communities. Some of these measures include guaranteeing a return that is dignified, ensuring the safety and security of the returnees in their homes, and managing the restoration of basic services to these areas. Only a strong state can provide these conditions. For example, though Zentan allowed Western Rayayneh refugees to return to their homes, they still face the hardships of living in houses that were seriously damaged during the fighting between the two tribes and the question of who will repair the town's infrastructure. The state's role in leading national reconciliation, then, must include not only establishing security but also repairing the damage of the war and enabling the displaced to resume their regular lives.

TWO

Yemen

On November 23, 2011, Yemeni president Ali Abdullah Saleh signed a Gulf Cooperation Council (GCC)–brokered settlement that brought an end to his decades-long rule and Yemen's months-long political stalemate. After rejecting multiple compromise proposals from the opposition and the GCC in previous months, Saleh finally agreed to transfer presidential power to his deputy, Abd Rabbu Mansour Hadi, in a ceremony held in Riyadh and attended by Saudi Arabia's King Abdullah. Saleh officially stepped aside in February 2012, and Yemen began the daunting process of transition.

Saleh became the president of the Yemen Arab Republic, or North Yemen, in 1978. Under his leadership, North and South Yemen united in 1990, and when the South attempted to secede in 1994, Saleh fought and won a civil war, preserving a unified Yemen but causing deep social, political, and economic grievances in the South. Saleh's rule also endured despite a lengthy insurgency fought by the Houthis in the northern province of Saada. Between 2004 and 2010, Saleh fought six separate wars against the Houthi rebels. Saleh's iron-fisted rule went beyond military campaigns; he readily cracked down on his political opponents, and his reign was fraught with allegations of extrajudicial imprisonments, torture, and forced disappearances. Combining such repression with skillful political maneuvering, Saleh was able to retain power for thirty-three years.

Like his counterparts in Libya and elsewhere, Saleh initially responded to his country's Arab Spring demonstrations, which began in January 2011, with defiance and violence. When the protesters proved undaunted, he offered some concessions, but they were not enough to placate his opponents,

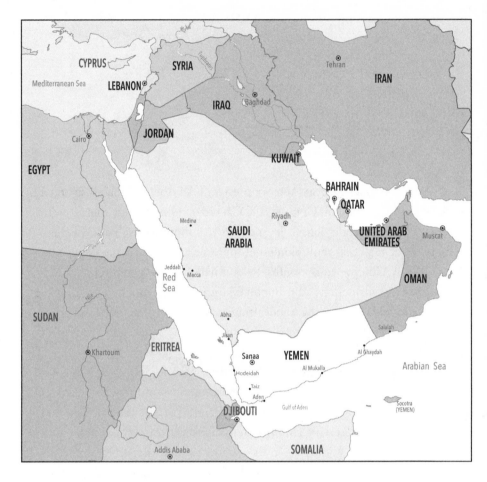

Fig. 4: Yemen in a Regional Context
Credit: iStock.com (adapted)

who had multiplied to include influential, and previously loyal, tribes and military commanders. For much of 2011, Yemen faced a tense military and political stalemate that threatened to deteriorate into a civil war. Saleh continued to cling to power in the face of intense pressure from his longtime foreign backers, the GCC and United States, even after being wounded in a bombing. Eventually, however, Saleh conceded that his long run as president was nearing its end. He only surrendered the presidency, though, after being assured that the GCC initiative called on Yemen's parliament to "adopt laws granting immunity from legal and judicial prosecution to the President and those who worked with him during his time in office."[1] The agreement also allowed the ruling party to continue as a major player in Yemeni politics without engaging in any serious reform. As a result, the GCC initiative neglected to address major underlying causes and conditions of the conflict in Yemen. It opted for regime renovation—rather than regime change—which carried with it the seeds of future instability. Sure enough, three years later, forces of the old regime that remained part of the political system allied with Houthi rebels to take over Sanaa and other districts of Yemen by force, igniting what could become a vicious and protracted civil war.

Like Libya, Yemen has yet to advance significantly toward national reconciliation, but unlike Libya, it has laid the groundwork with an extensive national dialogue, discussed in chapter 5. In August 2013, Yemen's transitional government apologized to both southerners and residents of Saada province in the North for the state's military campaigns against each region. Additionally, the government planned compensation funds to help with reconstruction and provide reparations to victims of political violence. While these are all important and positive steps, implementation is far from assured, and Yemen has major gaps in the areas of accountability and institutional reform. None of the crimes committed by Saleh and his regime during their rule and the 2011 uprising have been prosecuted, and Saleh continues to lead his party, the General People's Congress (GPC), which remains unreformed and retains great influence.[2] These concerns played a significant role in the Houthis-Saleh alliance that took over Yemen in September 2014 and provoked a military intervention from neighboring Saudi Arabia in 2015, as discussed later in this chapter.

Yemen faces significant challenges in attempting to remedy the intense polarization it has experienced since its revolution. Indeed, the country faces several difficult issues, including security reform, good governance, and development. There are three major challenges specific to Yemen, however, that will have a major impact on the success of the country's reconciliation: the demand for secession in the South, the Houthi rebellion in the North, and the 2015 civil war. No stability, civil peace, or national reconciliation can be achieved in Yemen if these three key problems are not solved in a sustainable way.

The Southern Cause

The People's Democratic Republic of Yemen, also known as South Yemen, existed from the end of British rule of Aden in 1967 until the South's unification with the North in 1990. Upon the North's capture of Aden in the 1994 civil war, the South's leadership, including former president Ali Salim al-Beidh, fled the country.

There seems to be widespread agreement even among northern Yemenis that southerners endured serious social, economic, and political injustices under the Saleh regime, and that their suffering must be acknowledged. These injustices have been significantly exacerbated during the 2015 Houthis-Saleh civil war where cities like Aden experienced serious damage to infrastructure and high numbers of casualties. Certainly, the mistreatment of the South under Saleh's reign escalated after the 1994 defeat. Examples include the sacking of twenty thousand military personnel immediately after the end of the war, layoffs of large numbers of public-sector employees, and the subsequent marginalization of southerners in state institutions. Even in the industrial sector, the number of factories operating in the South dropped from seventy-five prior to 1994 to only three at the time of writing. Furthermore, southern activists claim that large properties were confiscated and given to army generals, especially those who had participated in the war, under privatization policies adopted by the Saleh regime.[3]

A settlement with the South continues to be a serious challenge to Yemen's long-term stability. In April 2012, Yemen's Socialist Party, the former ruling party of South Yemen, released a statement on what it called the "determinants and outcomes for dialogue and the resolution of the Southern issue." This document outlined twelve confidence-building measures to create an environment conducive to dialogue, among them the granting of martyr status to southerners killed in the 1994 civil war, the return of seized properties to their original owners, and the rehiring of employees and military personnel who were forced into early retirement in 1994.[4]

Still, southerners themselves disagree on two major issues: what would constitute a fair solution for the South and who should rightfully represent southerners in a national reconciliation process. This disagreement even divides members of the southern separatist movement known as al-Hirak, or simply "the Southern Movement."[5] After Saleh's removal, Yemen saw three possible answers to the southern question emerge. The first calls for complete separation from the North and is represented primarily by the last president of the South, al-Beidh. The second, represented by two of al-Beidh's predecessors, Ali Nasir Muhammad and Haidar Abu Bakr al-Attas, supports continued unity with the North under a federal system—with a referendum on whether to maintain unity or secede after a few years.[6] The third option, with no prominent southern advocates, calls for addressing the South's grievances under the prior, unified political structure, without expanding southern autonomy.

Yemen's UN-sponsored National Dialogue Conference (NDC) determined that Yemen should embrace federalism. Following the conclusion of the NDC, a committee agreed in February 2014 that Yemen would become a federal state consisting of six different states, four of them in the North—Azal, Tahama, Saba, and Janad—and two in what was the South—Aden and Hadramout—prior to unification (see fig. 5).[7] Traditional leaders of the Southern Movement like al-Beidh, who did not participate in the Sanaa-based NDC, rejected the federal system and, in particular, the division of what was South Yemen into two federal states. In their view, this would prevent any future formation of a state in the South. In any case, a federal system is a model that Yemen has never tried. Advocates of federalism argue that Yemenis should give it a chance, especially given that both prior models—separation and forced unity—failed miserably. Southerners should not be confident that separation from the North would solve their problems. It did not do so in the past, and al-Beidh himself entered into unity with the North when the collapse of South Yemen became inevitable. Meanwhile, northern Yemenis should realize that the government in Sanaa inflicted

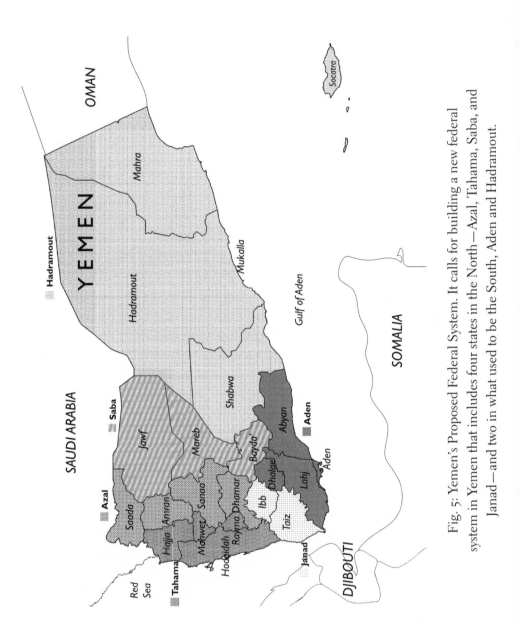

Fig. 5: Yemen's Proposed Federal System. It calls for building a new federal system in Yemen that includes four states in the North — Azal, Tahama, Saba, and Janad — and two in what used to be the South, Aden and Hadramout.

historical injustices against their fellow Yemenis in the South and consider federalism as an opportunity to compensate for these injustices. There is no doubt that the civil war has even hardened the southerners' position, especially that the causes of such a war come from the North, Saleh, and his Houthi allies. Nevertheless, the southerners should not resort to punishing their fellow Yemenis in the North by shattering the country into two states. It is ultimately not the entire North that contributed to the destruction that southerners experienced in the civil war. Northern Yemenis too had their share of suffering under the Houthis-Saleh coup and the destruction emerging from the civil war.

With this in mind, a transparent dialogue within the South, even after the conclusion of the broader national dialogue and the end of the civil war, is needed to deal with the new federal system and to resolve the issue of southern representation in the larger national reconciliation process. Successfully defining southern Yemenis' goals will provide a significant boost to the larger national dialogue and, subsequently, national reconciliation.

Furthermore, the southerners should distinguish between unity by force—as happened in the 1994 war—and unity or federalism that comes by choice. What the southerners have experienced since 1994 is a forced unity under Saleh's regime but not genuine unity with broader Yemeni society in the context of a democratic and pluralistic process. The new Yemeni state must work to represent a break from the country's pre-revolution past. As southerners participate in the country's transition and help shape a government founded on mutual consent, they should withhold judgment on the federal system and continued unity with the North.

The Houthi Conundrum

The origins of the Zaidi Shi'ite Houthi movement trace back to the early 1980s and a religious movement centered on Zaidi religious leader Hussein Badreddin al-Houthi.[8] The Houthis have evolved into a militia based in the northern governorate of Saada. A rejection of American hegemony is key to the group's resistance agenda. Saleh's government launched the first of several wars meant to crush the Houthis in 2004, when he accused them of aiming to topple the central government and implement Shi'ite religious law. The group, however, proved resistant to state efforts to uproot it, enduring a total of six campaigns against it between 2004 and 2010, and apparently continuing to grow in size, though estimates vary widely.

Like the southerners, the Houthis have their own set of grievances. They believe that Saleh's regime subjected them to hardships, including political and religious discrimination; economic marginalization; a lack of government services in Houthi-controlled territories; the exclusion and removal of Houthi preachers and imams; the confiscation of Houthi mosques (especially in the districts of Hajja and Thamar); the suppression of Houthi rituals, particularly the feast of al-Ghadeer, and the imprisonment of some individuals for their participation in the feast; and the issuance of fatwas by some religious leaders designating the Houthis infidels and sanctioning war against them as a jihad.[9]

While al-Hirak in the South has a definite set of options—separation, federation, or unity—the Houthis have struggled to communicate their political agenda clearly. In fact, many Yemenis believe that the Houthis have purposely remained vague about their goals because they are more ambitious than many think. In particular, many Yemenis believe that the Houthis' primary interest is to rule Yemen, not just to seek redress for historical grievances. In any case, when I conducted field research in 2012, determining what exactly the Houthis wanted was perhaps the most difficult task. The Houthis did set down specific conditions for their participation in Yemen's national dialogue. A May 2012 document lists their ten demands, including recognition of the just cause of the South and the North, ensuring a comprehensive agenda for the national dialogue, releasing political prisoners, and rejecting any outside intervention in the dialogue.[10] Beyond participation in the dialogue, however, the Houthis' ultimate objectives remain ill-defined. When I pressed a number of Houthi interviewees, including one of their most senior representatives in Sanaa, on the movement's political goals, their answers tended to be hazy: "We want to be treated like other Yemenis."[11]

The vagueness of the Houthis' political agenda, and other Yemenis' suspicions of the group's real objectives, represent major obstacles to successful reconciliation. Indeed, there are fears that the Houthis hope to revive the political legacy of Yemen's Zaidi community by restoring the imamate that ruled much of Yemen for over a thousand years until its demise in 1962. The Houthis have also been accused of receiving financial and military support from the Iranian government and of advancing its agenda. Iranian support for the Houthis against the Saudi airstrikes in March 2015 is not a secret and confirms the connection—though not the scale of the relationship—with the rebel movement. Of course, if the Houthis do have an Iranian orientation or seek to reclaim control of the country, this would seriously endanger reconciliation, as it would set them on a different track from the rest of the country. National reconciliation would then mean accommodating external agendas, something not traditionally involved in national reconciliation efforts.

Suspicions about the Houthis were confirmed on September 21, 2014, when they stormed Sanaa and seized control of the entire city without any resistance from the Yemeni Army or other security units. Most Yemenis believe that Yemen's security forces permitted the Houthi advance under instructions from former president Saleh, who maintained relations with them after stepping down. Saleh and the Houthis, former adversaries, appeared to have forged a new alliance that targeted common enemies—President Hadi, the Sunni Islamist Islah Party, and General Ali Mohsen al-Ahmar. General al-Ahmar, who led the six wars against the Houthis, defected from Saleh's regime during the revolution that toppled it. In fact, a leaked phone conversation in January 2015 allegedly between Saleh and one of the Houthi leaders—Abdul Wahid Abu Ras, who represented the militant group in the country's national dialogue conference—shows that the Houthis were coordinating military and political activities with Saleh.[12] The new Houthis-Saleh alliance forced al-Ahmar to flee to Saudi Arabia and arrested some of Islah's leaders. In addition, the government of Mohamed Basendwa resigned, and President Hadi had little choice but to sign a "Peace and Partnership Accord" with the Houthis and other political parties.[13] The agreement gave the Houthis a stronger position in ruling the country, but they refused to abide by the security appendix that called for them to withdraw their fighters from Sanaa. Instead, the Houthis continued their advance into other districts of

Yemen, taking Hodeidah, Ibb, Dhamar, and Bayda' by force. Especially in the cities of Rada'a and Ibb, Houthi fighters clashed heavily with tribal forces and al-Qaeda affiliates. With their massive expansion, clashes with local tribes, and crackdown on political opponents, the Houthis in fact laid the ground for a brutal civil war that could extinguish the transition process or even tear Yemen apart, as is discussed in the following section.

The most significant Houthi-related obstacle to reconciliation will likely be convincing the group to relinquish its effective control over parts of the country's north and center, and to instead become a traditional political party. Indeed, by doing so, the Houthis would stand to lose power and even popular support. They may end up with limited representation in parliament, whereas they now control large areas of the provinces of Saada, Amran, Jawf, Sanaa, Hodeidah, Ibb, Dhamar, and Bayda'. Still, Yemen's other political parties will never accept the Houthis retaining their arms. According to Mohammed Qahtan, spokesperson of the powerful Islah Party, "The Hizballah model in Yemen is completely rejected. Under no circumstances should the Houthis keep their weapons and be part of the political process at the same time. We support recognizing their grievances, compensation, apology, whatever they need, but no weapons."[14]

There seems to be widespread acceptance among most political parties that the Houthis have legitimate social, political, and economic grievances. Rehabilitation of the Houthis' war-torn Saada district, and even an apology for the wars fought against them, may be achievable, but the Houthis must be willing to disarm and enter the political process.[15] There will never be a successful transition or effective national reconciliation process if the Houthis choose to continue to "rule without governing" or if they attempt to rule and govern at the same time. By dominating Yemen's political scene, they invite a protracted civil conflict where everyone—especially the Houthis—will lose. Yemen's various political parties, tribal forces, civil society groups, and the general public will never again accept one-party rule, by the Houthis or others, after having revolted against Saleh and overcoming the fear of defying dictatorships. The Houthis should understand that it is particularly difficult for them to play this role as they are publicly viewed as agents of Iran. Yemen's political parties may tolerate the Houthis' increased power for some time, but they will not accommodate it forever. Tribal forces in a number of districts responded with attacks against the Houthis in the very first months of their advance, and such attacks are likely to escalate in the future. The Houthis should make every reconciliatory gesture possible to avoid finding themselves in a civil war, the costs of which would be severe. Finally, it is in the interest of the Houthis and Yemen's other political parties to immediately enter into an inclusive reconciliation process that is built on a genuine partnership where the Houthis can have their historical grievances acknowledged, be compensated for them, and agree to disarm and become a political party on equal footing with all others.

Civil War

Once the Houthis took the capital of Sanaa in alliance with former President Saleh, it became abundantly clear that they aimed to take and hold the entire country and rule by force regardless of any actions by the Hadi government or other political parties. The Houthis-Saleh alliance possessed enough power to effectively overthrow President Hadi on September 21, and proceeded to crush any potential post-coup violence. Undoubtedly, the Houthis-Saleh coup has set the country down the path of a protracted civil war, with President Hadi ultimately hoping to counter the power of the alliance by seeking external intervention, particularly from Saudi Arabia. After Hadi's call for intervention, Saudi Arabia was able to put an alliance together and militarily intervene in Yemen to stop the Houthis-Saleh coup and restore Hadi's reign in Sanaa. Of course, Saudi Arabia had its own interests in mind as it has historically attempted to keep Yemen under its control. The Saudis view Houthis as Iran's proxy, and for them to take power in Yemen has always been a red line for Saudi Arabia.

The Houthis escalated their move against the state in early 2015, progressively taking over institutions of governance. On January 3, they officially rejected the federalism plan—one of the major recommendations of the NDC—and continued to push south toward the city of Taiz.[16] By late January, Houthi actions against President Hadi and his staff led them to effectively place him under house arrest, then dissolve Yemen's parliament on

February 6, forming a "security commission" to lead the country in the interim.[17] The GCC, Arab League, and many tribes within Yemen condemned the move as a coup.[18] Complicating matters, President Hadi escaped house arrest on February 21, escaped to Aden, and rescinded his resignation on the basis that it had been tendered under duress from the Houthis.[19]

International efforts continued to try and contain the crisis even as the Houthis consolidated their rule in Sanaa. The UN Security Council reaffirmed its support for the Hadi government as well as Yemen's sovereignty and unity.[20] Later, on April 14, 2015, the council issued Resolution 2216 calling on the Houthis to "withdraw their forces from all areas they seized," and "immediately and unconditionally relinquish all additional arms seized from military and security institutions, including missile systems."[21] Importantly, the resolution was issued under Chapter 7 of the UN Charter, which empowers the UN Security Council to take military action if necessary. UN envoy Jamal Benomar encouraged various Yemeni political parties to return to dialogue, though they eventually resorted to establishing a "National Salvation Front" to counter the Houthis and Saleh. For their part, the Houthis refused repeated proposals for dialogue, including GCC-hosted talks in Riyadh and an invitation from Benomar to meet in Doha.[22]

Instead, the Houthis-Saleh alliance aimed to institutionalize the coup, signing an agreement with Iran that allowed for twenty-eight flights between Tehran and Sanaa every week, starting on March 1.[23] Additionally, Iran agreed to build a two-hundred-megawatt power plant to addresses Yemen's electricity crisis.[24] The Houthis continued their expansion south, capturing Taiz and moving to besiege the main southern city, Aden, by late March.[25]

On March 25, Saudi Arabia announced the start of Operation "Decisive Storm," with a coalition including GCC member states, Jordan, Morocco, and others launching airstrikes against Houthis-Saleh forces and installations.[26] Hadi immediately fled Yemen for Riyadh as the Houthis continued their advance on Aden.[27] Inside Yemen, Houthis-Saleh alliance forces began to clash with "Popular Resistance" groups in a number of Yemeni cities (Aden, Taiz, Ibb, Dhalae, Mareb, and Shabwa). Tribal forces also joined the resistance against Saleh and the Houthis. With the onset of war, Yemen's transition has unfortunately fallen back into violence, with long-term impacts for the future rebuilding of the Yemeni state. Tellingly, the main UN coordinator of national dialogue and peaceful transition in Yemen, Jamal Benomar, resigned not long after the start of the campaign, on April 15.[28]

Why Did the Transition in Yemen Slide into Violence?

I visited Yemen in 2012, soon after the signing of the GCC initiative and Saleh stepping down. There was a power outage almost every hour in the capital Sanaa. I argued in the *New York Times* at the time that "Yemen can't do it alone," warning that the government must deliver on basic services like water and electricity for the Yemeni people to see value in the transition and in their uprising against the former autocrat, Saleh.[29] Three years on, the transitional government had been discredited by its failures in providing these basic services, unable to change the corrupt nature of governance that had built up under Saleh. This frustration lent appeal to the Houthis' populist slogans of "reducing fuel prices" and "changing the inefficient transitional government," providing the Houthi coup with a veneer of public support. As Adam Baron has noted, "It is a testament to the faults of Yemen's transitional government that even many Yemenis with deep aversion to the Houthis initially welcomed their takeover of Sanaa on September of last year."[30]

A second driver behind discontent has been the real and long-term objectives of the Houthi movement in Yemen. The Houthis fought their first war in 2004 in response to large-scale marginalization by Saleh and deep grievances dating back to the 1980s. However, there have always been questions about the real aims of the Houthis, and what they ultimately want to achieve. Their declared goals of reducing fuel prices and replacing an inefficient government do not justify the alliance with Saleh—their former oppressor—to take over Yemen, the army, and state institutions. Their signing on to the NDC recommendations and the post-coup "peace and partnership" agreement, only to break with both proposals, suggests that they have merely been playing for time.

Mohammed Azzan, a former member of the Believing Youth, the Houthi movement's youth arm, explains that the Zaydi-Houthi ideology legitimizes rebellion, including armed ones, against what they consider an "oppressive ruler." Imam Zaid Ben Ali, the founder in 744 of this ideology, outlined four steps for dealing with an "oppressive ruler": advising the ruler, warning the ruler, disobeying and rebelling against the ruler, and finally, if the first three steps do not work, then initiating an armed rebellion against the "oppressive ruler."[31] In other words, the entire Houthi move against Hadi and the takeover of Sanaa can be simply explained in ideological terms where the Houthis see him as an "oppressive ruler" and that their religious duty—according to their ideology and Zaydi founder—is to wage an armed rebellion against him.

Bruce Riedel presents a not completely different explanation. He wrote in *al-Monitor* that "many suspect their [the Houthis'] goal now is to restore the Zaidi Imamate that ruled North Yemen until the 1962 revolution."[32] In my conversation with many Yemenis in Sanaa, some believe that the group aims even beyond Yemen, much as the Houthis still insist that they seek to cooperate with other Yemeni parties in building a new civil state. In any case, the Houthis-Saleh coup raises serious questions as to whether national dialogue and peaceful transition is even possible given the real agenda of this alliance.

Third, historically, Saudi Arabia treated Yemen as one of its territories. Saudi intervened in internal Yemeni politics, advocated certain agendas, supported leaders like Saleh himself, and bought tribal loyalties within Yemen. This Saudi intervention in domestic Yemeni affairs angered many Yemenis including the Houthis, who probably reacted at some point in response to what they saw as "Saudi Wisayah" (Saudi Guardianship) of Yemen. Saudi Arabia on its end saw the Houthis' growing power as a challenge to Saudi's historical control of Yemen and opted to crush the Houthis before they got out of control. Saudi airstrikes are likely to exacerbate the crisis for Yemen rather than resolving it. Military intervention will overwhelm the transition process by creating deeper divisions within Yemeni society between those who support and oppose the Saudi strikes, destroy infrastructure and state institutions, and create long-term instability. Airstrikes are not in Saudi Arabia's interest either as instability on its southern borders means refugees, poverty, and a lack of security. There is no military solution to the crisis in Yemen, and Saudi airstrikes are likely to make things worse for both Yemen and Saudi Arabia.

Fourth, the failure of the international community to manage the transition in Yemen has significantly contributed to the collapse of the central government, making violence seemingly the only available alternative. In particular, the U.S. prioritization of the fight against al-Qaeda in the Arabian Peninsula (AQAP) has clashed with the goals of a peaceful transition. Although the youth in Yemen are not supporters of AQAP, they did not begin their revolution to fight the group but rather to change a corrupt regime and demand serious development in the country. Nevertheless, the transitional government mobilized its army to fight AQAP in the southern Abyan province even as the capital suffered from electricity outages and over 40 percent unemployment. Government "victories" only displaced AQAP to other remote areas in Yemen, while failing to address the economic and social crisis in Sanaa.

Fifth, the stalled transition reveals the limitations of the GCC initiative's approach of compromising justice for peace. The GCC initiative sacrificed justice and holding Saleh's regime accountable for past human rights violations in order to achieve a smooth exit by Saleh. However, the Yemeni experience has shown that compromising justice for peace can fail to achieve either. Saleh, still the president of the GPC, skillfully used his immunity against prosecution to launch a counter-revolution, this time in alliance with the Houthis. The ability of Saleh to sabotage the transition process gives another important lesson in transitions: the need to address the "deep state." The removal of Saleh while keeping the structure of the dictatorship intact left the transition vulnerable to the machinations of the deep state. In particular, Saleh's former officers maintained their loyalties to the former dictator, and through their positions, were able to sustain a civil war against popular resistance groups and Saudi-led airstrikes.

Sixth, no one can deny the impact of the regional Saudi-Iranian "cold war." Iranian financial and military support to the Houthis emboldened them to defy the state, other political parties, and neighboring Saudi Arabia. Concerns over Iranian expansionism on the peninsula have led Saudi Arabia to react swiftly and with massive airstrikes against the Houthis, regardless of the level of damage this action deals the transition process. Saudi Arabia prioritized what is seen as its own security over what could become a successful transition in Yemen. Vicious competition between the two countries will continue to inflict damage to Yemen's transition. This cold war has created several proxy wars in the region, and reaching an understanding between these two regional power will give hope to solutions in a number of places.

What This Means for National Reconciliation and What Can Be Done to Save Post-Revolution Transitions?

The most dangerous consequence of the Houthis-Saleh coup and the Saudi strikes against them is that force and violence have replaced dialogue and non-violent pressure for change. The coup has put any peaceful transition on hold and undermined the outcomes of the national dialogue conference. As Danya Greenfield puts it, "Sadly, the rebels' tactics affirm the power of the gun over the power of persuasion."[33] The Houthis' bullying of other political parties and the military response from the Saudi-led alliance is likely to leave deep divisions within Yemeni society that will take a long time to heal.

The coup and the resulting civil war may have structurally impacted national reconciliation by inviting the evils of sectarian divisions in Yemen. Yemen's conflict has never been about sectarianism, as the Houthis were originally motivated by economic and political grievances. However, in 2014, the regional context substantially changed. Parties that supported the Zaidi Shi'ite Houthis have been Iran, Hizbullah in Lebanon, and the Shi'ite majority government in Iraq. Hizbullah's leader, Hasan Nasrallah, delivered three speeches strongly criticizing the Saudi intervention in its first month, more than he would normally do in a year.

It is hard to fully explain Yemen's civil war strictly in sectarian terms as it is far more complex than just a Sunni-Shi'ite conflict. Such an oversimplification of seeing it solely through a sectarian prism would understate, for example, the power of the deep state or the role of the corrupt bureaucratic system in resisting change. Nevertheless, the sectarian dimension cannot be ignored. For ordinary Yemenis, this has created a clear polarization that will make national reconciliation particularly hard to achieve.

Civil war and its devastating effect on Yemen's infrastructure and state institutions has added additional layers of complexity to any future post-conflict reconstruction process, one closely linked to successful transition and national reconciliation. The clashes on the ground between tribes and popular resistance groups on one side and the Houthis-Saleh alliance, coupled with bombing by Saudi airstrikes, have caused significant destruction in the country that will require even more reconstruction. A successful reconstruction process will be directly linked to achieving a national reconciliation process.

Additionally, Yemen's civil war has caused deep mistrust among the various political players. Houthi actions in Sanaa—including arresting then-Prime Minister Khaled Bahah along with hundreds of political parties' leaders—have undermined any sense of trust and cooperation engendered by the ten-month National Dialogue Conference. It will be quite difficult for Yemeni political parties to trust the Houthis again, just as the Houthis will find it difficult to trust the parties that supported strikes by Saudi Arabia and other external powers. The victim of this mistrust at the end is Yemen's national reconciliation process.

Finally, the civil war reveals the limits of third-party intervention, such as by the UN, in transition and national reconciliation. Supported by almost the entire Security Council, the UN led the transition process and its national dialogue conference. Jamal Benomar involved himself in the smallest details of the dialogue, negotiating with all parties and forging multiple agreements at every step. Driven by a desire to achieve a grand agreement on the implementation of national dialogue recommendations and prove himself a successful mediator, Benomar ultimately compromised on major principles of the transition process. In particular, he tried to accommodate the Houthis' September coup by refusing to call it a "coup" and pressuring all parties to sign a new "peace and partnership" agreement to contain the effects of the takeover.

Certainly, we should not ignore Benomar's great achievement in managing the national dialogue process. He successfully led a ten-month dialogue that produced a roadmap for Yemen's future transition, one that will always remain a point of reference for future transition debates. Yet Benomar's ambitions blinded him to the need to stand firmly against one party taking over state institutions and sidelining their political opponents by force. Once one party resorts to force, the "neutrality of the mediator" should be discarded, as an impartial mediator should be committed to the fair means of a political process rather than simply the ultimate outcomes. The Houthis-Saleh alliance's use of arms negated the spirit of the national dialogue, and Benomar should have taken a clear position and not allowed his accommodation to be seen as legitimizing the coup.

Despite these challenges, there is still room to salvage Yemen's transition and national reconciliation. First, we must discard the idea that a coup can achieve a peaceful political transition. A coup cannot coexist with a genuine and inclusive transition or effective national reconciliation. This applies not only to the Houthis-Saleh coup but any other attempts by any party in the future.

Second, "Saudi Wisayah" of Yemen needs to shift to a genuine and equal partnership between the two countries on many issues including security and economy. A Saudi top-down approach and constant intervention in Yemeni internal affairs will help neither Yemen nor Saudi Arabia.

Third, the UN and any other third parties should take a principled position of refusing to accommodate a compromised transition. Impartial mediation should keep a strong commitment to the process and keep equal distance from all parties.

Fourth, Saudi-led airstrikes and the bombing of Yemen are not the solution either. War, especially airstrikes, exacerbates conflicts. Saudi airstrikes have certainly created new issues that will burden the transition process including displacement, damage to infrastructure, and increased sectarianism in Yemen. Saudi Arabia should keep in mind that many of these new issues, like displacement, will end up spilling over to its territory.

Fifth, both Saudi Arabia and Iran know that their power struggle has affected many parts of the Middle East and created proxy wars for which the countries in the periphery are paying the price. Forging an understanding in the centers of regional powers—namely Riyadh and Tehran—will significantly reduce tensions in the region. There have not been any direct talks between the regional powers as of June 2015, which leaves the door open not only for government talks but also for non-government talks, commonly referred to as track II diplomacy, to break the impasse.

Sixth, whether there is a war or not, the political process should never stop. It took the parties two months of vicious fighting to agree to a first meeting in Geneva for talks, under the sponsorship of the UN. Channels of communication, direct or indirect, should remain in place, and the search for a political process should be kept active.

Seventh, it does not matter whether one party makes more gains than others. What matters is a commitment to the process of treating all parties equally, with no prejudice. The Houthis are therefore an equal party to all others, and their rights must be guaranteed. Any attempt to control others is what should be rejected. Ultimately, the Houthis disarming and becoming a regular political party is what will keep partnership at the core of transition and national reconciliation in Yemen.

Eighth, Yemen's political process, under the GCC initiative, compromised justice for peace in order to facilitate Saleh's departure in 2011. Compromising justice should never be the case again. Saleh has no place in a future Yemen, and his political role should end immediately.

THREE

Tunisia

The Arab Spring began in Tunisia, where on December 17, 2010, Muhammad Bouazizi lit himself on fire in an expression of frustration at government repression and his economic plight. A wave of anti-regime protests followed and quickly spread to other Arab countries. Tunisia's president and dictator for twenty-three years, Zine El Abidine Ben Ali, fled the country on January 14, 2011, leaving his ruling Dustouri Party to try to pick up the pieces. By March, however, further protests had forced the party to disband and its members from their ministerial posts, paving the way for Beji Caid Essebsi's interim government to take charge. This government ruled the country until elections in October 2011 brought the National Constituent Assembly (NCA) to power.

Ben Ali had seized the presidency from his predecessor, Habib Bourguiba, in a bloodless coup in 1987. Bourguiba was himself an authoritarian and had ruled Tunisia since it gained its independence from France in 1956. While Bourguiba especially played a major role in making Tunisia one of the most socially progressive countries in the Middle East and North Africa, both men were extremely repressive. They left behind legacies of imprisonments, torture, censorship, and brutal crackdowns on their opponents. While Tunisians managed to topple Ben Ali in a matter of weeks, it will take them many years to rebuild and fully transition from more than five decades of dictatorship to sustainable peace and stability. Additionally, the removal of Ben Ali created deep divisions within Tunisian society, especially between supporters of the former regimes, including groups like Nedaa Tunis and al-Mubadara (The Initiative), and those who participated in the uprising, like Islamists, Ettakatol, and the Congress for the Republic

(CPR) party. Indeed, these tensions have led to several severe political crises in the years since Ben Ali's fall.

Despite these challenges, Tunisia's political transition has gone relatively well in the five years since the revolution, and the country has become the Arab Spring's beacon of hope. Since its revolution, it has held not one but two national dialogues that have helped Tunisia's leading political parties forge compromises on its constitution and transitional justice law in spite of significant polarization. Tunisia's new constitution, ratified in January 2014, was hailed as the most progressive in the Arab world. Tunisia's inclusive and pragmatic approach to its transition has allowed it to pursue each of the essential national reconciliation processes. Truth-seeking committees are starting to function, and in the meantime, former regime members suspected of past violations are being held for trial in humane conditions and with protection from torture. Various methods of reparations are being debated and applied, and a number of judges have been dismissed. Nonetheless, the vast majority of the work on each of these national reconciliation processes is yet to be done, and Tunisia must faithfully carry it out to best situate itself for long-term stability and success.

Tunisia seems to be grappling with fewer problematic issues than Libya or Yemen in its post-dictatorship transition to civil peace. Nevertheless, the country still has significant concerns that are hindering its pursuit of national reconciliation and a stable peace. Two examples of these issues are Protection of the Revolution Committees and Salafi-liberal polarization.

Protection of Revolution Committees

On January 14, 2011, Ben Ali escaped Tunisia. Without his iron fist controlling the country, a security vacuum developed. Fears of anarchy and disorder inspired individuals in many Tunisian neighborhoods to respond by forming what later became known as Protection of the Revolution Committees (PRCs). After an interim government headed by Essebsi was formed and restored order, security became less of a concern. The role of the committees thus became less significant, but many adapted to the new reality and registered with the Ministry of the Interior as NGOs, though they continue to call themselves PRCs. As of mid-2014 there were approximately fifteen registered PRCs in Tunisia, each containing a few dozen members.

The PRCs became a source of serious political controversy when many of their members were accused by the opposition of affiliation with the then-ruling Islamist political party, Ennahda. In fact, some Tunisians described the PRCs as "the armed wing of Ennahda."[1] The role of PRCs in Tunisia's post-revolution period became even more controversial when some of their members were accused of being part of a group that attacked and caused the death of Lutfi Nageth, a Tunisian politician affiliated with the then-opposition party Nedaa Tunis, in the city of Tatwain in October 2012. The cause of death is hotly disputed as the medical report stated that Nageth died of a heart attack, while the courts charged ten people with his death. Two of the ten were allegedly Ennahda affiliates, which reinforced the accusation that the PRCs represent the armed wing of Ennahda.[2]

The Tunisian government, which until January 2014 was headed by an Ennahda-led troika coalition, refused to dissolve the PRCs. Ennahda argued for maintaining the PRCs as they were registered with the Ministry of the Interior, had well-defined structures, and were acting in accordance with the law. According to Ennahda politician Said Ferjani, "The executive branch should never dissolve a registered organization simply because this will become a precedent for the government to arbitrarily dissolve other registered organizations. The judiciary, not political decisions, is the authority to terminate the work of a specific organization when violations happen. Who knows who will be in power next! Allowing such a precedent could be manipulated by upcoming governments to silence opposition."[3]

Despite his opposition to dissolving PRCs except through the judicial system, Ferjani conceded that the name of these groups, "Protection of the Revolution," has an exclusionary tone. He agreed that the name infers that the committees have a monopoly on the protection of the Tunisian revolution. Ferjani said, "Revolution is a continuous and cumulative project. It started decades ago and many people contributed to the revolution. There were those who died before they saw freedom. It is therefore not very accurate that some groups today monopolize the cause of revolution protection."[4]

An important dimension of understanding the politics of PRCs is the context of mistrust that engulfs Tunisia's transitional phase. This mistrust explains the opposition's concerns about the exact operations and goals of the PRCs. Suspicion of them was exacerbated by the Nageth killing. Additionally, PRCs clashed with the powerful Tunisian General Labor Union (UGTT), contributing to the buildup of tensions between that organization and Ennahda, and the deterioration of trust between the groups.

The concerns of the opposition about the existence of PRCs are totally understandable. The opposition, however, should assess whether dissolving the PRCs through a political decision would genuinely serve the long-term democratic transition in Tunisia. In fact, it is in the opposition's interests to channel efforts to dissolve the PRCs not through parliament but strictly through the judicial system. Dissolving organizations through the NCA or the executive will confuse the democratic process and prevent the separation of powers. Instead of lobbying the NCA and protesting in the streets, the opposition should focus on collecting solid evidence of illegal PRC behavior to present in court. This would make the PRCs more careful about behaving according to the law, lessening concerns that they would act as intimidators. Holding PRCs accountable to legal standards will only strengthen the democratic transition and rule of law, and contribute to creating common ground where all parties can work together.

Salafi-Liberal Polarization

Tunisia also faces at least one kind of polarization that is more extreme than in other Arab cases: the vast—and growing—divide between secular liberals and ultraconservative Salafi Islamists. In fact, polarization between Islamism and secularism in Tunisia manifests itself in many ways including between Islamist Ennahda and several secular left parties. However, what makes this polarization significantly sharper and a threat to the transition process in Tunisia is the involvement of Salafists who take it to a new level that includes the use of violence. Another layer of polarization also exists within the Islamists themselves, in particular between ultraconservative Salafists and the moderate Ennahda party.

Tunisian secularism is vibrant and unparalleled in the Arab world. Under Bourguiba and Ben Ali, Tunisia was, for example, the only Arab country to ban the hijab in state institutions. Its jihadi Salafis, meanwhile, demand a purely religious state and have shown their willingness to attack cultural activities they deem un-Islamic.[5] Thus, the two parties are both at extremes, one banning the hijab and the other attacking cultural activities. This is not to suggest that either one of them is right, but the sheer distance between these two cultural extremes makes the likelihood that they will coalesce around one vision for the state rather slim, while a confrontation, possibly even a violent one, is certainly a possibility and may very well be in the making.

Moreover, Salafis, who were imprisoned or driven underground before the revolution, have been growing in strength. Jailed Salafi leaders, including Abu Ayadh, the leader of Ansar al-Sharia in Tunisia, were released as part of the country's post-revolution amnesty. Ansar al-Sharia's annual conference in 2012 attracted roughly five thousand attendees, and an estimated fifty thousand were expected to participate in the 2013 conference in Kairouan before the government decided to prevent the conference by force and blocked the roads leading to the city.[6]

This huge ideological gap between liberals and Salafis has left the moderate Islamist Ennahda party, almost by default, to occupy the Tunisian middle. The upshot is that one can witness Ennahda figures being described — often simultaneously — as closet fundamentalists by liberals and as infidels and tyrants by Salafis. Rafik Abdul Salam, a former foreign minister of Tunisia and Ennahda leader, explained, "Salafis accuse us of being infidels [for not representing Islam well] and the Tunisian left accuses us of allying with the radicals [for not being tough enough on Salafis]."[7]

Salafi-liberal polarization is occasionally exacerbated by violent incidents, which raise serious concerns about the possibility of coexistence between the two groups amid the deterioration of security in the country. In the five years after the revolution, NCA members Chokri Belaid and Mohamed al-Brahmi were assassinated, tourists were targeted in bombings in the cities of Sousse and Monstir, the Bardo museum in Tunis was attacked in March 2015 leaving twenty-one tourists dead, and a number of violent clashes took place between the Tunisian Army and extremist groups in the Sha'anbi Mountains. Especially after the government labeled Ansar al-Sharia a terrorist organization, fears of an impending security crisis have become more pronounced. In February 2014, Interior Minister Lotfi Ben Jeddou announced that Tunisia's National Guard had killed Kamel Gadhgadhi, the Islamist extremist who was the chief suspect in Belaid's assassination.[8]

With the increased level of individual freedoms and openness in post–Arab Spring Tunisia, it is unlikely that either the radical Salafis or the liberal left will be able to marginalize or eliminate the other. Tunisians will have to learn that peaceful coexistence between different viewpoints is the best way to deal with this polarization. To replace polarization with sustainable coexistence on the one hand, and to effectively respond to violence on the other, Tunisians need to embrace a strategy built on three pillars: rule of law, socioeconomic development, and enlightenment.

Rule of Law: Tunisia's liberals must understand that Salafis, first and foremost, are Tunisian citizens. Like all other Tunisians, they have the full rights associated with their citizenship. They are free to assemble and advocate for their beliefs, and the state should protect them as long as they remain committed to non-violence. Ennahda leader Said Ferjani argued that "the state must deal with the Salafi violence firmly and all within the rule of law. This is necessary first for the state to establish and maintain order, and second to ensure the rights of the non-violent Salafis—the Scientific Salafis—to practice their beliefs."[9]

Socioeconomic Development: A major cause of the revolution and the subsequent radicalization and violence is underdevelopment. It is no surprise that the violence and clashes that occurred with the police in May 2013 took place in Tadamun, one of the poorest neighborhoods in Tunis. The state must face these realities and implement economic development policies in these areas.

Enlightenment: "Counter Salafism by Malekism," said Ferjani. While Salafism leans toward conservatism and extremism, Malekism focuses on knowledge, reason, and enlightenment. The majority of Tunisia's Sunni Muslims follow the Maleki school of Fiqh, or Islamic jurisprudence.

Kairouan, about one hundred miles south of Tunis, is the capital of Malekism, and Al-Zaytouna in Tunis is one of the Muslim world's first universities. Ferjani pointed out that "Tunisia defeated Fatemism and rejected Wahhabism by Malekism. Our Maleki ancestors would not accept their teaching being hijacked by Salafism today. Our ancestors taught us how to fight with knowledge and that is how we can face Salafism today."[10] Alia Alani, an historian at Manouba University and specialist in Islamic movements, explained that in 1803, the founder of Wahhabism sent a strong letter to the governor of Tunisia, Hamouda Basha, asking him to follow the conservative Wahhabist school of thought. It was said that the governor consulted the Maleki scholars at Al-Zaytouna and twenty of them drafted a response rebutting—from a religious point of view—the principles of Wahhabism.[11] Tunisia's long history of moderate Islam should be highlighted in order to combat extremism.

FOUR

Issues of Reconciliation

A Comparative Perspective

The issues that the three countries under study must tackle highlight a number of facts about the nature of transition processes and the prospect of Arab Spring societies' transitioning to stable peace and embracing national reconciliation. All three cases seem to follow the same principle: the sudden removal of power structures and the change process that follows generate profoundly polarizing issues which significantly threaten the likelihood of Arab societies' making such a successful transition. There does not seem to be a way to avoid this, and so Arab Spring societies must face these issues to enhance their chances to transition peacefully and avoid sliding into violence. Arab countries that have not yet experienced the fall of their dictatorships must be prepared to deal with similar issues in the future. Those attempting to remove authoritarian regimes must also prepare to address a number of highly polarizing issues that could simply lead to widespread anarchy.

There is no one set of issues that challenges reconciliation, peace, and stability following regime change. Rather, they vary widely and depend on the historical context and specific conditions of each country. Nevertheless, a pattern of similar issues, at least to a limited extent, should not be ruled out. In fact, disarmament—though in different forms—has appeared as an issue in all three countries that experienced regime change and has proven to be a major challenge. As described in the preceding chapters, the magnitude of the disarmament problem differs vastly from one place to another. The most severe problems with disarmament have been in Libya, where former revolutionaries have refused to give up their arms and have presented themselves as an alternative, or at least a parallel, power to the formal state. In Yemen, the Houthi rebels have been unwilling to accept disarmament as an issue on the agenda of the National Dialogue Conference. In fact, the Houthis expanded their power, influence, and control over territories after Ali Abdullah Saleh stepped down. During Saleh's reign, the Houthis were in control of the province of Saada, but less than three years after Saleh's exit, they took control of large parts of Yemen including Amran, Jawf, Sanaa, Ibb, Hodeidah, Aden, Taiz, and other provinces. There is no doubt that failure to disarm the Houthis after Saleh's removal from power led to the 2015 civil war where the rebels thought they could control the country with their heavy weaponry. In Tunisia, the Protection of the Revolution Committees (PRCs), though they were not armed, became the center of a national controversy when they refused to disband after the removal of Zine El Abidine Ben Ali's regime and continued to operate freely in the country. Polarization grew much stronger when the Ennahda-led government rejected dissolution of the PRCs and the opposition treated them as Ennahda's "military wing."

One common theme that emerged in all three cases highlights the power of the deep state and the ability of old regimes to wage counter-revolutions. It is obvious that the removal of Saleh, Muammar Qaddafi, and Ben Ali did not dismantle their influential networks within all state institutions. These networks remained active and able to respond to revolutionary forces, transition, and change. Yemen provides the prime example where Saleh's connections with army generals facilitated the September 21 coup and allowed the Houthis to take over the capital without any resistance. In Libya, Khalifa Haftar, one of the generals that participated in the 1969 Qaddafi coup, was also able to form an alliance of militias and wage a civil war against the militias of the February 17 Revolution. He even pressed to abolish the Political Isolation Law passed by the General National Congress that prevented old regime figures from holding public office. Supported by the House of Representatives, Haftar later became the head of the army. Even in Tunisia, with its peaceful transition, former regime elements used their networks within the state to form a new political party—Nedaa Tunis—and win the elections and the presidency in December 2014. Although not one of the cases studied in this research, Egypt's experiences emphasize the same conclusion with the deep state's responding to the democratic process by removing an elected president from power, Muhammad Morsi; releasing former regime figures from prison; and arresting most of the youth leaders of the 2011 uprising against Hosni Mubarak. This comparison shows clearly that counter-revolution is a reality—not a myth—and that former regime elements could come back in different forms and sabotage the entire transition process. Deep states are not dismantled by the mere removal of autocrats, and systems that were built over decades remain a major obstacle to transition, peace, and change.

Nevertheless, it is critical to avoid blaming old regimes for all the problems that countries face in their transition to civil peace. Many of the issues that generate polarization and prevent reconciliation are actually the product of the transitions themselves, and in many cases, they are the product of the agents of change. These issues are new to the countries as they emerge after the removal of the old regimes. It is inaccurate to state that Libya's transition is struggling only because of Qaddafi. Indeed, most of Libya's polarizing issues, namely disarmament, the culture of the victor, and displacement, are the products of the revolutionaries themselves. Revolutionaries—or militias, as some call them—and other actors played a critical role in pushing the country into a new civil war. Revolutionaries in Libya have generated polarization and caused more damage to their revolution and to the entire transition process than the former regime and its loyalists. Many revolutionaries developed an interest in the status quo because a transition to a stronger state would decrease their power. Indeed, the influence and resources they currently enjoy provide little incentive to aid the transition to a strong state where they would become accountable to central institutions. Resisting integration has become a pervasive pattern among many revolutionaries who prefer to maintain their own power.

Civil wars, on the other hand, emerged as facts in two cases: Yemen and Libya. This confirms the longstanding argument about the nature of transitions being complicated, chaotic, and sometimes violent. If unable to handle transitions, societies could very well slide into violence so something that begins as a non-violent call for change—as in Yemen—may eventually end up with a brutal civil war, and even drag neighboring countries, such as Saudi Arabia in Yemen's case, into the chaos. Civil wars have a devastating impact on transitions, and in the cases of Yemen and Libya are likely to overwhelm the reconciliation process for years if not decades. Civil wars generate new issues and create new divisions that may shatter a society's social fabric. The Houthis in Yemen were partners in the National Dialogue Conference, but it will take years of intensive reconciliation work for them to regain the trust of the rest of the political parties. Similarly, Libya Dawn and Operation Dignity have caused serious damage against each other, and they too will require massive reconciliation before they can work together to rebuild Libya.

Transitioning to civil peace and national reconciliation is not a linear process. Countries do not follow the same transitional trajectory and do not necessarily make steady progress all the time. They often go "one step forward and two steps back," making progress in one area and suffering setbacks in others. Transitioning to civil peace, in other words, is a complicated process and can go in any direction at any point. Yemen, for example, made slow progress in tackling issues of national reconciliation. Tunisia moved significantly faster, while Libya has actually regressed for most of the first four years since the removal of the Qaddafi regime.

Transitioning to sustainable reconciliation is a process of trial and error in the post–Arab Spring societies. That is, all three countries, to varying degrees, have demonstrated a lack of indigenous expertise in dealing with issues of polarization and reconciliation. This is expected, as Arab societies in general have experienced a state of stagnation in the past half-century and have not produced scholars well versed on how to deal with the challenges of transition and reconciliation. Lack of expertise in transition and reconciliation has been apparent in many areas including, but not limited to, disarmament, demobilization, and reintegration (DDR); displacement and refugee repatriation; national dialogue; security reform; transitional justice; and institutional reform.

Yemeni, Libyan, and Tunisian societies need to pursue one major solution to dealing with these challenges. They need to confront rather than

Table 1: Mapping Reconciliation in Post-Revolution Transition in Yemen, Libya, and Tunisia

	Libya	Yemen	Tunisia
Issues of Reconciliation	• Disarmament of revolutionaries/militias • Displacement (refugees and internally displaced persons) • Civil war • Polarizing narrative: "Culture of the Victor"	• The Houthi rebellion and takeover • The South Yemen issue	• Salafi-Liberal polarization • Protection of Revolution Committees • Marginalization of specific areas, like the west
National Dialogue	• No national dialogue as of September 2015 • Top politicians and community leaders have attempted to initiate dialogues • Intra-revolutionary violence and civil war have prevented any substantive progress	• Ten month, UN-sponsored National Dialogue Conference (NDC) in 2013–2014 • Was broadly representative with 565 participants; only al-Hirak boycotted • Produced approximately 1,400 recommendations, but implementation has been lacking	• Two domestically driven dialogues; led by civil society and transitional presidency • Included over a hundred political parties and civil society organizations • Produced transitional roadmap, paved the way for elections, and laid foundations for a constitution and transitional justice law
Truth Seeking and Grappling with the Past	• A strong desire to pursue the full truth • Forty-two years of controversies, abuses, and unanswered questions to be investigated • Debate over how far back to delve: 2011 revolution, Qaddafi's rule, independence?	• A tendency to ignore the past • Regime and opposition elites alike are worried about their actions being exposed • Concern over possible social unrest in a tribe-dominated society • Debate over possible starting points: 2011 revolution, 1994 civil war, Saleh's rule?	• Established Truth and Dignity Commission to investigate the past • Less concern about social tensions; no tribal structure and many knew those responsible for torture • Settled on a 1955 start date after considering the start of Ben Ali's and Bourguiba's terms

(continued)

	Libya	Yemen	Tunisia
Victims and Reparations	• Large numbers of victims due to Qaddafi's wide-ranging social policies • Financial resources available but moral reparations are just as important after trauma • Victimization is ongoing due to continued tribal violence and civil war	• Many victims but extreme lack of funds • President Hadi has apologized for Saleh's wars against Saada and the South • Transitional government began reinstating purged southern military personnel and compensating families that lost land • Saleh received immunity and was permitted to remain involved in politics • The ruling party remained in place without undergoing any reform • No real progress on prosecutions, a transitional justice law, or lustration as of September 2015	• Consensus that victims need compensation • Lack of financial resources, though numbers of victims are relatively small • Issue is politically sensitive because most of the victims are Islamists • Tunisia has considered providing lump-sum payments and government jobs, both of which are problematic • Individual accountability is to be applied through special courts according to the transitional justice law • The former ruling party was dissolved, but parliament ultimately did not exclude past regime figures from politics
Dealing with the Former Regime: Accountability and Lustration	• Excessive pursuit of accountability has bled over into revenge and retaliation • Militias have imprisoned, tortured, and tried former regime figures • The justice system is corrupted and overwhelmed • Political Isolation Law has resulted in an extensive and damaging purge		
Institutional Reform	• Very little progress due to violence and civil war • Revolutionaries have sought to purge the judiciary • Comprehensive reform of the bureaucratic system is needed	• President Hadi attempted to reform the Ministries of Defense and Interior but with negative results • NDC recommended extensive, wide-ranging reforms • Implementation challenged by former regime's power and Houthi takeover	• Pursuing vetting is the approach to reform • Progress in reforming the security, media, administration, and judiciary sectors • New, independent institutions have grown out of civil society (e.g., Committee against Torture)

avoid issues that threaten to derail transitions to civil peace and sustainable reconciliation. These issues must be handled, however, in an inclusive and transparent manner. A comprehensive national dialogue can provide a vehicle for dealing with these issues. It will be an extremely difficult process for many Libyans, for example, to reconcile with Qaddafi loyalists. Still, Arab Spring populations must know that regardless of how difficult it is to participate in a dialogue with elements of former regimes, they have no choice but to bridge the chasms and attempt to move forward. Of course, reconciliation will have to include only those members of the former regimes that were not directly involved in human rights violations. Others will also be included in reconciliation, but within a framework of transitional justice and restorative justice, as the following chapters of this book explain.

PART II

Approaches of Reconciliation

FIVE

National Dialogue

National dialogue, as defined by the United States Institute of Peace, is "a dynamic process of joint inquiry and listening to diverse views, where the intention is to discover, learn and transform relationships in order to address practical and structural problems in a society." Such forums aim to expand political, often post-conflict, negotiations beyond political and military leadership with the aim of being more inclusive of society in general. Indeed, according to Katia Papagianni, national dialogues involve a cross-section of both victims and aggressors in an effort to "move away from elite-level deal making by allowing diverse interests to influence the transition negotiations." While dialogues are meant to aid the process of healing and reconciling differences between formerly opposing sides, the process also grants non-elites the opportunity to influence government decision-making at the local and possibly national levels.[1]

Because national dialogues are meant to involve broad swaths of society, it is difficult to determine how best to select participants, as well as the appropriate numbers. Generally, a broad cross-section is preferable, yet direct voting on participants is often too time-consuming and labor intensive to be practical, particularly in a post-conflict or transitional environment. Participants in most dialogues are therefore chosen by caucus-type constituencies or appointed. As a consequence, national dialogues are not completely grassroots, yet may still faithfully represent society at large. At a minimum, as described by the United Nations Development Programme (UNDP), a national dialogue "brings together a diverse set of voices to create a microcosm of the larger society." Significantly, extremists often form a part of this microcosm, and therefore another question arises about how national dialogues should include such figures. One popular solution is to begin the dialogue only with moderate parties, meaning those who are willing to work toward resolution without conditions, before adding in holders of more extreme views. In this way, moderates can work to strengthen public support for the dialogue before those tending toward extremism join the process.[2]

Because national dialogues usually take place after conflicts, it is important for participants to be committed to the process of dialogue, rather than seeking retribution or victory. Certainly, "dialogue is the implementation of a deliberative method. It is important for the public to discuss and deliberate."[3] To accomplish this, it is helpful for the public to cultivate a feeling of ownership over the process and become invested in the dialogue. Natalia Mirimanova suggests bringing together people who "have a common ground that is unrelated to the conflict, such as a profession, gender, generation, societal role, etc." This can help create solidarity across lines of conflict, as well as enhance the feeling of working toward a common goal. Because dialogues are intended to alter thinking about others as enemies in the interest of moving forward peacefully, holding common goals is important.[4]

The timing of national dialogues is also critical. Indeed, participants cannot be expected to focus on common goals and reorient their thinking toward one another while violence rages on. The UNDP argues, "Dialogue requires that basic conditions be present first. When violence, hate, and mistrust remain stronger than the will to forge a consensus, or if there is a significant imbalance of power or a lack of political will among the participants, then the situation might not be ripe for dialogue. Moreover, participants must feel free to speak their minds without fear of retribution, or rejection."[5] There is rarely a specific moment when timing is optimal for national dialogue, but if the above conditions are met, it is likely that a productive dialogue can be launched.

In addition, dialogue processes must be governed by specific rules and values. Maria Jessop and Alison Milofsky identify joint ownership, learning, humanity, inclusiveness, and long-term perspective as important organizing principles, and describe transparency, authenticity, patience, equality, and flexibility as additional essential features. Likewise, though national dialogues necessarily involve free-form discussions, they are not disorganized processes. Instead, post-conflict dialogues must be taken seriously, as they are "highly structured" processes that require "expert facilitation by dialogue practitioners familiar with the context of the conflict."[6]

Further aiding in the organization and promotion of the success of national dialogues is the clear definition of its mandate. Organizers must be specific about the exact goals of the dialogue to ensure that participants can work effectively toward such ends.[7] Certainly, dialogue is more than a process; it is meant to effect change. "People participate in dialogue, not only because they like it, but because they want results. If people participate in a dialogue that subsequently produces no results, then dialogue will begin to abuse its limits as a method, and people will become disillusioned, with the consequent risk not only to the dialogue process itself but to the system as a whole."[8] To maintain faith in the dialogue process, tangible goals must be sought and suggestions implemented.

Many goals of dialogues, which often include changing how people think and the ways they resolve conflict, are intangible and difficult to measure. Although no party "wins" in a national dialogue, new ways of handling conflict and seeing adversaries can emerge. As Papagianni puts it, "In some cases, the dialogue processes may not reach their formal goals but may still manage to avert conflict and to convince political actors to continue engaging with the political process. In other cases, national dialogue may reach all their formal goals but essentially fail because they have not included the major political forces of the country and to maintain a level of support for the political process among the public." In this respect, national dialogues require patience and often involve a long-term commitment, as such processes can last "anywhere from ten minutes to ten years."[9]

Perhaps the most difficult question regarding national dialogues is how to link the progress they make to institutional reforms that will perpetuate peace. Indeed, part of the challenge is transferring what is learned in such forums and applying it to constructive action on the ground. Mirimanova explains, "In order to contribute to peace and achieve the goal of conflict transformation, dialogue projects need to be complemented by advocacy and active promotion of structural change. Such projects are built on a dialogue foundation and yet evoke critical thinking in broader society, and promote a change in institutions and norms." Certainly, conflicts begin most often due to structural problems and therefore can only be fully resolved when these are considered and amended. Ultimately, in the UNDP's words, "dialogue is not a one-size-fits-all strategy, it is not a panacea for resolving all the world's crises. . . . Rather it represents just one tool in policymakers' toolbox . . . one that is especially useful when the parties to a conflict are not ready yet for formal negotiations." Dialogue therefore should be used in conjunction with other methods of conflict resolution to ensure successful change and the perpetuation of peace and stability.[10]

National dialogue in countries that have undergone regime change during the Arab Spring will have to consider all of these elements and challenges. Indeed, in framing national dialogues, Tunisia, Yemen, and Libya must determine the proper timing; select appropriate participants, specifically when it comes to the inclusion of revolutionaries and members of former regimes; ensure that participants are representative of and enjoy legitimacy with their constituencies; and, most importantly, develop a mechanism for translating agreements to action on the ground. There are no easy ways to resolve these issues, especially in a post–Arab Spring era that has been characterized by the absence of security, a lack of strong leadership, and overall uncertainty about how to transition from dictatorship to civil peace. This period of confusion has made national dialogues even more challenging, and it will likely affect their outcomes.

This chapter argues that Yemen, Tunisia, and Libya have taken three different approaches to national dialogue, and that these distinct approaches are likely to influence—and, in some cases, have already influenced—the overall transition process. Yemen relied primarily on a structured and UN-assisted national dialogue. Meanwhile, Tunisia opted to develop a home-grown national dialogue driven mainly by local civil society organizations (CSOs). With the assistance of the UN envoy Bernardino Leon, Libya was able to hold peace talks among the various parties of the civil war but not an inclusive national dialogue that involves Libya's political and civil society mosaic. Among these three approaches, Tunisia's model is likely the most effective approach to help end the polarization that has engulfed societies undergoing political transition following the Arab Spring.

Yemen

Within the framework of the Gulf Cooperation Council–engineered power transition deal and with the vigorous support of the UN and its special envoy, Jamal Benomar, the Yemeni government launched its widely representative National Dialogue Conference (NDC) on March 13, 2013. This start date was chosen "to commemorate the martyrs who fell during the 'Friday of Dignity' massacre, which was carried out in Change Square by Saleh's snipers."[11] Setting such a start date sent a message affirming the new government's commitment to upholding the goals of Yemen's revolution. The NDC lasted for ten months, finishing its work on January 25, 2014. As a nationwide reconciliation exercise, the primary goal of the conference was to bring various parties together to create a roadmap for Yemen's post-uprising transition and to develop solutions for the most serious problems it faces. Although the NDC encountered tremendous challenges during its ten-month duration, it was successful in recommending a series of sensible solutions to some of Yemen's most deep-seated conflicts. The Houthis-Saleh coup in September 2014 does not make the conference any less successful as its recommendations—or roadmap—will remain a point of reference guiding debate and providing a foundation for any future settlement of Yemen's 2015 civil war.

With 565 participants, the NDC reflected the diverse makeup of Yemen's political landscape. Some organizations and parties chose their own representatives (within guidelines), while the women, youth, and civil society representatives were chosen by committees. The resulting list of delegates was produced by Benomar in collaboration with the Yemeni government and various political parties. President Abd Rabbu Mansour Hadi had the final say on the NDC's composition. Most Yemeni political parties participated in the conference, including Ali Abdullah Saleh's General People's Congress (GPC) with 112 members; the Southern Movement, or al-Hirak, with

85 members (though one branch of al-Hirak, led by Ali Salim al-Beidh, re-fused to participate); the Yemeni Congregation for Reform, or Islah Party (a Muslim Brotherhood affiliate), with 50 members; Ansarullah, or the Houthi movement, with 35 members; the Yemeni Socialist Party with 37 members; the Justice and Building Party with 7 members; the Ba'ath Party; the Nasser-ist Party; and a new Salafi party called the Rashad Union. To ensure even more wide-ranging popular input, members of the NDC conducted field visits in April and May 2013, meeting with nearly "11,000 personalities repre-senting officials and civil society from across Yemen."[12]

By engaging in inclusive and continuous dialogue throughout its ten-ure, the NDC was expected to discuss and provide solutions to Yemen's most serious issues and persistent challenges. A successful NDC, in terms of providing solutions and engaging in their implementation, would result in sustainable national reconciliation. The NDC agenda was quite ambitious and included not only issues of conflict but also the nation's state-building and development agenda. In addition to the question of southern seces-sion and the Saada issue involving the Houthis in the North, the NDC discussed national concerns such as displacement, terrorism, human rights violations including forced disappearances, problems of state-building, de-termining the principles and foundation of the constitution, the electoral system, legislative and judicial authority, good governance, and develop-ment. The NDC was tasked with considering the identity of the nation itself and related issues such as its name, religion, national language, whether the source of legislation would be secular or Sharia law, and international commitments.[13]

Despite being the first of its kind in Yemen, and indeed in the entire Arab world, and despite facing serious social and political challenges, the NDC made a substantial contribution toward ensuring the success of Ye-men's transition process. If its recommendations and proposed solutions are implemented even after the 2015 civil war, the NDC will certainly have succeeded in bridging the divides of Yemeni society and bringing parties one step closer to sustainable reconciliation. The dialogue culminated with a final report that contains approximately 1,400 recommendations. With the exception of the committee for the southern issue, all committees on other subjects completed their work and filed definitive final reports. One of the NDC's most noteworthy contributions was to set the stage for an agreement on the structure of the state. On February 2, 2014, the Regions Defining Committee, which was commissioned by the NDC, approved a federalist structure consisting of six regions, four in the North and two in the South. This would be the first time that Yemen has adopted a federal system, demonstrating the failure of a two-state structure and of a system of forced unity, both of which the Yemeni government has implemented in the past. Observers consider federalism to be the system most likely to provide a sustainable solution to the issue of southern secession.[14]

Also helping to resolve issues between the federal government and the South, the NDC reached agreements to address the grievances southern Yemenis have suffered following the country's unification. Specifically, on August 21, 2013, the government expressed contrition "for the war of the summer of 1994 and what the previous government did against the southerners, considering that a historic mistake that cannot be repeated." The government also apologized "to residents of northern Saada province over repeated military campaigns that Saleh's administration launched against rebels there between 2004 and 2010." Importantly, the government not only granted emotional and symbolic support to the troubled areas in the North and South, but also provided much-needed material assistance. An agreement was reached to establish "two compensation funds . . . one to help reconstruction of the country's northern and southern regions . . . while the second would compensate victims of political violence."[15]

On the central issue of institutional reform, the NDC's State Building Working Group reformed the justice system in September 2013. It determined that 15 percent of the Judicial Supreme Council will be academics, while 15 percent will come from the lawyers' syndicate. Judges will be elected and confirmed by parliament, not appointed by the executive. In addition, the NDC reached an agreement to create a truly independent anti-corruption body to fight the rampant corruption that engulfed the entire state's bureaucratic system under Saleh.[16]

The achievements of the NDC went beyond the pressing political problems facing Yemen's transition, however. It addressed social issues that have long been ignored. The NDC reached an agreement to abolish early child-hood marriage and advance the rights of women, including granting them 30 percent representation in public office. Furthermore, "The National Dialogue also broke down important social barriers, and delegates empha-sized an important cultural shift with conservative Islamist leaders [sitting] in working groups led by women and older tribal sheikhs engaged on equal footing with youth leaders challenging traditional norms."[17]

Despite the remarkable progress of the NDC and the helpful solutions it proposed, Yemen's transition process remains far from complete and con-tinues to encounter serious challenges. A major obstacle is a nationally ac-cepted solution to the issue of the South. Obviously, the southern issue was not resolved, though the NDC attempted to address it. Ultimately, the con-ference was unable to develop a formula that would unite all stakeholders toward a single solution. Muhammad Ali Ahmed, chair of the "8+8" sub-committee (it included eight northerners and eight southerners) to resolve the southern issue, walked out of the talks on November 27, 2013. He said, "The decision to withdraw from the talks came after we exhausted all politi-cal efforts to reach a just solution for the southern question." Equally con-cerning is the boycott of the NDC by key southern leaders, despite exten-sive negotiations about joining the dialogue. Iconic leaders of the southern movement like Ali Salim al-Beidh, Haidar Abu Bakr al-Attas, and Ali Nasir Muhammad, all of whom were presidents of South Yemen, rejected partici-pation and instead demanded complete separation from the North.[18]

Equally threatening to Yemen's long-term stability is the Houthi problem, discussed in chapter 2. Although the Houthis participated fully in the NDC, helping to draft several agreements dealing with northern issues during the conference, implementation has proven to be another matter. Conflict in the North continued to worsen, and after the conclusion of the NDC, the Houthis expanded from Saada to adjacent territories, in particular the prov-ince of Amran, before taking over Sanaa and much of central Yemen in September 2014. The Houthis raised the slogan of implementing the rec-ommendations of the NDC, but on the ground they built alliances with the former dictator, Saleh, and together waged their coup against the state, causing a civil war and external military intervention by Saudi Arabia.

One major criticism of the NDC has been the role of external actors, as the UN was heavily involved in the process. The "wide[ly] held perception that [the NDC was] an externally lead process with an international rather than an indigenous local agenda" harmed its credibility.[19] Reservations over the role of external actors focused mostly on questions about the model's sustainability and the absence of local ownership of the dialogue process. Another major criticism of the UN intervention in Yemen has been that Benomar accommodated the Houthis-Saleh alliance on September 21, 2014, and continued to push the parties for an agreement regardless of its content. It seems as if Benomar was driven by the need to save his mission; in order to do so, he continued to accommodate the coup and refused to take a position against the use of force by two parties against the rest of the Yemeni political parties. In other words, his agreeing to work with the Houthis-Saleh alliance despite their use of force led to his compromising what should be an impartial mediation process.

Tunisia

Tunisia successfully elected its National Constituent Assembly (NCA) to serve as a transitional legislative body soon after Zine El Abidine Ben Ali fled in November 2011. Most of Tunisia's political parties managed to win a number of seats, securing representation in the NCA. The existence of a democratically elected and generally representative assembly with a mandate to manage the transition process raises questions about the necessity of a formal national dialogue. The national dialogue process, however, plays a different and important role for countries undergoing political transition, making it essential even in the presence of a formally elected body like the NCA.

Powerful decision-makers who are not currently sitting in government positions or in the NCA often have opportunities to participate in national dialogue. Rachid Ghannouchi, for instance, the iconic leader of Ennahda, who is not an NCA representative, leads his party's national dialogue negotiations. He is fully empowered to make decisions and compromises that Ennahda representatives in the NCA are not able to make due to political considerations and concerns about reelection. As Houda Cherif, a politician and member of the political bureau of the Republican Party (in 2013), which was a main part of the national dialogue, put it, a national dialogue "is the dialogue of the decision-makers." The involvement of top leaders from major political movements makes national dialogues smoother and much more likely to arrive at decisions that will be accepted by their constituencies. Similarly, the participation of political parties not represented in the NCA is as important. It allows them to feel included along with their constituents, and therefore they are more likely to accept the government's policies and feel that their interests have been taken into consideration in the decision-making process.[20]

Furthermore, national dialogues can raise public awareness of the issues at stake and prepare the population for the implementation of new policies following the dialogue. In contrast, most NCA debate is conducted behind closed doors, and so the public is not fully aware of the issues at hand or how they will likely be resolved. Most importantly, unlike in the NCA, participation in a national dialogue is voluntary, and parties can withdraw at any time. The participating parties are not obliged to develop any specific outcomes. These dynamics create a more relaxed environment, which enables constructive and honest discussion that is more likely to lead to consensus.

Tunisia has had two national dialogue initiatives since its revolution. The first was launched by President Moncef Marzouki in April 2012. It focused mostly on three objectives: agreeing on a roadmap for national elections and drafting a new constitution, coming to a consensus on the rejection of violence as a political tool, and ensuring prioritization of the country's economy. The other national dialogue was launched by the Tunisian General Labor Union (UGTT) in October 2012. Most of Tunisia's political parties accepted the UGTT's initiative and joined the conference. Although Ennahda and the Congress for the Republic (CPR) did not participate in the first meetings, they later attended the dialogue. In total, approximately sixty political parties and fifty CSOs participated in the national dialogue conference, which concluded in May 2013. The UGTT national dialogue initiative was successful in achieving a better understanding of Tunisia's political challenges and their potential solutions. The national dialogue reduced social tensions; forged agreements on major issues such as a civil state, Islam as a source of legislation, and the building of a constitutional system; ensured the independence of the judiciary; addressed media freedoms; produced a roadmap for the transition; and formed a follow-up committee to oversee implementation of the dialogue conference's suggestions.[21]

It is unusual for a trade union to play such a large political role in a national dialogue, confirming that national reconciliation models should always adapt to different contexts. Established in 1951, the UGTT became a dynamic force in Tunisia due in part to its historically significant political role, which began in the resistance against French colonization in the early 1950s. Indeed, leaders of the UGTT were prominent organizers of the national movement against France. Even after Tunisia's independence in 1956, the UGTT continued to play a significant role in Tunisia's politics, at times butting heads with the Bourguiba and Ben Ali regimes, while at other times contributing to government formation.

The experience of the national dialogues proved essential in ending the political standoff between the opposition and the troika government after the assassination of Nationalist political leader Mohamed al-Brahmi in July 2013. The ensuing protests and opposition boycotts demanded that Ennahda step down and threatened to derail Tunisia's transition process just as it was about to make meaningful progress. Staving off potential disaster and making use of the cooperative environment created by the national dialogue conferences, UGTT President Hussein al-Abbasi mediated a compromise. The Ennahda-led troika agreed to transfer power to a technocratic government after further progress had been made on the constitution and other key areas. The troika, and Ennahda in particular, gave up a degree of political power, yet doing so through a negotiated agreement mediated by Tunisia's civil society marked a great achievement for the country's democratic transition.

Despite the remarkable successes of the UGTT's national dialogue and mediation efforts, there have still been lingering criticisms about the union's role. The main complaint focuses on the trade union's involvement in national politics. According to Marwan Hubaita, a leader in the CPR, "UGTT should concentrate on the rights of the workers not politics."[22] Said Ferjani added, "There is an inflated role for the UGTT as it is expanding at the expense of the sovereign space of the state. Meaning, the UGTT is taking from the sovereignty of the state."[23] Although CSOs are fundamentally different from political parties in their traditional role and composition, they could easily become part of the political conflict, rather than maintaining a facilitation role, if their political involvement becomes too controversial. During its mediation efforts, the UGTT and its president were accused many times of siding with one party—usually the opposition—and thereby of losing its neutrality and role as facilitator. In the highly political context of national dialogue, the dialogue's facilitator, as in the case of UGTT, could easily be pulled into the dispute, seriously threatening the continuation of the dialogue itself.

One other observation that Tunisians should keep in mind about their national dialogue is the fact that it is an elite dialogue, that is, only political parties and the elite in general within Tunisian society have been involved in these debates. Those elites opted to make compromises and attempted to avoid confrontations in order to keep the transition moving forward and to avoid what they saw of violent transitions in the region, particularly in their neighboring Libya. This is actually an important tactic that helped the dialogue succeed. Tunisians, however, need to be aware that a considerable amount of work is still required, especially in terms of consensus building at the grassroots level, to ensure that this dialogue is not merely an elite deal but rather an actual reality that all Tunisians can live and own.

Despite criticisms, the Tunisian approach to national dialogue remains worthy of attention due to its sustainability. Indeed, because it has used a homegrown model, initiated and fully managed by local civil society, the Tunisian process allows parties of the dialogue as well as its facilitators to claim ownership of the process and have a stake in its success. The national dialogue in Tunisia is a product of the work of the Tunisian political parties along with CSOs, all of whom are likely to invest more in protecting the dialogue's outcome due to their involvement in and ownership of the process.

Libya

Although national dialogue is vital in almost all post-conflict situations, it is especially important in Libya as that country emerges from four decades of dictatorship during which Libyans grew accustomed to being told what to do rather than taking part in what ought to be done. Two-way communication was never part of the political system under Muammar Qaddafi, as he refused to tolerate voices other than his own. In such an environment, civil society remained stunted. Therefore, after the Qaddafi government fell, Libya faced a major cultural shift in addition to tremendous political challenges, making the need for consensus-based, popular solutions more urgent than ever. National dialogue can provide a forum for such solutions.

Because the Libyan revolution was short and spontaneous, it lacked an ideological framework that could guide it and the country's subsequent transition. Indeed, the Libyan revolution was truly leaderless and centered on a single goal: the removal of Qaddafi. Only after the collapse of the regime did Libyans begin grappling with the question of what kind of state they hoped to build. They were confronted with the challenges of disarmament, resettling of refugees, lustration, economic recovery, and others. In the absence of a philosophy to guide and shape the transition, the process of dealing with these challenges became arbitrary and chaotic. A national dialogue process could help provide structure in this environment, uniting people to overcome instability and factionalism. To be productive, the dialogue process must involve all those who participated in the revolution to discuss and debate their visions for how to move forward with Libya's transition. As Sami Esaadi, a Libyan Islamic Fighting Group (LIFG) leader during the fight against Qaddafi, explained, "More than two years since the revolution, we only have the constitutional declaration of August 2011; there are no other documents to guide the next stages. There is no literature, theory, concepts, or clear philosophy for how to build a state. That is why we definitely need to have a national dialogue between all Libyan parties to discuss important national issues. There are many unanswered questions, such as who will participate in the dialogue, what will be the issues discussed, and what will be the priorities of the state in the reconstruction phase, for example, justice or security."[24]

Moving from Qaddafi's fall and the subsequent collapse of the state directly to elections carries profound risks for the country's transition and national reconciliation. Ideally, a national dialogue process would be launched

before a new government was elected to take power, but timing is a difficult issue. In the months following Qaddafi's ouster, many Libyans did not
feel ready to discuss reconciliation. When Sheikh Ali Salabi, an influential
Libyan religious figure, met with Ahmed Qaddaf al-Dam, one of Qaddafi's
cousins, in Cairo seven months after Qaddafi's death to discuss prospects for
national reconciliation, the meeting was widely criticized by Libyan media,
political parties, and the general public. Another participant, a colleague of
Sheikh Salabi, said that his brother called him and said, "You are no longer
my brother. How dare you meet those war criminals and talk reconciliation with them?"[25] In 2015, with Libya facing a new civil war, emotions and
tensions remain high, which makes dialogue both difficult and essential. If
a referendum were held, the majority of Libyans would likely choose laws
that lead to exclusion and elimination rather than uniting and rebuilding
the country. The 2013 Political Isolation Law is a clear—and dangerous—
example of such an outcome. National dialogue provides an important opportunity for Libyans to learn about the risks posed by such laws as well as
their potential consequences for national unity.

Furthermore, national dialogue offers a means for various elements of
Libyan society to redefine their relationships and make decisions collaboratively on divisive issues. Sensitive topics such as the power of revolutionary militants and their disarmament can only be dealt with through the
framework of a candid and constructive national dialogue. Indeed, the state
lacks the political power and presence on the ground to limit the control of
military councils like those in Misrata and Zentan, much less disarm such
militias by force.[26] A meaningful national dialogue, however, could provide
neutral ground for discussion and likely bridge the gap between the official
Libyan state and these parallel mini-states, helping to lead to an agreement
about the need to enhance state capacity.

Taghyeer (change) Party President Guma El-Gamaty is insistent on
the crucial importance of a dialogue process for national reconciliation in
Libya. He said, "We need to have a national dialogue over the status of
the revolutionaries and their role in the new Libya. . . . Their weapons
are an obstacle for security and order. The military councils are presenting
themselves as the protectors of the revolution. They claim to possess the

legitimacy of the revolution; that's what the former regime did, ruling with what was called 'revolutionary legitimacy.' National dialogue between all segments of Libyan society will be able to resolve these challenges to genuine national reconciliation."[27]

Fortunately, both the state and revolutionaries are fighting for the same goal: a united country that does not allow the recurrence of past regime crimes against its citizens. Their approaches, of course, differ dramatically, and there is a major risk that the prevailing atmosphere of mistrust and suspicion could turn these differences violent. To avoid conflict in the future, a united government should speak with the revolutionaries, rather than only communicating the state's vision for the country. The central government must also gain a clear understanding of the revolutionaries' demands and goals. Esaadi said, "The state should not force the revolutionaries. That would only be counterproductive. The state needs the revolutionaries, and vice versa; the country faces security challenges that only the revolutionaries can deal with. The starting point should be that the revolutionaries recognize the state's legitimacy and the state recognizes their contribution."[28] A national dialogue would be the perfect venue for helping to bring about an understanding of such mutual contributions.

Many strategies can be implemented to encourage Libyans to embrace national dialogue as the preferred forum to discuss and settle their political differences. As of January 2015, there is still no government-sponsored national dialogue process in Libya. There are two governments and peace talks among the fighting militias sponsored by the UN. An inclusive national dialogue would involve not only the revolutionary forces from both sides but also other non-armed political parties, civil society, and the former regime figures who are not linked to corruption or any human rights violations. The absence of such a forum has essentially derailed the transition process and generated frustration among Libyan citizens who hope for a return to peace and stability. The absence of dialogue has created an environment of mistrust and exacerbated polarization. Former prime minister Ali Zeidan suggested the launch of a wide and representative national dialogue in August 2013. In Zeidan's words, "It is a question of forming a commission made up of Libyan personalities from civil society who will initiate a debate around the issues of the future constitution, national reconciliation, displaced persons, disarmament or security." His comments were immediately criticized, as some tribal groups claimed that they had not been consulted in discussions about a national dialogue. Unfortunately, the initiative failed, and Zeidan left office in March 2014 without having launched a national dialogue.[29]

Frustrated by the absence of meaningful efforts to bridge the divides among Libyans, a number of political and community leaders launched an alliance in January 2014 that defined their primary goal as the establishment of a serious national dialogue and achievement of national reconciliation. Under the banner of the Libyan National Group for Civil Democracy, the coalition was composed primarily of government officials who served in various capacities after the collapse of the Qaddafi regime. Fatima Hamroush, a former minister of health, played a significant role in forming the alliance and bringing its members together after the fall of Qaddafi, despite resistance from some Libyans who considered talking to former regime elements taboo. Shortly after launching their national dialogue and reconciliation initiative, many Libyans, including members of the diaspora, joined. The initiative called for "national dialogue for civil democracy and reconciliation as the first priority in any solution for the Libyan case for peace, security and state sovereignty." Debate among participants resulted in agreement on a number of measures: (1) initiating a national dialogue among Libyans of different political backgrounds in order to agree on a common framework to cooperate with and strengthen the Libyan Army, police, and judiciary; (2) developing a framework for the implementation of transitional justice in Libya to achieve national reconciliation; and (3) implementing international human rights to guarantee fairness and justice among Libyans in conflict. Bearing these primary goals in mind, the alliance aimed to "inspire a culture of forgiveness amongst Libyans, who fought against each other in exceptional circumstances, to rebuild a sustainable future together." Despite the pioneering nature of this initiative and the significant effect it had on the participants, the impact at the national level remained limited. The civil war that erupted in 2014 has had a devastating impact on this and other national dialogue efforts, as Libya's primary focus has become the war, not peaceful transition.[30]

Libya's failure to conduct a meaningful national dialogue and descent into civil war has encouraged external actors to call publicly for talks among Libya's warring parties. In other words, though the civil war has disrupted local efforts to hold such a dialogue, it has nevertheless emphasized how badly one is needed, as most alternatives have failed. This dire need is so apparent that Algeria has pushed for a Libyan national dialogue, even seeking help from Tunisian Ennahda leader Rachid Ghannouchi to convince Libya's Islamists to join such a conversation.[31]

Meanwhile, the UN has undertaken a major initiative to lay the foundation for a Libyan national dialogue. In September 2014, shortly after he was appointed, the UN envoy to Libya and head of the United Nations Support Mission in Libya (UNSMIL), Bernardino Leon, was successful in launching peace talks between the primary parties of the civil war: the House of Representatives (HOR) supported by General Khalifa Haftar and Operation Dignity, and the General National Congress (GNC) supported by Libya Dawn's coalition of various militias. Leon sought to initiate and coordinate talks along several tracks, including the dueling parliaments, political parties and activists, municipalities, women's groups, militias, and tribes. Different rounds of the assorted tracks took place in Geneva, Ghadames (in Libya), Morocco, Algeria, Belgium, and Tunisia. With the ultimate goal of the resumption of Libya's transition and political process, the UN-sponsored peace talks aimed to achieve a number of specific intermediate measures, including an immediate nationwide ceasefire, security arrangements to end the fighting, a phased withdrawal of armed groups from cities, building confidence between the parties, and forming a national unity government.[32]

After almost a year, however, the peace talks have managed to produce only extremely limited progress. In March 2015, for example, UNSMIL announced that representatives of municipal and local councils had agreed to support the ongoing political dialogue and establishment of a unity government; call for a ceasefire, the withdrawal of armed groups from all Libyan towns, full respect of the rights of detainees, and the return of refugees and internally displaced persons; condemn media incitement of hatred and violence; and enhance the participation of women in the political dialogue. Also in March 2015, the political leaders participating in the peace talks affirmed their commitment to preserving Libya's unity and integrity, and to the political process and security efforts.[33]

Nonetheless, some analysts view the fact that Leon was able to bring a large number of diverse actors, most importantly the GNC, to the negotiating table for serious discussions as a significant achievement. Similarly, analyst Mohamed Eljarh hailed the participation of local municipal councils as a positive development. Eljarh also noted, "The formation of a committee tasked with restoring trust and cooperation between the various parties that took part in the dialogue is an encouraging step in the right direction." This committee would look into the issue of prisoners held by warring factions, examine the situation of internally and externally displaced families, and coordinate efforts to ensure basic services and aid can reach affected populations in war-torn areas.[34]

Despite its limited tangible achievements, the UN peace talks in Libya remain necessary. Peace talks are important as they present an alternative to the vicious civil war that has prevailed in Libya and frozen its transition process. Even the mere existence of a dialogue process gives Libyans some hope for a different outcome than what would be determined by the machine gun. Furthermore, peace talks, even if unsuccessful, still create a foundation for additional future peace efforts, whether by the UN or other, perhaps regional, players. Most importantly, the peace talks provide a unique opportunity for the warring parties to interact in a different setting than the battlefield. Such interactions can put a human face on enemies that the respective combatants would not otherwise see, as they generally communicate only through violence.

But, of course, that is not enough. Libya needs more than the institution of a parallel process to its civil war consisting merely of meetings among rival factions and local activists. Unfortunately, the obstacles to a successful dialogue that could bring an end to the civil war are enormous. The challenges to the UN-led peace talks have existed on several levels.

First, the GNC, supported by Libya Dawn, initially refused to take part in the negotiations because it viewed the UN as biased since the HOR is considered the internationally recognized government. As Amanda Kadlec put it, "The GNC has little incentive to cooperate as long as it perceives the

Tobruk Government as enjoying a starting advantage on the international stage."[35] Nonetheless, the GNC ended up joining the dialogue, participating in at least five sessions during February, March, and April. In late April, however, it strongly and publicly rejected a draft proposal that Leon put forward, claiming that it was not "an objective, comprehensive, balanced solution," but rather a "return to point zero."[36] Furthermore, Libya Dawn rejected Leon's invitation to participate in the security track of the dialogue process, claiming that "it aims to increase division between the rebels and the leaders and weaken them for the benefit of the coup," referring to Haftar's camp. Libya Dawn went so far as to demand that the UN withdraw Leon and call for demonstrations against "Leon, the United Nations and all the conspirators against our people and our blessed revolution."[37]

Second, Operation Dignity repeatedly challenged the UN's efforts. It also rejected Leon's invitation to participate in the security track, complaining that he "was treating it as just another militia," not as part of Libya's official armed forces. Furthermore, Operation Dignity significantly undermined the credibility of the peace talks by continuing to bomb Libya Dawn–held territory, including Tripoli's Matiga Airport, including in the days just prior to a new round of talks and Leon's releasing draft agreements.[38]

A third challenge has been the actual representation of the broad alliances at the talks. As Amanda Kadlec has argued, "The HOR and GNC are far too fractured among themselves to act as unified bodies in discussions." It is unlikely that the GNC is truly representative of all the Islamists within Libya Dawn or Ansar al-Sharia in Benghazi. Likewise, while HOR negotiators engaged in peace talks, Haftar's forces, with whom the HOR is allied, escalated the conflict several times, including by bombing a Libya Dawn stronghold, Misrata, reflecting a severe lack of coordination within the alliance.[39]

Another hindrance to Libya's peace talks is the parties' seeming lack of readiness to engage, compromise, and solve the country's national challenges, or what can be described as the conflict's ripeness for resolution.[40] One year after the eruption of the civil war, the parties are still insistent that they can completely defeat each other. While Haftar is threatening to eliminate what he refers to as "all terrorism" from Libya, Libya Dawn is holding strongly to the Political Isolation Law that targets Haftar, among others. Indeed, both parties view the confrontation as a zero-sum game, making the UN mission to broker a peace deal particularly difficult.

Lastly, in addition to the internal politics, the regional dimension has appeared to play a significant role in solidifying the parties' resistance to solutions. Both sides are enjoying significant support from regional players, and as a result, they are in no rush to end the war. This support has facilitated the parties' pursuit of their objectives of eliminating each other, and has enabled them to refuse to compromise or even seriously engage with UN peace efforts. Operation Dignity and General Haftar have received rigorous financial and military support, specifically from Egypt, the United Arab Emirates, and Jordan—countries that have taken a counter-revolutionary role and invested heavily in defeating revolutionary forces like Islamists in Egypt, Libya, and elsewhere. Emirati and Egyptian fighter jets have at least twice intervened to back Operation Dignity, bombing Libya Dawn and other Islamist forces in different parts of Libya. Similarly, Libya Dawn has received needed support from parties on the other end of the regional equation—those who claim to be supporting revolutionary forces—particularly Turkey and Qatar. This firm regional support provides the warring factions with incentives to continue fighting, rather than to seek a compromise or diplomatic process such as the UN effort.

Given these complexities, there is obviously no easy way to break the deadlock between the parties' positions and engage them in meaningful peace talks. Nevertheless, there are still steps that could be taken to mitigate the conflict and provide a window of hope for a peaceful solution. In a February 2015 report, the International Crisis Group suggested deemphasizing "legitimacy" in favor of "participation in the UN-led negotiations and on behaviour on the ground," being more direct in confronting the parties' regional backers, and maintaining and strengthening the implementation of the UN arms embargo. Mohamed Eljarh has recommended localizing security issues as a measure that could contribute to improving the overall security situation in the country. He explains, "Development of local leadership and ownership of security problems arising from non-state actors linked to particular cities could prove effective. . . . Democratically elected local municipal councils are best situated to respond to the needs of local communities throughout Libya."[41]

The UN has focused heavily on managing the peace talks among the Libyan parties, which is important but not sufficient to produce a successful agreement. Looking at the regional dimension of the Libyan civil war, the UN has had no choice but to proactively engage with the centers of powers in the Middle East that support each party and encourage the war to continue. Libya's civil war cannot be separated from the regional revolution/counter-revolution confrontation, and any sustainable solution will have to be coordinated on that level. Therefore, the UN's forging understandings with regional powers will significantly affect the course of events in Libya and could very likely lead to an agreement. The UN should draw on the Lebanese experience of ending a fifteen-year civil war through what was ultimately a regional understanding, the Taif Agreement. The agreement was not in any way an ideal one, but it ended years of brutal conflict. Libyans should not have to fight fifteen years to reach a similar conclusion. Of course, Libyans could come together and put an end to their civil war independently from their regional patrons, and an entirely Libyan solution to their crisis would definitely be more sustainable than one that was linked to regional affairs, but would they really do that? At this point, the parties in Libya have not shown any serious indication that they are interested in ending the civil war on their own, and for this reason, a regional approach could help significantly to force the parties to move to at least consider negotiating.

There are still other ways that the UN can push Libya's civil war toward resolution, such as tightening the country's arms embargo. UN Security Council Resolution 1970 prohibits all countries from providing any arms to Libya. Seriously enforcing such a resolution will force the parties to answer questions related to their supplies. On the other hand, the UN can allow for certain exceptions for forces that are neither participating in the war nor associated with any of the combatants but are genuinely working toward restoring security and the authority of the central government.

Oil has proved to be a vital means of sustaining Libya's civil war, as many militias have sought to control specific facilities and engage in export

activities to fund themselves. A number of warlords have benefited personally from such activities, encouraging them to perpetuate the conflict, as
discussed in chapter 1. The UN therefore should investigate the actual beneficiaries of oil exports from Libya and act in a way that prevents oil sales
from bankrolling the civil war. Militias' exporting of Libya's oil is considered
illegal, and the UN would certainly be justified in taking measures that
prevent countries and non-state actors from engaging in such trade. Even if
the UN is not fully able to regulate Libyan oil exports, it could certainly take
measures to make the militias' illicit activities more difficult.

Finally, it is important to recognize that there is only so much that the
UN can do to put Libya back on the path to stability and a successful political transition. It is ultimately the Libyans who must make this happen—or
not. They should realize that the removal of the Qaddafi regime presents a
prime opportunity to rebuild a new Libya that has a place for all of its citizens. They should learn the lesson of other civil wars around the world that
there is no winner, especially when regional forces can ensure that balance
of power among the parties is restored whenever one nears a total victory. If
the current warlords do not realize this, the silent majority should take the
initiative to put Libya on a different track. The militias on either side cannot
fight forever unless the public is feeling indifferent about the war. In particular, Libya's civil society—though it is a young sector that became active
only after the defeat of Qaddafi—has huge potential to take on a proactive
role and provide alternatives to the civil war. Civil society could mobilize
a spirit of rejection of a meaningless civil war that will only drain Libya's
resources and deepen societal wounds that will take generations to heal.
Solutions from within Libya are the ones that would ensure sustainability
and lead to genuine national reconciliation in the country.

No matter how complex it would be to hold a national dialogue, Libyans
have no alternative to negotiating compromises to their disagreements in
an open and inclusive nature. No party will be able to eliminate its rivals,
and sooner or later, they will have to sit down with each other. A number of
measures can be taken to maximize the likelihood of government and public involvement in and support of a representative process. Public awareness campaigns can play an instrumental role in educating people about

national dialogue. Radio and television programs, for example, provide a space for healthy and constructive debate, promoting greater understanding of the issues at hand and narrowing divisions on particularly polarizing subjects. Furthermore, these programs can educate the public about the risks and benefits of different proposed solutions. For example, supporters of the extreme Political Isolation Law may have been unaware of the grave risks that came with it, leading them to voice their approval without understanding its pitfalls. National dialogue and a process of public debate can make clear the dangers of social divisions and continued marginalization of entire segments of Libyan society. This, in turn, can lead more Libyans to be willing to entertain different methods, and perhaps engage in compromise, to defend their revolutionary gains.

National Dialogue: Comparative Aspect

National dialogue has emerged as a pillar for post-regime transitions in Yemen and Tunisia. The correlation between progress in such transitions and the use of national dialogue is striking. Tunisia, with its robust and civil society–driven national dialogue, has made the most substantial progress in transitioning toward national reconciliation, civil peace, and pluralistic politics. In fact, Tunisia became the first Arab Spring country to negotiate and reach consensus among all political parties over its constitution. Yemen, with its structured, internationally assisted, and partially boycotted national dialogue, made significant but limited progress toward solving post–regime change challenges to transition.[42] Yemen's national dialogue produced over 1,400 recommendations to solve the country's problems, with some implemented on the ground—in particular those related to security reforms. Ultimately, however, the Yemeni process failed to produce agreement among all southern parties on how best to resolve political issues in the troubled area. Furthermore, Yemen's national dialogue did not deter one of its party members—the Houthis—along with its former ruler—Saleh—from launching a coup and taking over the state. Libya, by contrast, has yet to hold a sustainable national dialogue at all, and it is sliding deeper into instability, uncertainty, chaos, and civil war. The UN-assisted peace talks among the warring parties is a starting point, but an inclusive and representative national dialogue is desperately needed for Libyans to forge a new social contract. This correlation between successful democratic transitions and the use of national dialogue, as in Tunisia and to a lesser extent in Yemen, is not coincidental—it cannot and should not be overlooked.

In terms of outcomes, it is obvious that Tunisia's national dialogue did help the competing political parties to forge a new social contract that has held well as of 2015. In Libya, successful UN-led peace talks could very well pave the way for a wider national dialogue to take place in the future. The 2015 civil war in Yemen should not undermine the importance of the experience of its NDC, which ended with a roadmap for addressing its national problems and challenges in the transition process. The recommendations of the NDC provided a point of reference and a foundation for any future peace talks among Yemeni warring parties. All parties, including the Houthis, even in the midst of the civil war in 2015, keep referring to the need to implement the NDC's recommendations. It is interesting that the Houthis' first slogan, raised when they rebelled against the transitional government in 2014, was the demand to immediately implement the recommendations of the NDC. In 2015, each party was accusing the other sides of not adhering to these recommendations. Thus, the NDC will continue to shape the future politics of Yemen despite the civil war that put implementation on hold.

National dialogue is particularly important in the context of these countries that experienced largely leaderless and non-ideological uprisings during the Arab Spring. Indeed, in this period, Arab populations responded to decades of repression without the guidance of charismatic leaders and without clear political ideologies to inform what types of new states they wanted or how best to build them. More difficult than toppling regimes in Tunisia, Yemen, and Libya was the question of "where do we go from here?" once the former regimes crumbled. People of all ideological leanings participated in the uprisings, including Islamists, nationalists, Socialists, and Ba'athists, to name a few. With so many competing voices in one revolution, a national dialogue about what the new state should look like becomes necessary. For instance, in the Libyan context, the citizens that spent the last forty-two years submitting to a despotic leader now have no choice but to engage in a deep and comprehensive conversation so they can work together to determine which political system suits them and which political parties will represent them. There is no single way to form national dialogues and complete transitions in the Arab Spring countries. Certainly, each of the three countries under study faces a variety of different problems. Some issues, however, such as the question of whether Sharia should be the source, or merely a source, of legislation, have recurred in all three. Such wide-ranging issues are best addressed in the context of inclusive national discussions.

This country analysis has revealed two approaches to national dialogue: an adaptable homegrown model, and a structured and externally assisted national dialogue. Tunisia's experience demonstrates how homegrown, grassroots, and civil society–driven national dialogue functions. The UGTT played an instrumental role in initiating, facilitating, and implementing national dialogue agreements. It showed a strong political presence during all phases of the process, and equally importantly, it intervened vigorously when a crisis developed. Major strengths of this model are its sustainability and ownership. Tunisians feel that the national dialogue is their own product, one that needs to be protected and nurtured. Yemen's structured and internationally assisted national dialogue also scored significant successes and to a certain extent aided in restoring a degree of peace and national structure in the post-Saleh context. The Yemeni dialogue delivered solutions and transition roadmaps, provided a viable alternative to violence up until the 2015 coup, broke social boundaries, and shattered traditional gender roles, while also, perhaps most critically, bringing together various Yemeni stakeholders despite vast differences in their political agendas. Unfortunately, Yemen's national dialogue could not withstand the Houthis-Saleh counter-revolution, which raises questions over its sustainability and to what extent the Houthis really believed in dialogue despite being one of the main parties participating in it. It should be noted, however, that while Yemen succeeded in holding meetings and forging compromises, the outcomes remain merely symbolic as long as implementation is not carried out. Obviously, the 2015 civil war has put everything on hold but it did not eliminate the recommendations that the dialogue reached. An additional criticism of the Yemeni approach is the leading role of the UN, an external player, in setting the agenda, selecting the parties, and overseeing the proceedings. As a result, concerns over the sustainability and local ownership of such a national dialogue are understandable.

National dialogue in the three countries sheds light on the potential and limitations of third-party intervention, the UN in these cases. In Tunisia, there was no role for the UN, and the parties on their own were able to hold a solid national dialogue and reach sustainable outcomes. A proactive UN mediation in Yemen significantly helped in the creation and management of the ten-month representative NDC and in the parties reaching consensus over a roadmap to deal with Yemen's national challenges. Despite this, the national dialogue proved to be less sustainable than it should have been. The UN at some point became a party with a vested interest, and that is when Benomar continued to negotiate with the Houthis despite their coup. Committed to an impartial mediation process, the UN envoy should have taken a firm position against a coup that put the president, prime minister, and other political party leaders under house arrest. UN intervention in Libya, on the other hand, may be able to assist the warring parties in reaching an agreement, but would likely be challenged to hold and lead a wide, inclusive, and representative national dialogue in Libya. UN envoy to Libya Bernardino Leon should learn from the lessons of Yemen and allow a wider role for the parties to lead the process. All parties should come to the dialogue with a guarantee of being treated equally. Once a fair and impartial mediation is promised, the UN in Libya should certainly take a position and refuse to be used by one of the parties to cover its tendency to dominate the scene.

Civil society emerged as a major player in the implementation of national dialogues and in helping them to succeed. Tunisia's UGTT surprised observers with its resilience in overcoming the tremendous challenges that faced the country's national dialogue. The initial refusal of two major political parties—Ennahda and CPR—to join the UGTT's initiative did not deter the UGTT from moving forward, and eventually Ennahda and CPR joined the dialogue. The UGTT also successfully mediated serious political crises between the troika government—which Ennahda and CPR led—and the opposition. Civil society groups, along with youth and women, played a vital role in supporting Yemen's NDC. In total, 120 members out of 565 represented youth, women, and civil society groups, and they played an important role in the conference's various working groups. CSOs debated, proposed solutions, and mediated in an effort to narrow gaps among rival political parties. CSOs have earned the role of an equal partner in any future national dialogue process. The fact that many of these organizations play a non-partisan role positions them well to serve an intermediary function among rival political parties, which is sorely needed in the often-heated political environments of countries undergoing political transitions.

The above country analysis highlights important values and principles for national dialogue processes to succeed. Chief among these is the principle of equal partnership among all participating parties.[43] This does not mean that each party should be granted an equal number of seats, but that all parties to the dialogue, regardless of their relative size or strength, should have the right to voice their positions without fear of intimidation. The exclusion that underpinned the value system of the former dictatorship must be replaced with a spirit of inclusion, forgiveness, and acceptance of the other, and no one party should be able to control or dominate the process.

The study of Yemen and Tunisia in particular reveals that national dialogue must be inclusive and open to all active political parties to succeed, regardless of the political or ideological orientation of the varying groups. Any political party that denounces violence and accepts the equal participation of others should be given a seat in a national dialogue process. In Yemen, this should include all active political parties representing the country's various constituencies such as the GPC, Islah, the Socialists, the Nasserists, the Ba'athists, the Justice and Development Party, parties from the South, the Houthis, and even the jihadist militants of Ansar al-Sharia, if the group is willing to lay down arms and become part of the political process.[44]

We have seen that parties do not hesitate to use national dialogue processes for their own political gains. For example, parties use tactics like issuing sets of conditions as the "price of their participation." These parties hope that they can achieve political gains in advance while also appealing to their constituents as tough negotiators who can be trusted with the party's cause. The Houthis and the Socialist Yemeni Party each issued a list of ten conditions that had to be met before they would participate in the dialogue.[45] This practice of setting public and explicit pre-dialogue conditions will only impede a successful dialogue and hold parties to rigid positions that they may later find difficult to abandon, even if the national interest requires it.

Finally, factors that generally affect national dialogues, like timing and the selection of participants, proved not to be major issues in these cases. Starting national dialogues early, rather than late, suited Yemen and Tunisia quite well, while Libya continues to slide into instability in the absence of an inclusive and representative national dialogue. Participants were selected by political parties and civil society groups in Tunisia, while a combination of organizers and political parties vetted the participant list, with final approval by President Hadi, in Yemen. No serious issues related to timing or selection of participants arose in Yemen or Tunisia.

SIX

Truth Seeking and Grappling with the Past

The past few decades have been a dark chapter in the histories of Libya, Yemen, and Tunisia. The respective general publics had very little agency and limited impact on the directions of their own countries. Repressive regimes and their cronies were the dominant players and the only ones who really knew what was happening behind the tightly secured doors of the presidential palaces. As a result, there are many unanswered questions in the minds of these countries' populations that will plague their collective memories as long as they persist. Ignoring the instances of torture, forced disappearances, marginalization, and the many other forms of repression that Arab Spring societies have experienced over the past half-century would jeopardize—rather than facilitate—a healthy transition to a new era of civil peace. Transitional justice mechanisms, and particularly truth-seeking measures, can help with that process. As Libyan analyst and writer Abdullah Elmaazi put it, "Transitional justice helps in healing festering wounds and in acting as a national cleansing process. If Libyans are to fail in cleansing themselves of the heinousness of their past they will forever be beset by incessant ruminating."[1] Indeed, the general goal behind transitional justice, as expressed by Julie M. Mazzei, is to "establish a clear break with a country's past and lay the ground for a rights-based political future."[2] Choosing to suppress the past instead of facing it would leave the door open for future instability.

This chapter argues that dealing with the past through a robust and transparent truth-seeking process is an integral part of the transition process for Arab Spring countries. While truth seeking has limits, is vulnerable to politicization, and introduces risks, Arab societies in transition still need to pursue the truth about those dark chapters of their histories to learn from mistakes, clearly break from the past, and prevent grievances and grudges from shaping their futures. In particular, Arab societies need the truth to end polarization, establish unifying narratives, and sanitize their collective memories. Most societies emerging from civil conflict and regime change have to deal with their pasts in one way or another, and the Arab Spring societies are certainly no exception. In recent decades, truth seeking has become a commonly employed practice for societies seeking to grapple with their pasts. Truth commissions have been established in more than twenty countries that have gone through similar experiences as Libya, Yemen, and Tunisia.

Engaging in a truth-seeking process can produce a variety of benefits for countries in transition. Proponents of truth seeking argue that it promotes peace in eight primary ways. It is considered to be therapeutic — by acknowledging and facing past atrocities, people can begin to heal and work toward reconciliation. In El Salvador and Honduras, for example, Mike Kaye finds that the open discussion of past repression, exoneration of falsely convicted "terrorists," and identification of disappeared individuals promoted reconciliation. Second, efforts to uncover the truth can help to promote justice by exposing crimes and their perpetrators, making adjudication possible, especially when these efforts enjoy significant international support and attention, as in El Salvador, the former Yugoslavia, and Rwanda.[3] Third, establishing a public record contributes to the construction of a common history that acknowledges past crimes, which helps people move beyond the past and toward reconciliation. Relatedly, educating a society about past crimes can help it to prevent their repetition. Fifth, truth commissions in particular contribute to institutional reforms by shedding light on their flaws and abuses, and by providing specific recommendations to prevent such failures from being repeated. Sixth, the aforementioned promotion of justice helps to support the rule of law, a critical component of democratic societies. Finally, new information leading to the imprisonment and exposure of human rights violators can both preempt the commission of further atrocities and deter their occurence.[4]

Especially for the shattered and polarized Arab Spring societies, truth seeking has great potential. In assessing truth commissions, Eric Brahm finds that they "are as much as anything about nation building in which exposing the gruesome details of the past helps to usher in a new democratic era and advance the cause of human rights through peaceful coexistence." Truth commissions have indeed contributed to the type of easing of social divisions that Arab Spring societies desperately need. One of the major tasks of the Truth and Reconciliation Commission in South Africa, for example, was the promotion of national unity by establishing "the truth in relation to past events" and providing as "complete a picture as possible" about past events. Furthermore, truth commissions in Latin America have succeeded in establishing "the official presentation of an authoritative history, which counters the former regime's account," as well as "listening to, and validating, the stories and the human dignity of the victims." Based on the experience of Argentina's National Commission on the Disappearance of Persons, Emilio Crenzel advocates for "constructing a public truth about the crimes as soon as possible, immediately after the fall of state terrorism regimes."[5]

Although past truth-seeking experiences have been successful, especially in establishing national narratives, Arab Spring societies should be wary of their limitations and avoid overestimating what such processes can realistically accomplish. For example, truth commissions in Latin America struggled to bring about long-lasting institutional and structural reforms. Indeed, commissions have often hesitated to give the names of perpetrators to courts, and these courts have often been reticent to prosecute those responsible for crimes, making institutional change difficult. El Salvador's experience showed that "it takes constant monitoring and pressure—not simply a short-term spotlight—to ensure some measures of compliance with recommendations regarding accountability." Despite the ability of truth seeking to contribute to the rule of law, limitations remain severe. One scholar even maintains that "all that a truth commission can achieve is to reduce the number of lies that can be circulated unchallenged in public discourse."[6]

Another constraint of truth seeking is that dealing with the past and discovering what really happened may not be an easy thing for societies that are just ridding themselves of decades-long dictatorships. New information can lead to different types of social conflicts, especially if victims of torture, for example, decide to pursue revenge against newly revealed persecutors.

This is especially important for the three countries in question as Arab culture recognizes revenge as a legitimate way to respond to historical wrong-doings. However, no matter how hard it is for the victims and their families to deal with painful memories, truth seeking remains the healthiest way to come to terms with the past and move forward to begin a new society that is free from human rights violations. Genuine national reconciliation requires, as Mazzei puts it, the establishment of "a narrative regarding the past—to acknowledge victims as such, perpetrators as such, wrongs committed against innocent as such—and to assist in establishing this as the (new) dominant discourse."[7]

Libya, Yemen, and Tunisia have had similar experiences of state repression over the past three to four decades. All three experienced numerous human rights violations and have a number of unanswered questions about who exactly is responsible for perpetrating them. Each country must decide whether to face these questions or ignore them. Unfortunately, Arab Spring societies have yet to clearly demonstrate how they want to address their pasts to prevent them from harming their futures. Even more troubling is the fact that significant segments of these societies openly oppose any investigations of the past for fear of what they might reveal and instead insist that a mentality of "what happened in the past remains in the past" is the only acceptable basis for moving forward.

Libyans, Yemenis, and Tunisians share not only long histories of injustice but sincere aspirations to transition to stable, peaceful, and prosperous countries. How they decide to handle their pasts will affect both the processes and outcomes of their transitions. Thus far, as this research shows, each country has chosen its own approach, and they are therefore on different trajectories. What follows is an overview of how each country is handling this aspect of its transition and the resulting implications.

Libya

Forty-two years of repression and assaults on basic human dignity means that forgetting or avoiding the past is not an option for Libyans. They are now working to disengage from the identity imposed on the country by Muammar Qaddafi, one centered in equal parts on Qaddafi himself and on his societal vision of Jamahiriya, or state of the masses. In the process, Libya's past is influencing their efforts to define and shape a new identity. For many Libyans, Qaddafi's reign represents their defining historical memory. It is what Vamik Volkan calls a "chosen trauma" or "the shared mental representation of the historical traumatic event," which becomes a significant marker for the large-group identity.[8]

To overcome this collective trauma, Libyans are making a deliberate attempt to focus instead on what Volkan calls "chosen glories"—historical bright spots around which Libyans can collectively rally.[9] Libyans have elected to discard Qaddafi and his Jamahiriya and instead identify with Omar al-Mukhtar, who led Libya's resistance to Italian colonization from 1912 until his death in 1931.[10] In the streets of Tripoli, pictures of al-Mukhtar are so numerous that one could be forgiven for thinking that he led the country's 2011 revolution himself. By contrast, King Idris, who ruled from 1951 until Qaddafi's 1969 coup, is barely mentioned. Libyan discourse has very clearly embraced the demonization of Qaddafi and the glorification of al-Mukhtar while largely neglecting the country's monarchical past. Libyans have attempted to eliminate anything reminiscent of the Qaddafi era. Walking through Tripoli, one can see that cars' license plates—which used to be marked with "Jamahiriya"—have been defaced by their owners. Similarly, Libyans have blotted out or cut out completely the large picture of Qaddafi that still appears on the Libyan dinar.

As they grapple with their past, Libyans must decide how far back they want to look and how much of their history they want to unearth. The starting point for any investigation has serious implications for the scope of both the prosecution of human rights violations and the exclusion of former regime elements from political life—what is known as lustration. Discussions with various factions reveal that Libyans are struggling to determine which of the following key events from their country's past should serve as the cutoff point for their truth seeking:

- *September 1, 1969*: Muammar Qaddafi's successful coup against King Idris. Generally, hardline Libyan politicians demand that the investigation of past crimes start from this date. Opening the entire span of the Qaddafi regime to investigation could be problematic. Over Qaddafi's forty-two years in power huge numbers of Libyans were involved with the regime in some capacity and could therefore be found complicit in broadly defined crimes.

- 1973: Qaddafi's declaration of his "Popular Revolution" and the formation of his General People's Committees. This program was part of what he called the Third International Theory, the manifesto of direct democracy outlined in his Green Book.
- 1977: Qaddafi's official dissolution of the Libyan Arab Republic and establishment of the Socialist People's Libyan Arab Jamahiriya. It was at this point that Qaddafi began most vigorously applying what he called "revolutionary justice" to crack down on his domestic opponents.
- 1980: Qaddafi's redistribution of wealth, including the expropriation of all funds in excess of one thousand dinars in Libyans' bank accounts.
- *February 17, 2011*: The outbreak of the Libyan revolution against Qaddafi.
- *March 19, 2011*: The start of NATO airstrikes. Any regime official who defected after this date, when it became clear that Qaddafi could not survive, was arguably acting more out of self-preservation than principle.

Settling on a starting point is quite challenging, as each proposed date has ramifications for multiple internal and external stakeholders. Mahmoud Jibril, Libya's interim prime minister in 2011 and 2012, defected from the Qaddafi regime in the very early days of the revolution. It is in his interest, along with the interest of all those who defected before the NATO bombing, to push for March 19, 2011, as the starting point. On the other hand, the National Front for the Salvation of Libya, which fought against Qaddafi starting in the 1980s, does not differentiate between the periods before and after March 19, and therefore demands the truth about both. Families of the victims of various atrocities want, first and foremost, a starting point that includes their respective traumas. Regional players also have an interest in this debate. Chad's president, Idriss Deby, recently demanded the truth about Qaddafi's intervention in his country, as well as compensation for its losses in the war. Additionally, Lebanon has been pushing for a truth-seeking mission on the fate of Imam Musa al-Sadr, who disappeared after meeting with Qaddafi in 1978. In other words, the starting point for truth seeking in Libya is closely linked to the politics of transition, and any starting point is ultimately likely to be a reflection of the country's balance of power.[11]

Still, there are certain key events in Libya's recent history that cannot be ignored. These historical flashpoints, both from before and during the 2011 revolution, continue to destabilize Libya. At least for the following events and related issues, Libya must undertake a serious and comprehensive investigation sooner rather than later.

The first such event is the Abu Salim prison massacre. Human Rights Watch estimates that 1,270 prisoners were killed in Abu Salim prison in 1996 after they protested against mistreatment and human rights violations. To ensure that those responsible are held to account, the victims' families formed an influential pressure group called the Association of Families of the Martyrs of the Abu Salim Massacre. At its 2013 annual meeting, held in January in Tripoli, the association released a set of demands. They included honoring the Abu Salim martyrs, both by commemorating the massacre annually and including it in school curricula; returning the victims' bodies to their families and making a public, published apology and financial reparations to them; public disclosure of the entire truth of the massacre, including who was killed, who participated, and any circumstances or events leading to the massacre; and the full application of the law, specifically the trying of those suspected to be involved and the punishment of those found responsible for the killings.[12]

Another controversial issue is Law No. 4/1978, or the "Ownership Law." One of the first demonstrations to take place in Tripoli after the fall of Qaddafi was led by people whose homes and properties were confiscated under Law No. 4/1978. The 1978 law, which codified the principle of "the house to its resident," resulted in a wave of Libyans' appropriating other Libyans' homes. Questions of legitimate ownership subsequently became quite complicated, as those who seized homes were able to sell the houses on to others; in some cases, ownership has been transferred several times. The current owners, in many cases, paid for the homes, while the original owners have never been compensated. The scope of the problem is difficult to quantify, but in 2012, a lawyer interviewed by the UN High Commission for Refugees estimated that full restitution in Tripoli alone could mean the eviction and resettlement of three-quarters of the city's 2.2 million residents. Absent a solution, one can now see Tripoli houses marked with graffiti as the "sacred property" of a given family subjected to the Ownership Law. Some of the original owners are willing to wait for legal redress, but others have resorted to vigilantism, evicting the current "owners" at gunpoint.[13]

Libya is also facing a number of historical regional rivalries. Many of Libya's existing conflicts have deep historical roots, which complicate the process of reconciliation. The ongoing rivalry between Misrata and Bani Walid, for example, goes back at least as far as 1920, as Misrata holds Bani Walid accountable for the killing of anti-colonialist leader Ramadan al-Swaihli. In September 2012, almost a century later, Bani Walid defied a resolution by the Libyan General National Congress (GNC) demanding that it surrender wanted individuals because it believed the list was created by Misrata and its allies. Bani Walid was convinced that it was Misrata pushing for the resolution and that it was passed by the legislature only under pressure from the Misratans. In response, Misrata brigades—along with brigades from Souq al-Jumaa, Tajoura, and Azzawiya—led a twenty-five-day siege of Bani Walid that ended with the city's fall and left approximately one hundred dead and hundreds wounded. To add insult to injury, victorious Misrata fighters displayed a big poster of al-Swaihli and painted slogans citing his name throughout the city, firmly situating the violence within the cities' historical rivalry.

A more recent flashpoint is that of revenge and retaliation. Libya's past is replete with unresolved grudges. Many of Libya's Islamists, for example, were tortured and abused in Qaddafi's prisons. During the revolution, many diverse factions unified around the goal of removing the regime, but this temporary unity was too fragile to survive even until that goal was accomplished. General Abdul Fattah Younis, Qaddafi's minister of the interior, who defected on February 22, 2011, and ultimately became head of the rebel army's general staff, was assassinated on July 28, 2011. It is generally believed that former jihadis were behind the slaying. After Qaddafi's fall, many such old issues came to the fore. Post-revolution Benghazi, for example, has seen widespread attacks on security offices and police stations. The targets were understood to be members of the former regime still serving in Benghazi's police. People believed that those behind the attacks were either former jihadis who were tortured by Qaddafi's security forces or possibly former regime loyalists who wanted to take revenge on defectors. The number of targeted assassinations, however, increased from dozens in 2012 to hundreds in 2013 and 2014. In addition, the targets came to include not only former regime officers but also military officers, customs officers, and even prominent February 17 revolutionaries. Hence, simply accusing groups like Ansar al-Sharia no longer made sense because in many cases the assassinations did not serve their agendas. The resulting widespread fear has led many Libyans to believe that there is a third party at play, conducting an old strategy of creating a problem so it can then offer to solve it. What *is* clear is that the assassinations are fueling Libya's civil war as the militias accuse each other of being behind the killings.[14]

While vigilantism is a legitimate concern, Hussein al-Buishi, the head of Libya's Truth and Reconciliation Commission, has argued that "knowing the truth in Libya won't cause social unrest, simply because those who worked with the regime and were involved in violations are known to everyone—to the victims and to Libyan society. They didn't hide during Qaddafi's time, and now they're known to almost everybody." Furthermore, Libya's Grand Mufti, Sadeq al-Gheryani, believes that knowing the truth is necessary in order to apply justice and, eventually, forgive and reconcile. Specifically regarding trials, he said that "the judge should not ask the parties to engage in peace and reconciliation before stating the facts and identifying the rights of each party first. Only then the judge should encourage the parties to forgive and reconcile."[15]

Finally, there is an array of unanswered questions lingering from the Qaddafi era. There are many dark spots in the last four decades of Libyan history. In addition to individual cases of torture and disappearance, there is also the broader truth of what happened to the country under an opaque and impenetrable regime. Libyans want to know, for example, why their country waged a war on Chad for almost ten years (1978–1987) and what could justify the deaths of over seven thousand troops in a war Libya ultimately lost. In another episode, Libyan Arab Airlines Flight 1103 was flying from Benghazi and crashed in Tripoli in December 1992, killing all 157 passengers. Some Libyans now allege that Qaddafi orchestrated the incident to be able to claim to the world that the sanctions on Libya had deprived passenger jets of necessary parts and maintenance, thus causing civilian deaths. Regardless of the real causes of the crash, Libyans genuinely want to know what happened, and the truth is necessary for them to have closure. Similarly, Libyans deserve to know the truth about the 1988 bombing of Pan Am Flight 103—the "Lockerbie bombing"—which killed 270 civilians. Libya was accused of perpetrating the bombing, and in 2003, it signed a settlement with the victims' families that paid them $2.7 billion in exchange for the lifting of sanctions. A Libyan intelligence agent was convicted of the bombing, but in March 2014, Al Jazeera released a documentary claiming that Iran and a Palestinian group were behind the attack.[16] Unfortunately, the list of similar mysterious tragedies during Qaddafi's rule is long, ranging from the Abu Salim massacre to the infection of four hundred children with AIDS between 1999 and 2007.

Yemen

Yemen similarly faces a number of major issues from its past as it tries to build a better future. For Yemenis, uncovering the truth about abuses by the government and other power-holders, the fate of the disappeared, and the wars Ali Abdullah Saleh waged against the Houthis is particularly important. Saleh first came to power in the Yemen Arab Republic (North Yemen) in 1978. An attempted coup and assassination attempt by Nasserists followed soon after, triggering the first of several waves of executions and forced disappearances.[17] In 1990, Saleh's Yemen Arab Republic peacefully united with the Socialist regime of the People's Democratic Republic of Yemen (South Yemen), which had seen its own bloody internal war in 1986.

When South Yemen attempted to secede in 1994 amid disputes over power- and revenue-sharing, war erupted between the North and South. The war ended with the North's capture of the southern capital of Aden in July 1994, resulting in forced unity, the flight of the South's political leadership, and another round of forced disappearances. Saleh also sacked thousands of former South Yemen army officials and seized their land. Sanaa has since marginalized Aden and the entire South economically and politically. As a result, the South has significant grievances that are major threats to post-Saleh unity. Based on their past experience, many southerners continue to insist on secession from a government in Sanaa that they do not trust.

Under Saleh's thirty-three-year reign (1978–2011), as well as under the Socialist regime in the South (1970–1990), many members of the opposition disappeared without explanation. Even in times of relative peace and stability under Saleh, political prisoners were held for long periods, tortured, and exiled, while others' whereabouts remain unknown. A campaign of state terror and the disappearances of political opponents are all deeply ingrained in the Yemeni collective memory. The failure to deal properly with past grievances has fed instability in a transitioning Yemen. Resentment and alienation persist among the families of the disappeared and the supporters of their cause, some of whom recently graffitied the faces of their lost loved ones throughout Sanaa as part of a 2012 protest campaign. Additionally, since unification, Yemen has faced a persistent rebellion by Houthi militants in its northern provinces, including six bloody wars between 2004 and today. The country has also struggled with a persistent al-Qaeda–linked jihadist presence.[18]

It is unrealistic to expect these memories of oppression and conflict to fade simply as a result of the signing of the Gulf Cooperation Council (GCC) initiative in Riyadh. The alternative to forgetting the past—as expressed by the GCC immunity laws—should not necessarily be understood to mean public trials and the execution of former regime officials. A middle-ground solution could be what Desmond Tutu, chair of the South African Truth and Reconciliation Commission, called the "third way."[19] The idea is to find a balance between the draconian Nuremberg process and national amnesia, as South Africa did, while leaving the specifics up to Yemen.

Like Libyans, Yemenis are torn on what time frame any truth-seeking efforts should focus on. When asked for their opinions on the appropriate starting point for a truth commission, interviewees gave answers that included the following:

- Starting with the September 21, 2014, coup of the Houthis-Saleh alliance against the state and the truth behind it;
- Limiting truth seeking to the eleven-month uprising that began in 2011 in order to make the duration more manageable;
- Starting with the first war against the Houthis in 2004, as this would help ensure that the Houthis take part in the national reconciliation process;
- Beginning with the 1994 war with the South, as this was the major war that resulted in Yemen's unification and is related to the present-day southern cause;
- Starting with the first unification of the North and South in 1990, as that date marks when the South and the North came together on a voluntary basis;
- Going back to 1978, when Saleh came to power, as Yemenis deserve to know the full extent of the crimes for which Saleh was responsible; and
- Beginning with 1962, which marked the death of Imam Ahmad bin Yahya and the resulting civil war between Saudi Arabia–backed royalists and republicans supported by Egypt.

Clearly, Yemenis hold widely differing opinions about the proper point of departure for truth seeking. Yasin Saeed Noman, head of the country's Socialist Party, recognizes such diverse viewpoints but suggests that 1990 would be most reasonable. Earlier abuses—for example, the Nasserists' executions and disappearances of 1978—could be treated on a case-by-case basis. While 1990 could be used as a starting point, the rights of the victims before that should be recognized and dealt with accordingly, Noman explained.[20]

Not everyone agrees that national reconciliation should include digging into the past at all, however. Vice chairman of the General People's Congress parliamentary bloc Yaser al-Awadi argued, "Yemen's political legacy shows that reconciliation was built on burying the truth, not openness. In the past, there was a victorious party and a defeated one. This time, both parties are equals, with no victorious and no defeated. This makes it more necessary for the two parties to move on and look toward the future, not the past."[21] Those opposed to uncovering past abuses fear that, in a tribal society like Yemen, knowledge of past crimes and their perpetrators could lead to social strife. Indeed, outbreaks of fighting in Yemen are often motivated by traditional tribal practices of retaliation and revenge.

The problem, however, is political as well as social. Most of Yemen's current leaders are part of the very history that would be investigated. Opposition leader General Ali Mohsen al-Ahmar, for example, led military operations against the Houthis in the North; later, the Houthis demanded that al-Ahmar be held accountable for those "unjust wars" as a condition for their participation in the 2013 national dialogue. Yemen's failure to hold al-Ahmar accountable gave the Houthis further incentive to launch their 2014 campaign against the government. Moreover, the Islamist Islah Party, the most powerful party in the opposition Joint Meeting Parties, was part of Saleh's government during the 1994 war with the South. During the 1980s, Islah Party head Mohamed al-Yadoumi served under Saleh in the notorious state security apparatus, which was allegedly responsible for torturing political prisoners.

Despite lingering suspicions about the wisdom and practicality of truth seeking, Yemenis should not shy away from trying a different approach this time. Yemen's ongoing conflict is itself evidence that previous efforts at long-term conflict resolution—which have not incorporated truth commissions—have failed. Truth seeking is a springboard to begin a process of acknowledgment, apology, forgiveness, and, importantly, the application of broader transitional justice laws. Abdulhakim Helal, a Yemeni journalist and managing editor of al-Masdar Online, suggested that "forgiveness is necessary for national reconciliation but should be preceded by truth and confessions." Mahmoud Nasher, a civil society activist from southern Yemen, explained that the state owes its people two things: the truth and an apology. He argued that the regime "should apologize to the entire Yemeni people . . . and not just to political prisoners or other segments of the society. The entire nation should know what happened, as knowing reinforces the rights of citizenship among the people."[22]

Certainly, acknowledgment of and apologies for past wrongdoings would go a long way toward building popular support for national reconciliation, increasing Yemenis' trust in the country's post-Saleh leadership, and making any political settlement more credible in the eyes of the Yemeni people.

Tunisia

Having been led by autocratic regimes since gaining their independence in 1956, Tunisians have never experienced rule by a transparent government. Some of the events of the past six decades were extremely controversial and continue to divide Tunisians today. Entering the post–Zine El Abidine Ben Ali era represents an opportunity for Tunisians to reflect upon and come to terms with what has occurred, and to heal and move forward. They do not have to unanimously agree on these issues—or forge a national accord over them—but the mere process of acknowledging the issues and reflecting upon them will aid the larger national healing process.

Rafik Abdul Salam, a former foreign minister, says that Tunisia needs a new reading of its contemporary history, a reading that is free of imposition and dictation. He explained, "The past should be reviewed not by political elites but by historians who are able to read history objectively and independently. Such an objective reading of the past would recognize, for example, accomplishments made by Bourguiba as well as acknowledge the denial of the rights of nationalists, leftists, and Islamists, during those times. We need to look at Tunisia's history since its independence in 1956."[23] The issues that remain the most salient for Tunisians, serving as powerful dividing forces and rallying cries, include Habib Bourguiba, the Youssefist issue, the Qafsa mining uprising, and systematic repression, including forced disappearances and political imprisonments.

Habib Bourguiba ruled Tunisia for the first three decades of its independence, from 1956 until 1987. Was Tunisia's founding president a reformer and "modern state builder" or simply a tyrant? This question continues to divide Tunisians even fifteen years after his death. No national consensus exists over his role in Tunisia's contemporary history. Some Tunisians view him as a reformer who made education his first priority, built a modern state, and even advanced women's rights. He was given many titles such as *al-mujahed al-akbar* (the greatest fighter) and "nation builder." Others, however, consider him an absolute dictator who monopolized authority, established a one-party system centered on his *Dustour* (constitution) Party, and fiercely cracked down on political dissidents. He marginalized Tunisia's Islamic religious establishment, fought pro-Nasser nationalists, went after his opponents known as the Youssefists until their leader was assassinated in 1961, and suspended the Socialist Party after an assassination attempt against him in 1962.

Today, Bourguiba's legacy fuels divisions and rivalries among various political parties in Tunisia. His supporters formed six new political parties after the collapse of Ben Ali's regime and then united in one bloc, calling themselves the Dustouri Front. In addition, Beji Caid Essebsi, one of Bourguiba's pillars of power as a former interior and defense minister, founded Nedaa Tunis to represent Bourguiba's philosophy. In fact, the Dustouri Front and Nedaa Tunis have competed over who best represents Bourguiba's vision. Especially after their electoral victories in late 2014, it is obvious that Nedaa Tunis and Essebsi have become the recognized representatives of Bourguiba's philosophy. Meanwhile, Bourguiba's opponents, especially the center-left parties Ennahda, Ettakatol, and Congress for the Republic, had sought to purge those who served in the Ben Ali and Bourguiba regimes from public office using the "revolution immunization law" (*qanoon tahseen al-thawra*). The former opposition argued that Ennahda, along with its ally the Democratic Alliance Party, was using the immunizing law specifically to exclude Essebsi and other Ben Ali loyalists, while Essebsi used Bourguiba's legacy to appeal to those loyalists and build his political constituency. It could also be argued that one form of Tunisia's political rivalry has roots in the contrast between Bourguiba's liberal-oriented project and Ennahda's Islamist one. It should be noted that Ennahda and other Islamists suffered significantly under Bourguiba. The post-revolution period is the time to put the practices used against them into perspective.

Finally, to understand how divisive Bourguiba remains for Tunisians, one should contrast him with another political figure, Farhat Hashad, who plays the totally opposite role as a unifying figure in Tunisian politics. Hashad, who took a leadership role in liberating Tunisia from French colonialism in the 1950s, also gave his people the Tunisian General Labor Union (UGTT). As discussed in the national dialogue and civil society chapters (chapters 5 and 10), the UGTT led one of Tunisia's national dialogues and has played a significant role in defusing political crises through its robust mediation initiatives among rival political parties.

Another matter from its past that Tunisia will have to resolve is what came to be known as the Youssefist issue. Salah Ben Youssef was one of the prominent leaders of the Tunisian National Movement during the end of France's rule and a leader of Tajamu Dustouri, the party that came to power following independence. After he clashed with Bourguiba and was removed from the party, he went into exile in 1956, and in the years that followed, his supporters were arrested, tortured, and executed in Tunis. In 1961, Ben Youssef was assassinated in Frankfurt, Germany; no one knows exactly who killed him. During this period, the aforementioned Essebsi was Bourguiba's minister of interior. Therefore, how the Youssefist issue is settled will have a major impact on the role that Essebsi and the entire Bourguiba-loyalist alliance will continue to play in Tunisian politics.

Addressing this issue concerns far more than those individuals who were accused of orchestrating what Bourguiba used to call the "Youssefist Conspiracy." Bourguiba deliberately marginalized the entire western region of Tunisia, where the bulk of the Youssefists came from, to punish his opponents. Both Bourguiba and Ben Ali used this tactic of penalizing the families and regions of their challengers. As Tunisia embarks on a new phase, its western region demands amends for its past oppression and the development of the region.

Tunisians of the Qafsa region are also seeking answers. In 2008, phosphate miners and other residents of the region protested peacefully against Tunisian authorities, demanding improved labor rights and serious development in their marginalized, exploited region. Ben Ali's police force responded with an aggressive security campaign against the city of Rdayyef, the core area of protests, to put an end to the uprising. The government did not allow media to cover what was happening. Many protestors were imprisoned and killed, while others just disappeared. No one knows exactly what happened in the uprising, and it remains a question that begs for answers in Tunisians' collective memory.[24]

Forced disappearances, such as those that occurred during the crackdown on the Qafsa mine uprising, are a major issue. According to former prisoners who were incarcerated for years by Ben Ali, he perpetrated at least twelve cases of forced disappearance.[25] The tactic was used on active regime opponents as well as the remains of executed prisoners. A number of those executed during Ben Ali's regime were buried without the knowledge of their families. Now their families are understandably insisting on receiving the remains of their loved ones so they can carry out proper Islamic burials. All are believed to have been executed during the 1980s and 1990s, and their families still do not even know where the bodies are. Failing to bring resolution to these cases would leave Tunisian society with an open wound.

Some former detainees believe that the regime was responsible for the death of a total of approximately 150 political prisoners. Of this number, some died while imprisoned and under torture, and the rest died after they were released due to medical conditions stemming from their lengthy imprisonments during which they were denied serious medical care. Former prisoners have conducted lengthy protests since the revolution, demanding that the government acknowledge their suffering and provide them with a meaningful rehabilitation program. Some were imprisoned as long as sixteen years, and as a result, are destitute and lack skills that allow them to integrate with society.[26]

As part of grappling with these divisive issues, Tunisians have faced the difficult question of how far back into their history to delve. Defining the starting point for investigating the past has implications that are important for Tunisians in general, but especially for their political parties, who have advocated for different starting points based mainly on their political agendas. The debate about the past in Tunisia revolved around two possible starting points:

- *November 7, 1987*: Ben Ali's assumption of power. Bourguiba supporters advocated for this starting point in order to exclude his era from scrutiny and to prevent anyone from investigating what really happened during his rule.
- *January 1, 1956*: The year Bourguiba assumed power. Initially March 20, 1956, Tunisia's Independence Day, was suggested as the starting point, but in order to preserve the positive connotations of that date, January 1 was offered instead. In any case, those who were in the opposition during Bourguiba's time in power, such as Ennahda, Ettakatol, and the Congress for the Republic, pushed strongly for this earlier starting point. It would not only serve justice to their cause but also put their political rivals, especially Nedaa Tunis and Beji Caid Essebsi, under examination.

Tunisia, unlike its regional counterparts, has begun to make some progress in seeking the truth about its past. The country's transitional justice law, ratified in December 2013, mandated the creation of a Truth and Dignity Commission, which, according to the International Center for Transitional Justice, is to "investigate gross human rights violations that were committed by the state or those who acted in its name and under its protection" since July 1, 1955. After soliciting nominations, the responsible National Constituent Assembly committee carefully selected fifteen commissioners from various societal segments and professional backgrounds to lead the commission's work, which began in the latter half of 2014 and is to last for at least four years.[27]

While delving into the past remains controversial and carries some risk, many Tunisians do not think that revealing the truth will cause or inflame social tensions, and anecdotal evidence supports their stance. Oula Ben Nejma, a lawyer and member of the committee that drafted Tunisia's transitional justice law, reported that "one former prisoner came to me and said he was physically tortured by twelve interrogators. He said he knew all of the twelve including phone numbers of a number of them. He is not going to take revenge but asked that justice be applied so that he can put his ordeal behind him."[28] Said Ferjani, an Ennahda politician, agreed that exposing the truth was unlikely to cause social tension in post–Ben Ali Tunisia, and argued that it would help victims heal. Of equal importance, it would ensure that human rights violations will not be repeated in the future. He explained, "I was physically tortured by Ben Ali's security units. I know the individuals that tortured me. They once asked me if I hated them. I said, 'No, you are a small screw in an enormous system; if you don't do the torture, another officer would, my problem is with the system, not you.' Today, I don't demand those individuals be punished. I don't want financial compensation. I want only one thing: that torture will not happen again in Tunisian prisons."[29]

Libya, Yemen, and Tunisia: A Comparative Perspective on Dealing with Their Pasts

While engaged in a state of transition from dictatorships to civil peace or a democracy, Libya, Yemen, and Tunisia have many lessons to share with regard to the concepts of truth seeking and dealing with the past.

Dealing with the past is a must, though the specific approach should be determined by each country: No matter how a country removes an oppressive regime, whether through a popular uprising as in Tunisia, a bloody revolution as in Libya, or a negotiated agreement as in Yemen, it will have to deal with its past in one way or another. The past is an integral part of the transition process itself, and it will appear forcefully in different phases. Ignoring the past will only make the transition process more complicated as aggrieved parties, especially the victims and their families, fight tooth and nail to ensure that the truth is revealed and justice is served. Attempting to ignore the past will perpetuate the state of polarization in Arab Spring societies. The families of the victims of the Abu Salim prison massacre in Libya, the former prisoners who were tortured in Tunisia, and the families of the missing opposition figures in Yemen all have one voice demanding the truth about the past and compensation for their suffering under the former dictatorships. While dealing with the past is necessary for these societies to heal and move forward, the approach should be determined by each society. As

Desmond Tutu suggested, dealing with the past does not necessarily mean going to the extremes of Nuremberg-style trials or blanket amnesties. In between, there are numerous ways of dealing with past crimes. Dealing with the past should never be understood merely as retribution and trials, though that approach could be implemented in extreme cases where national consensus exists. Amnesty can also be effective, but only if embraced by those who suffered, particularly the victims and their families, not when it is a political compromise dictated by elites as in Yemen.

Selecting a historical starting point for truth seeking is difficult and divisive: A factor that has appeared in all three countries' transitions is the struggle to decide how far back into history a truth-seeking process should delve. In every country interviewees offered at least four different potential starting points, each of which would have its own implications for victim compensation, accountability for perpetrators, and the overall implementation of the truth-seeking process. Determining the starting point for such a process has significant potential to deepen social and political divisions within the societies, possibly even pushing the countries to slide into violence. What finally determines the actual starting point is the overall balance of power among the different political entities in the country. Libya's starting point, Qaddafi's assumption of power on September 1, 1969, was chosen for one major reason—the appearance of heavily armed militants at the doors of the GNC. These ex-combatants pressured the GNC to adopt Libya's controversial Political Isolation Law (discussed in detail in chapter 8), which excludes everybody who worked with the former regime since that date from the new government. Furthermore, the failure to pass an "immunization" law in Tunisia that would have excluded those who helped the former regime in the past from running for public office after the revolution was also a reflection of the power relations among the various political parties in Tunisia. Simply put, those who were part of the Bourguiba and Ben Ali regimes, especially Nedaa Tunis, were able to gather enough support to vote against such measures, opening the way for them to be key players in post-revolution politics.

Truth seeking is highly politicized: There is no such thing as an objective truth-seeking process that purely aims to support victims and penalize perpetrators. The experiences of all three countries show that truth seeking and dealing with the past is a highly politicized process subject to systematic manipulation by the various actors in their attempts to make political gains. This is very obvious in their responses to the question of whether they want to know the truth about the past.

Most of the Libyans I interviewed wanted to know "the full truth about the past." A major reason for their insistence on thoroughly investigating the past is that the former regime was fully eradicated and the truth about the past would help the current parties in power to further pursue the remnants of the regime and exclude all those who worked with it from public life. The pursuit of truth in this case is, to a certain extent, a reflection of the balance of power in the country.

Conversely, most of my Yemeni interviewees did not want to know what happened in the past but to instead focus on the future. Both the opposition and the former regime are part of the past in Yemen, and any robust investigation of what really happened in the past may lead to both Saleh's regime and the parliamentary opposition, especially the Islamist Islah Party, being held accountable for their past political behavior. For example, during the two-month-long 1994 war with the southern part of the country, during which human rights violations were allegedly committed, Saleh's regime and the Islah Party were allied in perpetrating the war. In addition, during the six wars that Saleh's regime fought against the rebellious Houthi movement in the North, General Ali Mohsen al-Ahmar was in command. He is the same general who defected during the 2011 uprising against Saleh, joined the opposition, and ended up protecting the uprising from a potential massive response from Saleh. It is no wonder that Yemeni opposition parties easily agreed to grant Saleh immunity from prosecution against crimes committed in the past in order to get him to step down.

Tunisian respondents, on the other hand, were torn. Some wanted to know the truth, some did not want the truth to come out, and some were primarily concerned about the risks involved. Once again, the country's stance on investigating the truth about possible crimes committed in the past is a reflection of power relations. Ben Ali fled Tunisia, but the majority of his cohort stayed behind. These figures have transitioned to new political parties like al-Mubadara and Nedaa Tunis, which emerged in 2014 as Tunisia's most popular party. Nedaa Tunis in particular opposed efforts to discover the truth about the past. Meanwhile, the transitional troika government—led by Ennahda, which endured significant repression at the hands of the former regime—aggressively pursued the investigation of the past. In Tunisia, truth seeking has been opposed by those hoping to avoid prosecution and supported by those seeking to exclude political opponents, creating a significant split on the issue.

Dealing with the past is necessary for redefining identity: The past for these populations represents imposed political identities by repressive rulers. Regardless of whether the populations actually subscribe to these identities, the top-down approach taken by authoritative rulers has left these populations without any sense of ownership over the identity formation process. Regime change in these countries presents a unique opportunity for these Arab Spring populations to renegotiate such identities on their own terms.

The Jamahiriya system that Qaddafi created is no longer forced on Libyans, and while they deconstruct that former identity, they will need to define what they want as its replacement. By the same token, Bourguiba's legacy remains divisive as Tunisians debate what sort of identity their newly participatory country should have. Likewise, southern Yemenis see unified Yemen as a project of Ali Abdullah Saleh, not part of their own legacy. They see Saleh's removal from power as an opportunity to redefine the relationship between South and North, either by seceding completely to rebuild a "southern identity" or by establishing a new relationship with the North that is built on the principles of full equality and partnership between the two regions. Yemen's National Dialogue Conference has addressed this challenge of redefining past identities by proposing a new federal system of six states, a model with which all Yemenis can identify. Instead of the forced unity imposed by Saleh, or the secession demanded by some radical southern voices, all Yemenis will have equal rights as partners within the larger Yemeni identity.

Dealing with the past helps end polarization by strengthening a collective memory and creating a unifying national narrative: Truth seeking is important for these transitioning Arab societies because it contributes to the consolidation of a collective memory and the development of a national narrative about the past. For Arab Spring societies to come to terms with their past, they will have to have a clear and well-defined discourse of the traumas they went through under the former dictatorships. Truth-seeking efforts will help them uncover the facts about the past and develop new national narratives. The narratives that prevailed in the past were the ones that the regime built. Failure now to reconstruct the truth would leave various parties to proceed on the basis of their own narratives and understandings of the past. The existence of conflicting narratives would lead to confused nations that are pulled in different directions. These societies will then have to deal with competing narratives that can lead to conflict and individual parties' imposing their narratives on others. All three countries have demonstrated this need while grappling with their pasts. In fact, Yemen made impressive progress on this level during its national dialogue conference. The participants openly discussed the country's crises and national traumas, especially the 1994 civil war and the six wars with the Houthis. The conference collectively declared that those conflicts were "unjust wars," and Yemen's transitional president, Abd Rabbu Mansour Hadi, publicly apologized for them.

Tunisians too are slowly coming to acknowledge injustices committed on the national level in their past, especially the persecution and assassinations of the Youssefists, the crushing of the Qafsa mining uprising, and the deliberate marginalization of the western part of Tunisia. Even the Libyan government has recently taken measures to rehabilitate the image and status of King Idris in its national history. When Qaddafi carried out his coup, he stripped King Idris of his Libyan citizenship and confiscated all properties belonging to the king and his family. As a result, King Idris and his family lived in exile until he died in 1983. In March 2014, the Libyan government officially restored his citizenship and that of his family members, and also began a process of identifying seized properties that should be returned to his family. Despite all three countries showing steps toward establishing understandings of their pasts, each of them still has a long way to go. The many still-unresolved issues lend themselves to competing narratives that divide people. Further recognition of these issues definitely contributes to ending polarization and achieving transitional reconciliation.

The recent civil wars in Libya and Yemen will further complicate truth seeking and national reconciliation. Civil wars in general are notorious for human rights violations. Yemen and Libya are not exceptions. Such violations have been noticed in both countries and have taken several forms including but not limited to arbitrary arrests, torture, assassinations, crackdowns on individual liberties, and indiscriminate shelling against displaced communities. When the dusts settles and Libyan and Yemeni societies resume transition and reconciliation again, the victims of the civil wars will want to know the truth about these violations. The longer these civil wars last, the more complicated they will make the national reconciliation processes in the future.

Finally, Arab Spring societies should understand that dealing with the past and knowing the truth about what happened is challenging emotionally and practically. Either because of being overwhelmed with other priorities or simply because of the politics of transitions, Arab Spring societies may be tempted to avoid the past and focus solely on the present and future. Avoiding the past and pretending that it never existed would be a huge mistake. An avoidance approach would lead them to remain entangled with the past and allow the past to continue to threaten the present and future, possibly even breeding conflicts and violence. The past must be faced, and Arab societies in transition must come to terms with what they went through. Dealing with the past will not erase atrocities committed decades ago, but it will minimize their impact on shaping these people's futures. In other words, past grievances and grudges will no longer serve as a motive for vindictive behavior. Breaking cleanly from the past and its problems will be a significant step in these Arab Spring societies' ensuring a healthy transition toward civil peace and national reconciliation.

SEVEN

Reparations

The brutal repression of former Arab dictators over the past three to four decades resulted in a variety of grievances. Indeed, many suffered injustices of all kinds, including torture, imprisonment, forced disappearance, assassination, exile, death under torture, execution without trials, and sacking from public office. These dictatorships also targeted entire groups collectively—not only individuals. In particular, some towns and cities were penalized through marginalization and the neglect of development projects as punishment for political opposition. As a result, the practices of old authoritarian regimes left their societies divided between those who benefited from allying with the authorities and those who suffered from acting against the rulers. Regimes in Tunisia, Libya, and Yemen have been removed, yet deep divisions within their societies remain, particularly between the former ruling class and the ruled, and have perhaps even deepened.

This chapter argues that now that these societies are engaging in transitions from dictatorship to civil peace, in order for them to forge a new social contract, the injustices of the past must be addressed. That is, an intensive reparations process must begin immediately to help victims come to terms with their pasts and prepare them to deal with the challenges of the new post-dictatorship era. Victims of past human rights violations require both moral and material support. Morally, their past suffering must be acknowledged, while materially, they should receive the support they need to secure a decent living, whether it be financial assistance or some sort of rehabilitation. The success in repairing past damages and helping victims to move forward will go a long way in diminishing the polarization that the former regime left between its loyalists and the opposition. If these states fail to help victims of the old regimes heal their wounds, the new governments will exclude them from the reconstruction of their societies, thereby deepening polarization and instability.

As explained by Naomi Roht-Arriaza, reparations are important in particular because they "are both material and moral: reparations for the body to enable survival, reparations for the spirit and the sense of justice, and some sense of a decorous and secure future for future generations." Material reparations include a variety of goods, such as "the restitution of access, and title to, property taken or lost, a job or freedom, a pension or a person's good name . . . [and] medical psychiatric or occupational therapy aimed at rehabilitation." Moral reparations, on the other hand, "may include disclosure of the facts of a victim's mistreatment or a loved one's death, disclosures of the names and positions of those responsible and of the patterns of repression. They may include official acknowledgement that government agents wronged the victims, and an apology. They may include, most importantly for many victims, that those responsible suffer consequences, whether criminal, civil, or administrative—that they are brought to justice, and removed from positions of power." Psychosocial assistance, though not sufficient in itself, as the case of Angola shows, should also be included in reparations programs.[1]

Perhaps most importantly, any provision of reparations should take the needs and preferences of victims into account. As Abdulsalam Ajetunmobi argues, "Consideration of justice's impact on the actual lives of victims is paramount." He finds that while only 12 percent of Sierra Leonean victims and 22 percent of families of missing persons in East Timor considered criminal prosecutions important, most felt a need for "non-judicial strategies, including forgiveness, material compensation, symbolic acknowledgement and recognition of their victimhood."[2] Similarly, East Timorese, Cambodian, and Rwandan victims have all expressed the importance of documented perpetrators admitting their wrongdoings for justice, reconciliation, and peacebuilding.[3]

In addition to being both material and moral, reparations are also both individual and collective. They are meant to recognize wrongs done to segments of society as a whole as well as to individual victims. A reparations program in Peru included the acknowledgment that some ethnic minorities and the poor had been treated as second-class citizens, and assurances that the state would protect their rights in the future.[4] The effect of reparations on individual victims also influences broader society, helping to demonstrate the government's commitment to rebuilding society after major conflict.[5]

In the context of transitions, as in the case of Arab Spring societies, some scholars maintain that a program of reparations "acts as a bridge between the past and the future. It combines the backward-looking objective of compensating victims with the forward-looking objectives of political reform. Thus, it helps the new state in reconciling itself with its past."[6]

Each of Tunisia, Yemen, and Libya has its own share of former regime violations, and these countries face similar challenges in dealing with the massive numbers of victims that dictatorships left behind. Each country's experience is discussed at length, including challenges and possible solutions. Finally, the end of the chapter analyzes—from a comparative perspective— reparations and how they contribute to successful transitions toward peace and reconciliation in the three countries under study.

Tunisia

Many Tunisians agree that those who suffered under Zine El Abidine Ben Ali, and to a large extent under Habib Bourguiba, should be compensated in some manner. Those who would receive reparations include victims of torture, imprisonment, and exile, as well as families of those who were tortured to death. It is highly unlikely that national reconciliation is possible in Tunisia without seriously engaging in the reparation of past injuries, especially those suffered under Ben Ali. During his rule, injustices took place on a large scale and involved not only opposition figures but their families as well. As Oula Ben Nejma, a member of the transitional justice drafting committee, explained, "Several political prisoners were able to resume their lives under Bourguiba, as the ruler believed in giving them a second chance. He even granted jobs to some Tunisians to facilitate their reintegration into the society and their abandonment of activism. Ben Ali, however, took a different tack and effectively banned any prisoners, their families, and even relatives from job opportunities in the public as well as private sectors. Ben Ali's philosophy was that not only should members of the opposition be penalized, but rather their entire clans as well."[7]

While there is currently no major disagreement in Tunisia about the principle of reparations, the approach to addressing past injuries remains hotly debated. No single tactic in the Tunisian case seems to have sufficiently addressed the problem. Disputes center on the efficacy of lump-sum payments, the advisability of providing public-sector jobs to victims of the former regime, and the overall type and amount of reparations that are reasonable.

At one point, the Tunisian government proposed making a one-time payment of 60,000 Tunisian Dinars (approximately $38,000) to victims of torture and imprisonment to settle their cases. The government backed away from this plan, however, after receiving sharp criticism from civil society.[8] The risk of such an approach is that beneficiaries would spend the money quickly and then turn again to the state for solutions. Indeed, such a single payment would be unlikely to provide victims with adequate compensation over the long term for the pain of being tortured and the opportunity costs of being imprisoned.

To avoid the potential problems associated with lump-sum payments, some Tunisians instead proposed providing victims of human rights violations with employment in the public sector. While giving the victims jobs to support themselves may sound like a sustainable solution, it has the potential to cause greater societal problems. Increased public-sector hiring can create a bloated bureaucracy, which would do more damage than good to the state. Furthermore, many victims, especially those who spent long periods in prison, do not have the right sets of skills or education to perform public-sector jobs. Such hires would therefore likely lead to a decline in government efficiency. In addition, in the case of Tunisia, a large majority of the victims of torture and imprisonment under the former regime were Islamists. If they were all to receive positions in the public sector, one segment of Tunisian society—Islamists—would, to an extent, take over the state and its bureaucratic system.[9]

Victims' expected amounts of compensation are, not surprisingly, quite high. No matter how much the state tries to make amends financially, the damage caused by the former regime can never be fully repaired. Indeed, how can money compensate a mother who lost her son or a man who spent over a decade in prison and lost his chance at an education and a decent life? Even when amounts of compensation are low, their provision can pose a huge problem for a country like Tunisia, which lacks resources to finance its transition process. Tunisia therefore must be innovative in addressing this dilemma. One way to decrease costs while still providing reparations is by combining moral solutions with material ones. For example, one man told Oula Ben Nejma that he did not want any money for his son's death but rather hoped that a street would be named after him.[10] Other possible means of reparation include state issuance of licenses to allow Tunisians to open businesses or the offer of a free education. Certainly, however, Tunisia will need to create a fund to pay reparations to victims, and should invite local and international donors to contribute to it.

Dealing improperly with victims and their families can be very costly. The Tunisian government suffered a series of setbacks while trying to resolve the question of the reparation and rehabilitation of ex-political detainees. Frustrated by the government's mismanagement of their situation, these former political prisoners conducted protests in front of the government offices in Tunis for over five months, demanding fair and speedy resolutions of their cases. Many were unable to easily reintegrate into Tunisian society due to their lack of income and skills after enduring long prison terms. The Tunisian Ministry of Human Rights gave them jobs in an attempt to resolve these cases, but the positions were menial and, for some, degrading. Former prisoners were offered jobs as janitors, doormen, and guards. Indeed, some of the protestors displayed a picture of a colleague who was tortured under Ben Ali and spent over ten years in prison working as a gardener. As one protestor explained, "This is very humiliating. We're not demanding that we become rich but we need a little dignity. This is very important for us." In another incident, "The Ministry of Human Rights sent one of the female prisoners for a maid job in the Manouba area. When she arrived at the house, she found the owner of the house was a former ruling party figure. Yes, the Ministry later apologized but it was too late."[11] The long-term social and political consequences of handling victims and their reparation improperly, therefore, are too serious for the government to ignore.

The good news for the Tunisian government is that the number of cases of severe human rights violations under the former regime is relatively small. There are only thirty-two recorded cases of torturing to death in Ben Ali's prisons, while the number in neighboring Libya reaches the thousands.[12]

A final dilemma of reparations in Tunisia is differentiating between compensation for individuals and for groups. Both Ben Ali and Bourguiba, to varying degrees, used collective punishment to suppress opposition. Neighborhoods, towns, and even entire regions were penalized for their residents' opposition to the dictators. Western Tunisia in particular is significantly underdeveloped in comparison to other parts of the country, due to the fact that opposition to the Bourguiba regime came from that region, and therefore the government used collective punishment in impeding development there. As a result, comprehensive reparations will require the state to implement special development programs in the previously marginalized areas to help them catch up to the rest of Tunisia.

Yemen

Reparations for damage caused to victims of past crimes in Yemen are essential for the success of building a national consensus that moves reconciliation and civil peace forward. Although it is impossible to undo past damage, failure to recognize the sufferings of the victims in Yemen and to compensate them will allow the issues of the past to generate further conflicts, disunity, and possibly renewed fighting. Therefore, to heal the wounds of victims and rid the transition in Yemen of past injustices, reparations should be awarded within a framework of transitional justice laws that address the victims' needs on two levels: compensation (moral and material) for the damage that happened in the past and holding perpetrators accountable for violations they committed.

There are several categories of victims of past crimes in Yemen. Forced disappearance was a problem dating back to the early days of President Ali Abdullah Saleh's arrival to power in 1978. At that time, a group of Ba'athists was accused of plotting to conduct a coup against Saleh, and when it failed, a number of the accused were executed, while the fate of others remains unknown even today. Forced disappearances also took place in the 1980s and especially in the 1990s during the war with South Yemen. The families of those who disappeared are still protesting, demanding the truth about the fates of their loved ones.

In addition to forced disappearances, large numbers of people were imprisoned and tortured during Saleh's thirty-three-year reign for opposing the regime's repressive policies. Likewise, wars against the South (1994) and the Houthis in the North (2004–2010) left many killed, wounded, or exiled, and others dependent, as they found themselves without anyone to care for their livelihoods. Particularly after the transitional president, Abd Rabbu Mansour Hadi, publicly admitted that these wars were unjust, redress for their victims and the families of those affected has become more necessary than ever. Reparations for victims of past crimes in Yemen are quite a complicated matter and are challenged on several levels. These challenges, if no serious solutions are provided, threaten to undermine the process of victims' reparation.

First, the nature of the settlement that led to President Saleh's leaving power is not conducive to justice or to victims' redress. Simply put, the Gulf Cooperation Council initiative granted the former ruler and his main advisors immunity from prosecution, in effect excusing the entire regime. Indeed, as a result, holding perpetrators accountable for their past crimes will not be feasible in post-Saleh Yemen, especially because the immunity clause was approved by the Yemeni parliament. In fact, in the legislature, the opposition, led by the Joint Meeting Parties, joined the former ruling party members in signing off on the immunity deal, making it impossible to bypass or ignore. While the initiative enabled "macro-reconciliation" at the national level, it failed to address individual reconciliation and in particular the sufferings of victims of the Saleh regime and their families. In other words, the power transition deal sacrificed responding to the grievances of the individual victims for the larger cause of solving the country's broader political crisis.

Establishing an effective transitional justice law that addresses the needs of victims has become particularly challenging. Given the former regime's immunity from prosecution, transitional justice in Yemen is generally referred to in terms of compensation to the victims and their families; nothing is said about historical truth, accountability, or the identification of perpetrators. Such an approach does not constitute transitional justice but rather buying the silence of the victims and their families. Even worse, a limited transitional justice law that addresses only financial compensation for the victims while limiting the ability to investigate crimes and prosecute suspects would establish a precedent in post-Saleh Yemen of human rights violations and corruption going unpunished. As the director of Human Rights Watch's Middle East and North Africa division, Sarah Leah Whitson, put it, "Redress is an essential component of justice, but a truth commission without the judicial power to learn the truth is an affront to victims. . . . Burying the mistakes of the past is a sure path toward reinforcing impunity."[13]

Reparations to victims of past crimes are made even more difficult due to Yemen's precarious financial situation. Certainly, the human rights violations of Saleh's thirty-three-year rule were massive and far-reaching, while the financial resources available to engage the victims and their families in effective redress programs are extremely limited. Yemen simply lacks the funds to tackle immediate development needs and restoration of basic services such as water and electricity, let alone reparations. On its national priority list, therefore, reparation programs may come toward the bottom. Limited or no support to victims of past human rights violations may complicate their mourning, add to their frustration and anger, and eventually lead to further instability and polarization. For example, in order for a tribal leader to encourage members of his tribe to forgo retaliation in favor of reconciliation, he would be expected to offer compensation to families who lost their primary breadwinners.[14]

The victims of past violations in Yemen have waited for decades for justice to be served. Now that their source of frustration—the former regime—

has been removed, they will not be willing to wait any longer. They need to see solutions delivered. To prevent losing the major gains made in the transition, victims of the Saleh regime want to see their grievances addressed immediately.

Libya

Victims deserving of reparations due to past human rights violations in Libya date as far back as 1969, when Colonel Muammar Qaddafi took power. Libyans suffered different kinds of victimhood under the Qaddafi regime. There are thousands of victims of assassinations, torture, forced disappearance, and execution without trial, as in the infamous Abu Salim prison massacre where 1,270 people were killed in two hours. In addition, there are victims of wars fought primarily for Qaddafi's personal motives, namely with Chad (1978–1987), where an estimated 7,500 Libyans were killed. Many Libyans are still wondering today why they fought a ten-year war with their neighbor.

Financial reparations are generally quite costly, and in Libya's case, they have the potential to be extremely expensive given that human rights abuses under Qaddafi were widespread and lasted for forty-two years. Further complicating the Libyan case, reparations require not only direct payments to those who were abused by the regime but also the resolution of serious property and ownership disputes. For example, repairing the damage from Qaddafi's Law No. 4/1978 (the "Ownership Law") will require the state to make whole both those whose homes were appropriated and those who subsequently bought those houses lawfully. Both of these parties have legitimate claims to the property, and the state must compensate whichever party was wronged under the law.

The good news for redress in Libya is the fact that it is a wealthy, oil-exporting country with a relatively small population of around six million people. The Libyan government should therefore be able to extend reasonable compensation packages for cases of past wrongdoing. In fact, state funds have already paid for medical treatment for almost all of those Libyans wounded during the revolution. Hospitals in Jordan, for example, received approximately 27,000 patients, all of whose fees were paid by the Libyan state.[15] Tunisian hospitals treated similar numbers and were also paid by the state.

No matter how large the amount of money set aside, however, financial resources alone will not be sufficient to fully repair decades of state abuse. Moral measures play a central role in providing redress for victims of the former regime. Some of the demands of the families of the victims of the Abu Salim massacre are a good example. When I attended the annual meeting of the families of the victims in Tripoli in 2012, I noticed that most of the demands focused on the recognition and acknowledgment of the massacre rather than financial aspects of reparation. They have asked that victims be remembered by the establishment of a memorial and by naming streets, schools, and other public places in their honor. They also request that the massacre be mentioned in school textbooks so that later generations learn about it, in the hope that such an atrocity will not be repeated.[16]

Moral recognition is particularly important for redress in the Libyan cultural context. Victims of torture place special importance on the acknowledgment of their previous suffering. When asked about the type of compensation they expected, a number of victims interviewed answered with the traditional Libyan saying, "Show me my rights, and then you can take them."[17] This means that they want their rights to be recognized first, after which they can forgive without demanding punishment or compensation. Indeed, for some victims, the acknowledgment of past sufferings seemed more important than financial compensation.

Finally, the Libyan case is even more complicated, as in their case, reparations involve not only victims of past crimes but also victims of current crimes. During the revolution that ousted Qaddafi, almost one million refugees fled the country for fear of violence and potential retribution, as many were perceived to be allies of the former regime. In addition, an estimated 64,000 people that fled their towns to other parts of Libya, also in large part due to fear of retaliation, remained displaced as of May 2014.[18] A large number of those refugees and internally displaced persons (IDPs) include family members of individuals who were in some way linked to the Qaddafi regime. Furthermore, prisoners believed to be Qaddafi loyalists were severely tortured in secret prisons held by revolutionaries who accused loyalists of aiding the former regime during the uprising.[19] With all of the suffering they have experienced because one family member was linked to the former regime, current victims of displacement and torture will demand reparations just as much as those who were victimized by the Qaddafi regime.

The cost of reparations for "current victims" might become even higher, as their suffering is ongoing. In fact, Ali al-Tawerghi, a representative of the Tawergha IDP camp in Janzour near Tripoli, argues that Tawerghans are now themselves the victims of atrocities. "Before we uncover the truth of past violations," al-Tawerghi said, "we need to uncover the truth of present violations. There is no transitional justice. There is only one justice, and that is the justice of the victor."[20] Victims of current violations also demand reparations. Ignoring the unjustified suffering of the "children of perpetrators" may produce a generation of youth frustrated with their country, as it has granted them only the bitterness of displacement. With that in mind, ignoring their experiences of victimization will contribute to "structural polarization" and instability when a new generation of almost one million refugees and IDPs are prevented from going back to their homes for crimes their parents are accused of committing.

Reparations: Comparative Analysis

Reparations to victims of past human rights violations are vital for successful transitions to peace and reconciliation. The preceding analysis of Tunisia, Yemen, and Libya shows a link between the dynamics of reparations to victims of past wrongdoings and stability, polarization, and civil peace. Failure to address the injustices committed against citizens of the three countries will reinforce frustration, exacerbate anger, and may eventually lead to acts of social unrest. Frustrated by the governments' slow response to their grievances, victims of past violations have taken matters into their own hands and acted on their discontent in all three countries under study. They have also expressed a willingness to escalate protests unless their demands are fully met. Therefore, discontent of victims will function as an impediment to unity unless they are incorporated into the reconciliation process.

There is a great risk that some Arab Spring societies will fail to address the needs of the victims of past crimes simply because those nations are overwhelmed with the massive challenges facing their transitions. The civil war in Libya and the Houthi rebellion in Yemen have caused those countries to prioritize security over any other transition task, no matter how important it is for their long-term stability. The Libyan people and decision-makers, for example, have practically forgotten about the families of the victims of the Abu Salim prison massacre in the midst of the civil war between Operation Dignity and Libya Dawn. Ignoring the needs and demands of victims over the long term will push victims and their families to oppose their governments, perhaps even by taking part in civil conflict, thus reinforcing those conflicts and further undermining the spirit of the transition process. It should be kept in mind that the Operation Dignity/Libya Dawn–led civil war has significantly exacerbated the reparation challenge by adding additional massive numbers of new victims that, when the civil war is over, will require reparations as well.

It is important to remember that, in all three cases, there is not one type of victim of past violations. The former dictatorships created multiple categories of victims as well as collective victims. The regimes' violations were massive, especially as they occurred over three or four decades in all three countries. Such a massive scale of violations obviously requires solutions on the same level, which makes the task of reparation enormous.

There is no easy way to repair the damage created by the practices of former regimes. However, the experiences of the three countries under study show that a variety of approaches will be required to address the grievances of victims and help them overcome past traumas. Such approaches include material and moral compensation, truth seeking (though it is opposed by certain stakeholders), and accountability for the perpetrators.

Truth and accountability are particularly helpful in healing the emotional aspects of the victims' need for redress. But Tunisia, Yemen, and Libya all demonstrated high levels of confusion over the use of these two approaches. This has led to further complications in the victims' mourning and healing processes. Yemen complicated the victims' healing process by granting former regime figures immunity from prosecution and allowing them to hold positions of power in the transitional government. Libya, on the other hand, experienced backlash due to excessive retribution against the perpetrators. Tunisia, by contrast, seems to have responded to victims' need for justice in a more sound and moderate approach, namely through legislating a transitional justice law that deals with both victims and perpetrators, though limitations exist.

Financial compensation is critical for reparation and for the countries' successful political transitions. Financing reparation, however, is more complicated than many realize. Resources emerged as a serious challenge for the governments' ability to finance reparations. Three major factors make funding reparations particularly difficult: the high expectations of victims, the overwhelming number of victims entitled to reparations, and the limited resources of new governments to engage in reparations programs. There is no easy solution to this financial challenge as new governments, with the exception of Libya's, simply do not have the funds to finance reparations. Possible solutions, however, may include international funding of transition processes, something that is already occurring, and placing reparations on the financial aid agenda. In addition, governments should focus on rehabilitation programs, granting privileges (e.g., business licenses) to victims, as well as providing moral reparations in the form of public acknowledgments of victims' suffering.

Victims' mourning and healing are further complicated by the absence of perpetrators' apologies for past injustices. Regime change during the Arab Spring led to a pattern of dictators' leaving power without emotionally settling their antagonism with their people in general and with those who were hurt in particular. Indeed, in Libya, Muammar Qaddafi was killed without having apologized. In Yemen, Ali Abdullah Saleh stepped down without acknowledging the thirty-three years of poverty that the Yemeni people experienced under his reign. In addition, Tunisia's Zine El Abidine Ben Ali escaped without apologizing for the political repression that Tunisians suffered during his tenure. The absence of apologies or acknowledgment of past injustices will encourage acts of revenge and deepen polarization, in addition of course to making victims' mourning and healing from trauma particularly complicated. As discussed in chapter 5, national dialogue and inclusivity can help to elicit some attitude of future togetherness and minimize polarization.

Arab Spring societies should be very careful to ensure reparations not only for victims of past crimes, but in some cases for victims of ongoing crimes. The absence of an effective national reconciliation process has led, particularly in Libya, to severe acts of revenge, imprisonment, torture, assassinations, and large-scale displacement, among other wrongdoings. Instead of repairing the damage caused to victims of the past, Libya has generated new victims and new damages in the post-Qaddafi era, pushing the country into a vicious cycle of victimization and retaliation. In other words, the victims of yesterday are the victimizers of today. The only way to break this cycle will be, again, to institute an inclusive and transparent national dialogue process that can bring the parties together to share fears and concerns, and proceed toward a stable future that they collaboratively put together.

Finally, no matter what approaches are proposed to effectively treat the wounds of the victims, those approaches will have to lead to dignified solutions that help victims move forward in their social environments. The traumas of the past are highly sensitive and require very careful handling; otherwise, intervention could make things worse. Treating reparations as merely financial compensation to solve a problem, for instance, may backfire, as some victims of past crimes care more about their experience than money. Conversations with victims from all three countries revealed that some are actually offended when their past pain and suffering is dealt with strictly on financial grounds. They cared as much about the understanding and acknowledgment of their experiences as they did for their livelihoods. A solution with dignity could serve as a very powerful tool to repair past injustices and contribute to ending polarization in their societies.

EIGHT

Dealing with the Former Regime

Accountability and Lustration

For Libya, Tunisia, and Yemen, dealing with former regime elements is an integral part of the national reconciliation process and necessary for successful transitions to peace and stability. The approach each country takes in handling their former regime apparatuses and members will have a major impact on the ability of these post-dictatorship societies to reduce and overcome their high levels of polarization. The process of dealing with former regimes has two inherently connected aspects: accountability and lustration. Accountability involves prosecuting perpetrators of past violations and is generally applied within a framework of a transitional justice law.[1] Lustration is the institution of policies and processes that regulate or prevent "the participation of people associated with the former regime in the successor political system."[2]

This chapter argues that Libya, Tunisia, and Yemen need to pursue accountability to curtail vigilantism and establish rule of law. However, they should be wary that excessive accountability through retributive justice may backfire by leading to further instability, complicating the transition process. In addition, as alluded to in the chapter on reparations, the three countries must incorporate restorative justice as part of the application of the principle of accountability. In studying East Timor, Rwanda, and Cambodia, Wendy Lambourne finds that when states focus on accountability and prosecutions without incorporating restorative aspects that can build relationships, they are "unlikely to overcome the societal divisions that undermine peace and security."[3] When it comes to lustration, Libya, Yemen, and Tunisia must tread carefully, with Libya in particular needing to revise or repeal its Political Isolation Law. Yemen must incorporate deep party reform as part of its approach to dealing with the former regime and its ruling party. A meticulous vetting process could also serve as a strong alternative to a lustration law.

Libya, Tunisia, and Yemen should prioritize accountability to curtail the individual acts of vengeance that can occur following a transition, especially when the fall of a regime is accompanied by the deterioration of the rule of law. In essence, if the state does not address justice, it runs the risk of widespread vigilantism.[4] Supporters of retributive justice find that the application of accountability has a positive effect on victims of past offenses. They argue that "only trials . . . lead to a full recognition of the worth and dignity of those victimized by past abuses. A post-conflict society thus has a moral obligation to prosecute and punish the perpetrators."[5] In El Salvador and Honduras, the lack of admissions by—and convictions of—perpetrators of human rights violations made victims and their families less willing to forgive and forget.[6] This is especially true in the case of the transitioning Arab countries where the number of victims of state repression is so high. Helping these victims to heal and move on will be important to comprehensive national reconciliation and the overall success of the transitions.

Bringing suspects to trial can also establish individual accountability, thereby limiting the amount of blame indiscriminately placed on all of the people associated with the former regimes for its abuses, which can exacerbate polarization and lead to violence.[7] The regimes that fell during the Arab Spring employed bloated public sectors, and most of those who worked within them never engaged in corruption or human rights violations. Those that are innocent should not have to live in fear of retribution for crimes they did not personally commit. Failing to establish individual accountability will perpetuate this fear and leave members of the old regime feeling vulnerable. Without assurance that no acts of revenge or injustices will be committed against them, they may seek to regroup in order to protect themselves, causing divisions and polarization to persist and harden. This is a major lesson from the Iraqi experience, where punishing the entire

Ba'ath Party through de-Ba'athification policies deepened structural divisions among the country's communities.

By pursuing accountability the transitional governments of Libya, Tunisia, and Yemen can assure their societies that autocratic rule is over, rule of law is being instituted, and crimes will no longer be committed with impunity. If these states fail to hold old regime elements accountable for their crimes, it will signal that justice remains lacking in these countries and trust in the entire transition process will erode. One of the biggest flaws of the Taif Agreement that ended Lebanon's civil war in 1989 was that it allowed warlords to transition back to civil and political life without being held even slightly accountable for their numerous war crimes. Lebanon's civil strife, divisions, and structural weakness persisted. The warlords remain among Lebanon's most powerful politicians to this day, and the fragile peace among their factions has been interrupted by a number of violent episodes over the ensuing twenty-seven years.

Accountability can reduce polarization and help transitioning Arab societies move forward, but it also has important limitations. One major challenge is conducting fair trials when they are fundamentally political. Indeed, "a human rights problem arises when the behavior the courts must judge is of a purely political nature, such as membership in a pro-authoritarian movement or publicly advertised approval of totalitarian ideas."[8] Convictions on the basis of speech or association would clearly be counterproductive to the establishment of new states that respect basic human rights. Additionally, the prosecution of former regime members risks provoking a backlash that could destabilize what are new, fragile governments.[9] Some scholars have argued that trying such cases can actually "obliterate and distort" the cause of truth seeking by allowing issues to become confused and the past muddled.[10] Accountability also faces the fundamental challenge that "the past—including the economic and ecological impact it has on the present and future—cannot be changed or undone, due to the non-retroactivity of causality. Nor can the cultural values, attitudes and behavioral patterns that have been cultivated under the old regime be undone, or at best undone only in the medium or long run."[11] Considering these limitations, Libyan,

Tunisian, and Yemeni societies should be realistic in their expectations and understand that accountability is only one piece of the larger national reconciliation process they all need. Nonetheless, accountability is necessary to mitigate the negative effects of former regime elements on the futures of these states, and to lay the foundations for the rule of law.

In countries where wholesale regime change has taken place, the new governments often complement the application of accountability with lustration. Lustration, depending on its form, can effectively put the entire former regime on trial rather than specific individuals. Under the most exclusionary variants of lustration, all person who served in the former regime are prevented from being part of the successor political system because of their involvement with the old regime, regardless of whether they are found guilty of violations. They are "guilty by association." The transitioning Arab Spring countries have confused lustration as being an aspect of transitional justice, as accountability is. Unlike accountability, however, lustration targets an entire group, not individuals, and disqualifies them through employment laws and electoral systems, not convictions. As one expert puts it, "Regulations like the political isolation law in Libya should not be seen in any way linked to transitional justice in the Arab region. It is an electoral system that regulates elections and who should and should not run. Transitional justice, however, is about prosecution of perpetrators for past crimes."[12] Libya and Tunisia have entertained exclusionary lustration laws that they label as "protecting the revolution" from the influence of former regime elements or even counter-revolutions. Libya's parliament passed the very controversial Political Isolation Law (PIL) by a vote of 164 to 4. Rather than protecting the revolution, implementation of the law may be setting the country up for deeper polarization, further divisions, and a possible counter-revolution or significant violence.

Lustration in the post–Arab Spring phase is problematic and could undermine the entire transition process by establishing a foundation for future violence. Major criticisms of lustration include that it can penalize individuals for acts that were not crimes at the time when they were committed, violating the rule of law. Similarly, when lustration policies bar former regime members from holding certain public positions because they were members of a former organization, due process is violated.[13] Another challenge of implementing lustration policies that could be especially problematic for Libya, Yemen, and Tunisia is that doing so would jeopardize the "institutional memory" of the state. As previously mentioned, the bureaucratic systems of the former regimes were very large, and it is the tens of thousands of civil servants that know how to run the state. Excluding those bureaucrats from the new system will undoubtedly have a negative impact on how the state functions. No matter how skilled the new personnel are, they will lack useful institutional knowledge and face steep learning curves. Lustration policies have also raised concerns over the "moral aspect of creating a new democracy on the basis of exclusion."[14]

Despite these drawbacks, lustration has some merits. One major argument in support of lustration is that "bureaucratic change is required in order to create a trustworthy and competent state apparatus."[15] In addition, lustration may "minimize the influence of the legacy of the non-democratic past on the democratizing present."[16] The revolutionaries that drove the uprisings in Libya, Tunisia, and Yemen, and the general publics at large, have exhibited strong support for such laws. Some of this is self-serving, but a larger portion of it seems to stem from a basic desire to ban the officials of the highly corrupt and abusive former regimes from any role in public life. Under these conditions, policymakers, regardless of whether they are convinced that lustration is in the best interests of their country, feel pressure to adhere to the demands of their constituencies. After all, their positions now depend on their ability to build trust with voters, not their loyalty to a ruler.

All of these factors suggest that there is no easy way to handle lustration in post-conflict situations, and that the Arab societies in transition will have to tread carefully. Each state should objectively assess its transition and attempt to determine to what extent lustration and accountability can contribute to stability and peace rather than disorder and violence. Libya, Tunisia, and Yemen have taken three different approaches to accountability and lustration. Yemen decided to forgo accountability and lustration by granting the former regime—Ali Abdullah Saleh and all the people who worked with him—full immunity against prosecution in exchange for his stepping down. Libya has pursued accountability and lustration to the extreme by instituting its PIL. The law precludes those who worked with the former regime from holding public office for ten years. Tunisia has developed and adopted a transitional justice law that targets only former regime figures who are linked to past crimes as part of its larger legal framework. Tunisia has also seriously considered approving a severe lustration policy titled the "Immunization of Revolution Law." The rest of this chapter discusses how each country is dealing with accountability and lustration, and then compares how the approaches are affecting their chances of achieving meaningful national reconciliation going forward.

Libya

To achieve national reconciliation, and thereby stability and civil peace, Libya must unequivocally apply the principle of accountability by holding individuals directly linked to past crimes responsible for their actions. This includes crimes committed under Muammar Qaddafi's reign and during the 2014 civil war. This is important not only for the victims and their families but also for a society that is undergoing a transition from a dictatorship to a new system of governance. Victims and their families are unlikely to embrace the new regime until they see their tormentors prosecuted, while the public will only begin to trust the new state when they see justice and rule of law being established. Furthermore, holding perpetrators accountable for their crimes will send a clear message to current and future rulers that committing human rights violations will no longer be tolerated. However, Libyans should be aware that applying accountability does not necessarily mean that a large number of former regime figures will be executed. Using accountability in such an extreme manner would likely backfire and lead to instability and further division. What matters is applying the principle of accountability itself, rather than focusing on the numbers of former regime figures that are held accountable to their past actions. In addition, Libyans should understand that retributive justice alone will not ultimately solve the issue of the old regime, but must be combined with restorative justice to achieve the desired civil peace.

In the first few years after the revolution, Libya took several steps toward holding members of the former regime accountable for their actions while in office. Over one hundred senior former regime figures were being held in Libyan prisons as of June 2015. In October 2013, approximately thirty-eight of them appeared in court in Tripoli, including former prime minister al-Baghdadi al-Mahmoudi, former foreign minister Abd al-Ati al-Obaidi, and former spy chief Abdullah al-Sanousi. In addition, Libyan authorities requested that Interpol issue warrants against forty other former senior officials who were still at large, including Qaddafi's cousin and former aide Ahmed Qaddaf al-Dam, former interior minister Naser al-Mabrouk, and Qaddafi's daughter Aisha.

Yet even merely punishing former regime figures has not been a simple task. One of the first challenges Libya faced in trying to establish accountability was the lack of a competent and functioning justice system to adjudicate the many crimes committed during Qaddafi's forty-two years in power. As it stands, Libya's justice system needs fundamental reform after having been marginalized and corrupted under the former regime. In fact, some of Libya's revolutionaries have insisted that the judiciary be purged before any trials take place. The resulting paralysis has contributed to the deterioration of security in the country.

The Libyan justice system's lack of credibility was exacerbated by the case of the former dictator's son, Saif al-Islam al-Qaddafi. Since he was captured in November 2011, al-Islam has been held by the Zentan Military Council, which has refused to hand him over to Tripoli, citing distrust in the central government's ability to properly safeguard him. The International Criminal Court (ICC) has also demanded al-Islam's extradition and rejected Libya's request to try him, due to concerns over Libya's ability to conduct a fair trial. As of September 2015, al-Islam's trial in Zentan had been suspended, a Tripoli court had sentenced him to death, and the dispute with the ICC had yet to be resolved.[17]

Another major challenge is the proportionately high number of individuals suspected of corruption and human rights violations. If everyone who committed a violation or corrupt act was held accountable, much of the old regime would have to be tried, which would preclude a successful transition. Rwanda faced this problem after its 1994 genocide. In that case, Rwanda detained 130,000 suspects and prosecuted over 2 million cases; the huge scale of the accountability efforts overwhelmed the country's judiciary system, leading to lapses in due process and even deaths due to overcrowding in prisons.[18]

While the political, security, and logistical issues are substantial, Libya's ultimate challenge in regard to accountability is how to pursue it without undermining national reconciliation in the process. One possible solution is to ensure that the principle of accountability itself is implemented, with the form and extent of implementation varying as appropriate. Applying the principle is important for establishing a new Libya where corruption and violations of human rights do not go unpunished. Nevertheless, accountability does not necessarily have to mean a Nuremburg-style approach, where everyone who was part of the former regime will be penalized on the basis of his or her association. Libyans will have to decide whether they want to fully pursue retributive justice, which seeks to punish perpetrators in proportion with their crime and can be summed up as "an eye for an eye," or instead embrace some form of restorative justice, which seeks to reconcile offenders to their victims and the community at large.

Some victims demand retributive justice against certain regime figures, viewing it as necessary to grant them closure and help them move forward. While retribution may provide limited psychological release to victims, Libyans will have to realize that achieving stability in their post-conflict context requires a restorative strategy that seeks to repair broken relationships and heal deep wounds within society. If Libya pursues restorative justice, regime figures may be granted an opportunity to acknowledge the suffering of their countrymen, apologize for their past wrongdoings, and seek forgiveness. Under either approach to justice, former regime individuals would have to relinquish all privileges they gained due to their positions.[19]

In addition to accountability, lustration has been one of the most divisive challenges to Libya's post-conflict reconstruction efforts. Suggested approaches have ranged from a complete ban on former regime officials' occupation of any public position, regardless of the level and nature of their involvement with the former regime, to their regulated incorporation into the new state's institutions. Revolutionaries were adamant that the law should encompass not only the former regime's senior leadership and security officials but also a broader class of officials deemed to have contributed to the regime.[20] They argued that the regime functioned as a whole, not just as individual units, and that even those not directly involved in the torture of prisoners, for example, helped to perpetuate the regime while offenses were ongoing.

Libya's revolutionaries ultimately got their way when the General National Congress (GNC), its hand forced by the militias holding it hostage at the time, adopted the PIL on May 5, 2013. The law imposed a ten-year ban from holding public office and other select positions on those who had previously held high-ranking positions—including ministers, police chiefs, and student union heads—at any point during the Qaddafi regime. Other criteria for possible exclusion include collaboration with the security forces, public praising of Qaddafi or his "Green Book," or having done business with the regime.[21]

Those pushing for the law in its most extreme form successfully demanded that it apply to officials who defected before and during the revolution, even those who had publicly split with the regime decades ago. Some proponents of the PIL argued that there is no such thing as defecting from the old regime, just smart political calculations by some former regime officials; they read the political map well and realized the regime was at its end. They jumped from the "sinking boat to a new one." The law should not be seen as targeting individuals but rather the way of thinking and acting under the former regime.[22]

Other political parties expressed a forward-looking rationale for the PIL. Muhammad Suwan, the president of Libya's Muslim Brotherhood–affiliated Justice and Construction Party, argued that "political isolation is more of a preemptive measure—not punitive—taken to protect the revolution and break off the relationship with the former regime. Those subject to the law are normal citizens, with a full set of rights and responsibilities, but they should be prevented from occupying senior government positions so that the former regime is completely removed from the leadership of the state."[23]

Proponents of the PIL came from various segments of Libyan society, and their calls for applying the law reflected their suffering under Qaddafi. Revolutionaries, victims of torture, and the families of the victims of the Abu Salim prison massacre stood among the strongest advocates for the passage and enforcement of the PIL. Many pushing for the law genuinely believed that only by adopting and enforcing it could Libyans protect their revolution and prevent a counter-revolution by loyalists of the former regime. Those who supported a corrupt and repressive regime, they argued, should not be rewarded with privileged positions in Libya's new system. Holding public office entails power, and former officials' access to state resources would potentially allow them to continue to work against the revolution.[24]

There were also less noble motives at work, among them political self-interest. Whatever some might fear, a counter-revolution is not on the horizon. The former regime and its allies are mostly in disarray; many fled the country or are now displaced inside Libya. In fact, the real threats to the country's stability and the revolution's achievements come from the revolutionaries themselves, as Libya's 2014 civil war has revealed. Transition politics, on the other hand, are very real and almost certainly played a role in the push for the law. The PIL has been used by some to exclude rival politicians and set the stage for political gains. Mahmoud Jibril, who was an economic advisor to Qaddafi in the years leading up to the revolution but then served as the head of the Libyan opposition's interim government for much of 2011, was specifically targeted. After the revolution, Jibril's National Forces Alliance won thirty-nine of eighty seats in the July 2012 GNC elections, more than twice the showing of the Muslim Brotherhood's Justice and Construction (or Development) Party.[25] Due to his pre-revolution governmental role, however, the PIL banned Jibril from political office. Both the Muslim Brotherhood and Salafis, on the other hand, were excluded from politics under the previous regime. Islamists have therefore been the major political beneficiaries of the isolation law, and this will likely continue in future elections. Despite some internal opposition, the Muslim Brotherhood ultimately backed the PIL and framed it, as noted above, as a preemptive measure to protect the revolution.[26] By and large, the PIL was passed due to pressure both from constituents who had suffered under Qaddafi and from armed groups lobbying for the protection of the revolution.

Whatever the motives underlying the PIL, however, the application of the now-passed law threatens to lead to protracted instability and complicate the country's fledgling national reconciliation process. Speaking to the UN Security Council in June 2013, Special Envoy to Libya Tarek Mitri said that "many of [the law's] criteria for exclusion are arbitrary, far-reaching, at times vague, and are likely to violate the civil and political rights of large numbers of individuals." Libyan law professor al-Hadi Bu Hamra similarly warned that the PIL will have a divisive and destructive effect on Libyan society: "Political isolation is a program that could undermine the core of national reconciliation and split Libyan society in half. The law poses a serious threat to the stability of Libyan society. It's the opposite of transitional justice, and applying the law will lead to the exclusion of a large margin of society—which will in turn create a power working against the state. It will significantly strengthen former regime loyalists and present a serious threat to the Libyan state."[27] Furthermore, GNC member Mohammed Toumi offers an alternative approach that is built on three major aspects: changing the name of the PIL to "protection of the revolution" law, excluding those who caused harm to public life before *and* after the 2011 revolution— whether as part of the Qaddafi regime *or* as revolutionaries—and emphasizing an individual's actual behavior as the main criteria for exclusion, not his or her position in the former or current regime.[28]

To draw the obvious comparison, the PIL is clearly reminiscent of the notorious U.S. policy of "de-Ba'athification" in Iraq. Paul Bremer, then head of the Coalition Provisional Authority in Iraq, made a fatal mistake when in May 2003 he issued orders that culled all members of Saddam Hussein's Ba'ath Party from the top ranks of Iraq's civil services and disbanded the Ba'ath-dominated military and security organizations. The purge stalled Iraq's reconstruction process, marginalized large segments of Iraqi society, and fueled sectarianism that has persisted to the present. The PIL in Libya will likely have similar results. Advocates of the PIL argue that Libya is different from Iraq as almost 97 percent of Libyans are Sunni Muslims, leaving little potential for a sectarian conflict. Libya, however, has other social fault lines that the PIL could aggravate. Tribalism and regionalism are likely to worsen thanks to the PIL. If the law disproportionately affects and excludes groups identified as regime loyalists, or *azlam*, it will only exacerbate existing rifts. "We're doing our best to contribute to the rebuilding of Libya," said a tribal leader who requested anonymity. "We don't want to keep being treated as Qaddafi loyalists; those of us who helped Qaddafi don't represent our tribe. We're reaching out to our fellow Libyans to build a new country. But if we continue to be excluded, we'll be left with only one option: looking for those who are also excluded and building new coalitions among the marginalized. We will be forced to fight back. Permanent exclusion is not an option for us."[29]

The risks of enforcing the PIL lie not only in damaging Libya's social fabric but also in wiping clean the Libyan state's institutional memory by excluding those with experience from running the state's institutions. Further complicating the situation is the fact that the GNC has not yet decided how exactly the law will be enforced, though the number of high-profile resignations that have taken place may be a signal the GNC will be strict. Jibril warned after the law's passage that almost half a million people would lose their jobs as a result, which he said would "destroy governing structures." In June 2013, Libya's Judicial Committees went on strike in protest of the law, which, according to political risk consultancy Menas Associates, is "likely to affect scores of judicial employees, from judges to lawyers and prosecution committee members. According to some estimates, at least half of the country's judges will be axed." Even Muhammad Magarief, president of the GNC and Libya's effective head of state, resigned from his post days after the law's passage; he had served as Libya's ambassador to India for two years before defecting in 1980.[30]

Clearly, the PIL is an exceptionally blunt tool with which to address the corruption and abuses that characterized the Qaddafi regime. The law punishes entire categories of people based on guilt by association, but it provides no real, objective yardstick to ensure that new public servants are upright and honest—that is, it does nothing to those who are corrupt but had no prior relationship with the regime. In other words, the PIL could just as easily result in new corrupt faces replacing old ones. For all these reasons, it is likely that Libyans will find the PIL, as enacted, unworkable. It is reasonable to expect that the PIL in Libya will have to be amended, supplemented with other laws, or even repealed entirely. While some damage has already been done, Libya can save itself a great deal of trouble by pursuing alternative approaches to such a draconian form of lustration.

The issue of personnel reform should really be taken up as part of a broad transitional justice framework that is informed by an inclusive national dialogue. Combined with the recommended truth-seeking efforts, a transitional justice law could target rights abusers and the corrupt regardless of whether they were involved with the old regime or the new government. Truth commissions and serious, evidence-based investigations are what Libya should use to "protect the revolution"—the goal of the PIL's advocates—by preventing compromised old-regime figures from taking on large roles in the new Libya. At a minimum, Libya should consider modifying its PIL. It could limit the PIL's enforcement and implement a comprehensive strategy to rehabilitate and reintegrate most regime-linked Libyans. For instance, while the PIL could be enforced to target only the very senior level of the former regime a parallel strategy would be implemented simultaneously to address the regime's broader power base. This strategy would have to focus on the absorption of those individuals—former regime members who were not involved in human rights violations—through development and national reconciliation programs. Such an approach would address revolutionaries' concerns by excluding very senior individuals, especially from the security forces, while at the same time allowing for the reintegration of most of those with lesser regime links.

A thorough vetting process for former regime elements could be another alternative to the PIL. Immediately after the fall of Qaddafi and in preparation for GNC elections, the National Transitional Council, which functioned as the de facto government during the fight against Qaddafi from February 2011 until GNC elections in July 2012, issued Resolution No. 16 for 2012, which established a vetting agency called the Commission for Integrity and Patriotism (CIP). The CIP was tasked with investigating the background of any candidate for a leadership position in the state (e.g., GNC membership) to ensure that the candidate had no history with the former regime or record of corruption. The commission was formed on a temporary basis and is set to dissolve when Libya's new constitution comes into effect.

Unfortunately, the CIP was overwhelmed with the number of cases that demanded investigation. For GNC elections, for example, the commission received five thousand candidate applications and was given only twelve days to allow or bar each from running. CIP General Manager Saad al-Deen said, "We were able to disqualify 250 cases. We gave approval to the rest, pending no new evidence linking them to the leadership of the former regime." There were, of course, many complaints over the nature of the commission and its work. "Our commission is named [the] Commission for Integrity and Patriotism," a commission member told the *Libya Herald*. "When we vote to disbar someone, it is means [*sic*] somehow he is not a patriot. It's a very difficult decision to take." A Congress member who was banned by CIP after his election to the GNC complained to the *Libya Herald*: "I was very surprised when the GNC Secretary told me the Commission had banned me. I was not even interviewed by the members. It's like they are above everyone. It's [the] Libyan version of democracy."[31]

While the CIP experience was far from perfect, the lessons learned could help Libyan authorities establish a reformed agency. Reforming the CIP could be premised on improved transparency, solid criteria for review, and a process for appealing CIP decisions in court.

Tunisia

Unlike Libya, Tunisia has thus far dealt with the former regime within the context of a broad transitional justice framework and electoral laws, and informed by the country's national dialogue. This systematic approach has been a strength of the country's political transition. Tunisia developed and enacted a robust transitional justice law that targets only those individuals of Zine El Abidine Ben Ali's regime that were involved in violations and corruption. Similarly, Tunisia's National Constituent Assembly (NCA) debated the issue of lustration and ultimately rejected proposals that would have disqualified former regime figures from running for office. Applying accountability and debating lustration within legal frameworks will contribute to Tunisia's stability and help it achieve a transition to civil peace.

Even as Ben Ali fled Tunis on January 14, 2011, Tunisia's security forces had begun taking steps toward holding him and his associates and family members accountable for the crimes they committed while in power. Within days, thirty-three members of Ben Ali's extended family and Rafik Belhaj, the former interior minister who many blamed for the violent police crackdown during the uprising, had been arrested. The army and justice department were directed to gather and preserve evidence for investigating the former regime.[32] Additionally, according to Salim Ben Hamidane, minister of state property and land affairs, the Tunisian government issued Decree Number 13 on March 14, 2011, ordering the confiscation of the properties of 114 of Ben Ali's family members, relatives, and assistants. The decree also called for the confiscation of any property that was gained due to the corruption of any of the same 114 people. Any property that was proven to have been obtained through inheritance was totally excluded from confiscation, including properties that belonged to Ben Ali himself.

In June 2015, however, a Tunisian court annulled the 2011 decree to confiscate the properties of Ben Ali and his people. The Tunisian government announced, while vowing to appeal the ruling, "The decision was issued yesterday to annul the decree," a minister, Hatem Eleuchi, told Mosaique FM radio. Despite the court ruling, which set back the effort to hold the former regime accountable, it is at the same time an additional indicator of Tunisians' growing democracy that the rule of law is guiding the transition and that the government is responding within the legal framework to appeal the decision. The minister added, "It's a shocking decision and we hope the court will take the right decision when it comes to the appeal."[33] Efforts to enforce accountability also included Tunisian authorities' banning approximately 460 people tied to the former regime from traveling outside the country. They were allowed to live their lives normally—though under careful observation—while awaiting the adoption and implementation of a transitional justice law.[34]

Tunisia built its strategy for dealing with former regime elements firmly on the development of a transitional justice law. Drafted in a civil society–led process, Tunisia's "Organic Law on the Foundations and Organization of Transitional Justice" was ratified by the NCA on December 15, 2013, with 125 out of 126 votes.[35] In addition to creating the Truth and Dignity Commission, as described in the chapter on truth seeking, the law mandates that specialized courts staffed with specifically trained judges consider cases "relating to serious violations of human rights" including murder, rape, torture, forced disappearances, and executions undertaken without fair-trial guarantees. These judges are also to adjudicate allegations of vote rigging, misappropriation of public funds, and other forms of financial corruption. The law targets only those individuals who are found to be responsible for corruption and human rights violations. Those suspected of such crimes are to be dealt with as individuals on the basis of specific charges, not merely for being part of the former regime. Importantly, mere affiliation with the former regime is not considered a crime, and the transitional justice law does not apply in cases where specific charges are not present. The law, which also contains provisions concerning memory preservation, reparation and rehabilitation, institutional reform, and reconciliation, is now being implemented by Tunisia's judiciary.[36]

Although the development and implementation of transitional justice laws are considered milestones in the effort to hold perpetrators accountable for past crimes, Tunisia's law has significant limitations. Mohamed Ben Aisa, a law professor at Tunisia University, expressed concern that politicians who were key cogs in the repressive regime but were not directly implicated in specific human rights violations or cases of corruption could not be prosecuted under the law. He noted that "some former regime figures are not known to be linked to specific violations, but they occupied senior level positions and were key politicians in Ben Ali's regime. How would the transitional justice law prosecute them? They did not apologize to the Tunisian people, they are not being prosecuted, but instead they are now invited to the national dialogue table!"[37]

Indeed, due to the narrow scope of the transitional justice law, many former regime politicians have avoided any sort of censure and become part of the new political system. Kamel Morjane, for example, who served as defense minister and foreign minister under Ben Ali, established the al-Mubadara Party, which earned 3 out of the 217 seats in the 2014 parliamentarian elections. Morjane even apologized to the Tunisian people for the wrongdoings of the former ruling party and vowed to begin a new page in Tunisia's political history. One of al-Mubadara's representatives in the NCA, Ameera Marzouk, explained that the new party is "not against accountability. We want everything to go through the transitional justice law. We are with a truth commission and all of its subcommittees. We are only against collective punishment. We are against treating those who served in the former regime as criminals only because of their position in that regime, not because of crimes they committed."[38]

Applying accountability to former regime elements that were not directly involved in corruption or human rights violations remains extremely controversial. On one hand, the principle of accountability seems compromised when pillars of the former system are invited to contribute to national dialogues and participate in post-revolution politics instead of being tried for being senior figures in a repressive regime. On the other hand, this could be what the post-dictatorship transition actually needs. Incorporating prominent regime members who are not directly linked to violations may encourage them to use their influence constructively rather than disruptively, as would have been likely if they were excluded.

Similar to other countries in transition, Tunisia has been tempted by the politics of lustration. Some of Tunisia's political parties advocated for a strict lustration policy to ensure a clean transition to a new system and a complete break from the corrupt former regime, while the potential targets of such a policy viewed its sponsors as purely seeking to make party gains and exclude others. Unsurprisingly, the parties that would likely have been harmed by such laws fought against lustration to allow for their survival in post-revolution politics. Thus far, the NCA has rejected the proposed laws and provisions that would have excluded former regime members from politics. It is unclear whether such measures will be considered again, though the chances of their being enacted are not great due mainly to a lack of sufficient popular support.

The departure of Ben Ali from power was followed by the collapse of his one-party system that used to dominate Tunisia. Ben Ali's party, the Constitutional Democratic Rally (RCD), was dissolved, and for approximately six months its leaders practically disappeared from Tunisia's political map. To prevent their return to politics, a number of parties including Ennahda, Ettakatol, and the Congress for the Republic (CPR) advocated for what came to be known as the "immunization of the revolution law," first in advance of the 2011 parliamentary elections, then again during the country's constitution drafting process. The proposed law would have prevented senior former ruling party figures and those who worked with Ben Ali from occupying a public office for at least five years. The debate over such a law became particularly heated when former regime figures revived their political careers by forming new parties, as both Beji Caid Essebsi and Kamel Morjane did. The law's advocates saw it as a tool to exclude political opponents, especially Essebsi's Nedaa Tunis, from new political arrangements.

Yet many prominent political figures spoke out against the immunization law. Said Ferjani questioned the effectiveness of the immunization law in protecting the revolution. He suggested that "even if you're able to remove the first layer of the former political party's leadership through immunization the problem will not be resolved. The second layer may be much worse and more corrupt than the first layer. The same logic applies to the rest of leadership layers. Where do you draw the line then? The solution is in fact in building a strong transitional justice law that targets corrupt individuals and perpetrators regardless of what category of leadership they exist in. With transitional justice you can immunize the revolution." Souad Abderrahim, an NCA member, echoed Ferjani's concerns. She explained, "We don't believe in exclusion. Practicing politics is a constitutional right for all Tunisians regardless of their political orientation. Those who committed human rights violations should be dealt with through the court. Anyone who does not have violations must be included in the political process, not excluded. Exclusion laws can also lead to counter-revolution among other possible negative outcomes."[39]

Khaled Kchier, a history professor at Tunis University, believes that it is also necessary to review the 2013–53 Organic Law of December 24, 2013, on transitional justice, especially articles 8 and 43 on lustration. He also agreed that lustration should be replaced with laws that target individuals involved with corruption and human rights violations rather than penalizing categories. He suggested that "after the fall of Ben Ali's regime, the state continued to function normally. All state institutions continued to operate at their normal pace: education, health, electricity, security, military, and the rest continued to deliver. This is important evidence that the bureaucratic system did not rely on the corrupt regime in its performance. Why should we then penalize those people and institutions that proved that they could deliver independently from Ben Ali's regime practices?"[40]

This strong rejection of the proposed lustration measures has helped to prevent them from passing in the NCA. When the immunization law first failed in 2011, its supporters still sought to prevent any of Ben Ali's administration from running in that year's parliamentary elections, but ultimately only those who had also been members of the RCD were excluded. The NCA debated the law during the drafting of Tunisia's new constitution in 2013, but they left the issue to be resolved as part of the 2014 electoral law. Article 167 of that law would have excluded any RCD members that held a government position under Ben Ali, and anyone that occupied a position within the RCD from that year's parliamentary elections. Although CPR, Ettakatol, and others solidly supported the article, Ennahda was ultimately split on it, and on April 30, 2014, the NCA voted it down. The repeated failure of immunization measures has clearly distinguished Tunisia's transitional experience from that of Libya. Instead of imposing extreme forms of lustration, Tunisia has pursued an inclusive path, rejecting exclusion as a viable option.[41]

Since the NCA's rejection of the immunization article, the issue of allowing former regime figures to run for public office has only become more prescient. In Tunisia's October 2014 parliamentary elections, Nedaa Tunis, led by members of the Habib Bourguiba regime, secured a leading 85 out of 217 seats, followed by Ennahda with 69 seats. Nedaa Tunis's leader, Essebsi, then won the presidency with nearly 57 percent of the vote in a December 2014 run-off election against the incumbent interim president, Moncef Marzouki. In January 2015, Essebsi nominated a Ben Ali–era official, Habib

Essid, to be prime minister and form a government. Former regime figures assuming control of two branches of the government has exacerbated fears of a counter-revolution. Said Ferjani of Ennahda characterized Nedaa Tunis's parliamentary victory as the regime returning "through the back door."[42]

Nedaa Tunis's rise is not necessarily a counter-revolution, but the concerns some Tunisians have about this possibility are understandable. Essebsi did not merely serve in the Bourguiba regime, but in 1965, he occupied the most sensitive position — minister of interior — when torture against political prisoners was widely practiced. Specifically, some Tunisians believe Essebsi was probably responsible for the highly disputed, alleged torture of members of the Youssefist movement that opposed Bourguiba in the 1960s. He later served as Bourguiba's foreign minister and minister of defense, and was a member of the rubber-stamp parliament during Ben Ali's early years as president. If Essebsi were to adopt his predecessor's policies of repressing political opponents and Islamists, he would likely find staunch regional support, especially from General Khalifa Haftar in Libya and President Abdel Fattah el-Sisi in Egypt. Although Essebsi frequently stated he would be a president for all Tunisians, there have already been times when he has seemed more focused on attacking Islamists than the more crucial task of rebuilding Tunisia's devastated economy.[43]

Nevertheless, Tunisians should not rush to assume that Essebsi, despite his background, necessarily represents a return of the old regime or a counter-revolution. Much has changed since 1965. Then, as minister of interior, Essebsi was beholden to the autocratic leader who appointed him. In 2014, Essebsi came to power through the votes of Tunisians, and his loyalty should be, first and foremost, to the people and the democratic process. It is in Essebsi's interest to emerge as a leader of all Tunisians, regardless of their political ideology, rather than to pursue a narrow agenda and monopolize the political scene by excluding others. Most of all, unlike in 1965, when his future as a young minister depended on proving his loyalty to Bourguiba, Essebsi, who turned eighty-eight in November 2014, should be focused on his own legacy. As Essebsi himself put it, "Do you think that a man my age will now dominate and restrict freedoms?"[44] Even with those assurances, the strongest guarantor against a return of the old regime's practices is still the Tunisian people themselves. State repression that was accommodated under Bourguiba and Ben Ali is unlikely to be tolerated now that Tunisians have broken the wall of fear. Society itself has changed, and it includes new political parties and a more powerful and assertive civil society.[45]

Yemen

Yemen has approached accountability and lustration completely differently than Libya and Tunisia. To this point it has not pursued either method of dealing with the former regime, allowing many of its members to maintain their roles or shift smoothly into new ones within the transitional government. This unfettered continuation of the former regime's participation in and influence on the successor political system—with no accountability, justice, or reform—raises significant concerns over the future of the country. In fact, allowing Ali Abdullah Saleh and his close aides to be part of the new political system eventually contributed to the disruption of Yemen's transition process, and in alliance with the Houthi movement, Saleh launched a coup against the state on September 21, 2014. Thanks in part to Saleh's support, the Houthis were able to take over the capital, topple the government, and eventually engage in a large-scale Yemeni civil war that also dragged neighboring Saudi Arabia into it.

Protests in 2011 divided the Yemeni military between Saleh loyalists, including the Republican Guards, Central Security, and the Air Force, and anti-Saleh units, which notably included the First Armored Division and its commander, Major General Ali Mohsen al-Ahmar.[46] This shift in the balance of power made it unlikely that either party would win a military confrontation decisively and resulted in a stalemate. The stalemate lasted for almost a year and served to polarize the conflict, with each side becoming steadily more entrenched. Any military confrontation would have likely led to a civil war the outcome and consequences of which neither party could predict. The subsequent stalemate paved the way for a compromise brokered by the Gulf Cooperation Council (GCC) countries. The GCC initiative removed Saleh from power in exchange for an "honorable exit" and legal immunity. From the point of view of the opposition, the Joint Meeting Parties (JMP), the deal saved Yemen from descending into all-out violence, making the compromise well worth accepting. Ultimately, however, the deal sacrificed the principles of justice and accountability merely to preserve a fragile peace. Discounting justice has concerning implications for Yemen's transition toward civil peace, and relevant measures must be taken to eliminate or minimize the damage that such an absence of justice is likely to cause.

The settlement did more than avert a civil war in Yemen, however. It also initiated a forward-looking transition by guaranteeing an inclusive process involving all opposition parties, represented officially by the JMP.[47] While the Yemeni parliament remained as it was, the deal produced a thirty-five-member unity cabinet divided almost equally between opposition and loyalist ministers. Furthermore, the deal solidified international consensus on the need for a transition in Yemen. As the Syrian uprising has shown, a divided international community can contribute greatly to the persistence of domestic instability, violence, and even proxy wars sponsored by opposing external parties.

Still, Yemen's power transfer left significant unanswered questions that may have negative implications for the country's future stability. The GCC initiative required that Saleh step down from his position as president but did not demand that he retire from political life altogether. As a result, Saleh was able to remain the head of his still-powerful party, the General People's Congress (GPC). With Saleh continuing to occupy a key political office, many Yemenis believe he is working to roll back the revolution by manipulating the domestic political scene and seeking to undermine the settlement outlined in the GCC initiative.[48] Saleh's role has complicated Yemen's national dialogue process and its efforts to move forward with its transition.

In addition, the GCC deal gave unilateral immunity to Saleh and his allies yet did not mention the opposition, leaving the door open for future disputes between the two parties. In particular, Saleh used a June 2011 attack against him in the presidential mosque as justification for prosecuting several members of the opposition, accusing them and certain tribal leaders of orchestrating the attack in an effort to assassinate him.[49] Granting full immunity to one party while allowing it to pursue legal action against the other makes it almost impossible for the country's parties to work together and trust each other.

Furthermore, the immunity clause's obstruction of accountability may fail to comply with international humanitarian law. Amnesty International considers the law in breach of Yemen's international legal obligations, saying, "Under international law, including the Convention against Torture and Other Cruel, Inhuman or Degrading Treatment or Punishment, to which Yemen is a state party, Yemen is obliged to investigate and prosecute anyone suspected of such crimes where there is sufficient admissible evidence." UN High Commissioner for Human Rights Navi Pillay criticized the law when it was in draft form, saying that if it became law, it would violate Yemen's international human rights obligations.[50]

It is also not clear what entitles the opposition representatives to make such immunity agreements for Saleh and his allies, as the JMP by no means represents all victims and their families. The GCC's immunity deal is, in any case, merely a partial solution, as it only shields individuals from prosecution inside Yemen—they remain vulnerable to prosecution on human rights charges in countries that claim universal jurisdiction. To achieve something close to a resolution of these issues, the country is in need of transitional justice laws that will guarantee all parties fair and equal treatment.

Finally, Yemen's political settlement has addressed justice only in terms of those who were directly affected by human rights violations. The focus has been on victims and their families in particular. Even on this subject, however, the process has raised questions. One activist noted that "the general public also suffered seriously during the eleven-month uprising and for decades under the reign of Saleh."[51] During months of street protests, almost all Yemenis underwent a loss of basic services including water and electricity, freedom of movement, and employment opportunities. This is in addition to the many who were exposed to extreme stress and, in some cases, trauma. While the political settlement may provide relief to those who were directly affected by the country's unrest, it fails to address the general suffering of the Yemeni people. An effective national reconciliation process will have to address this hardship in several ways, including the state's acknowledgment of that suffering and potentially an apology for the Yemeni people's experiences under the previous regime. Such acknowledgment and apology can have a powerful emotional impact and could be effective tools in helping move the country toward reconciliation.

Ultimately, the GCC initiative's tradeoff between peace and justice has led to what Johan Galtung calls "negative peace," or the mere absence of violence.[52] Negative peace tends to be fragile. It could crumble at any point during the implementation of a peace agreement. This actually proved to be the case when Yemen's negative peace enabled the former regime to regroup and, in alliance with the Houthis, launch a coup to take over the country and begin a large-scale civil war that is going to impact the entire transition and national reconciliation process. In order to achieve a "positive peace," which provides a foundation for subsequent political and social progress, the causes of instability must be dealt with. In Yemen, this process has barely started. Much remains to be done.

The power transition deal in Yemen guaranteed that no lustration laws will be enacted and that former regime figures, regardless of how involved they may have been in past human rights violations, will not be excluded from the new political system. Not only former regime elements but also the ruling party itself, the GPC, will enter the post-uprising era on a power-sharing basis with the opposition. While lustration in its extreme forms—as in Libya—is not conducive to reducing societal tensions, allowing implicated former regime officials to maintain positions of power in the successor system could be equally problematic. Without genuine personnel changes, it will be difficult for Yemen to move beyond the polarization of 2011.

Some of Yemen's revolutionary youth would like to see a democratic transition that excludes old-regime political figures. This is unlikely for a number of reasons. First, the very nature of the political settlement brokered by the GCC emphasizes power sharing between parties rather than a zero-sum settlement. Second, Saleh's GPC remains in control of key political positions, especially in the military and security apparatus, and has retained popular support within certain constituencies. Third, the former ruling party is the most familiar with the machinery of the state. As the ones occupying most public-sector positions, they know how to administer the country's civil service and are needed if the bureaucracy is to continue functioning. While seeing the value of a "ban on regime figures practicing politics for at least ten years," Mahmoud Nasher, a Yemeni activist, conceded that a "complete departure from the past regime cannot be implemented, as the leaders of the transition in Yemen [including some among the revolutionary forces] were part of that regime."[53]

Total exclusion of the GPC, then, is not a viable solution. Instead, giving the GPC an opportunity to take part in the rebuilding process should encourage the party to work within the system rather than outside or against it. Yaser al-Awadi, vice chairman of the GPC parliamentary bloc, suggested that "the former ruling party remaining as an important part of the Yemeni political landscape . . . will provide balance with the Islah Party. Without the GPC, Islah will dominate the political landscape and totally control the state's institutions."[54] Still, to play a constructive role in the transition to civil peace, the party must engage in wide-ranging internal reform. The GPC should realize that serious reforms would not only improve the chances of national reconciliation but would benefit the party itself as it seeks to adapt to a new political era. The GPC may even choose to look at how other countries' former ruling parties reformed in the face of dramatic political changes.

The GPC itself must decide which internal reforms to prioritize. One example of reform would be changing the party's name; many Yemenis will be reluctant to reconcile with a party whose name was long linked to repression, corruption, and human rights violations. "The name of the former ruling party is associated with an era that the Yemeni people want to put behind them and from which they want to move on," Nadia al-Sakkaf, a member of the National Dialogue Conference's presidency, noted. "Individuals can still practice their political rights, but the party itself should probably change." Making serious reforms to the party's charter is another option. Certainly, the GPC must objectively assess the policies and practices it implemented over the course of thirty-three years in power. In determining what went wrong, it can establish new party bylaws and regulations. For example, the GPC should adopt strict policies to fight the corruption that has plagued the party in recent decades. It may also want to consider removing a number of its leading figures, particularly the more notorious names associated with corruption and repression. The party must recognize that it owes the people serious sacrifices in order to be genuinely accepted as a part of Yemen's future politics. Al-Sakkaf suggested that "the best way to move forward is to completely remove the top regime figures from the entire political scene." She pointed to a proposal that was made in the early days of the uprising against Saleh to resolve the country's impasse, the "ten-ten initiative," which recommends excluding the top ten figures from both the government and opposition from the political process.[55]

Finally, the Yemeni opposition must realize that serious reform within the former ruling party would demand a commensurate response. The opposition must be willing to take part in an inclusive reconciliation process that would welcome a newly reformed GPC. Engaging in genuine partnership with the GPC would improve the prospects of a wider national reconciliation. Newly empowered revolutionaries should avoid repeating the mistakes of the former ruling party and steer clear of exclusionary policies and the monopolization of power.

Comparing Approaches to Accountability and Lustration

The cases of Libya, Tunisia, and Yemen all show that the approach a transitioning country takes toward accountability directly impacts both its present and future. Applying a reasonable level of accountability contributes to achieving broad national reconciliation as victims, perpetrators, and the public see that justice is being served and that the rule of law is taking force. Accountability in this sense functions as a marker between a dark and oppressive chapter in the country's history and a new chapter where no one, not even the regime or head of state, is above the law. Accordingly, large swaths of the populations in each country are demanding accountability as an important part of their transitions from dictatorships to more inclusive systems of governance. Even in Yemen, where the parliament granted immunity to Saleh and his cronies, many, especially revolutionary youth, are demanding that the state try them for their apparent crimes. Some Yemenis have even suggested that Saleh should be prosecuted outside the country under other jurisdictions that allow for the trial of foreign individuals accused of human rights violations.

All three countries have also demonstrated how prone the processes of both accountability and lustration are to becoming significantly politicized. Libya's revolutionaries are using the country's PIL to completely exclude anyone that worked with the former regime from government, even those who defected and played major roles within the opposition during the uprising. Politicization of accountability is clearly on display in the decision of Libya's House of Representatives (HOR) abolishing the PIL in order to allow General Haftar—who served for years in the Qaddafi regime—to be part of their state institution, namely appointing him the army chief during the civil war. Libya ended up with the PIL in Tripoli enforced by Libya Dawn and no PIL in Benghazi under Operation Dignity. Tunisia's troika government coalition lobbied for an "immunization of the revolution" law in hopes of marginalizing still-influential figures of the past regime. Nedaa Tunis, on the other hand, was successful in fighting the law that would have prevented its party leader, Beji Caid Essebsi, because of his past connections with the Bourguiba regime, from running for the presidency. Yemen's former regime used the negotiations to resolve the country's political crisis to secure immunity for itself, thereby pre-empting accountability efforts. The longstanding opposition coalition was complicit and has not called for accountability, hoping to preserve its prominent role in Yemen's political system going forward. There is no easy answer here, as objectivity and neutrality are generally illusory, but clearly the politicization of accountability and lustration can seriously hinder attempts to establish a credible system of governance that is based on the rule of law. Failure to overcome these hurdles could have severe ramifications for the future of these transitioning states.

While applying accountability can be logistically and politically difficult, Libya, Tunisia, and Yemen show that striking the proper balance is the greatest challenge. Both too little accountability, as in Yemen, and too much accountability, as in Libya, are quite problematic. Tunisia, however, seems to have gotten as close as possible to the right balance by showing a robust commitment to accountability within a legal transitional justice framework. This transitional justice law is homegrown, developed mostly by a network of locally based civil society organizations. As a result, there is significant support for the law in large segments of the population, increasing the likelihood that the transitional justice process will be sustainable and that Tunisians will work together toward national reconciliation.

Yet Tunisia has shown that even a well-developed transitional justice law that takes a proactive and measured approach to accountability can have limitations. If, like in Tunisia, such a law only applies to the overt commission of specific crimes and not membership and participation in a repressive regime, reviled faces of such regimes may escape punishment and remain politically active. This can understandably be quite galling to those who suffered under the former regime and want to see a complete break from the past. Nonetheless, that is the reality if accountability is to be implemented according to international standards. In such situations, removing figures that do not face criminal charges from the political scene must be done through political means—such as lustration.

Despite the popular support for lustration, especially in Libya, there is little evidence to suggest that it in fact contributes to peaceful transitions and national reconciliation. On the contrary, lustration, especially in its extreme form as in Libya, further polarizes communities and can derail transition processes. In the worst cases, it can lead former regime loyalists to regroup and seek to regain power, exacerbating serious security concerns and even facilitating a resumption of violence or civil war, as in the case of Yemen, where Saleh regrouped and forged an alliance with Houthi rebels to take over the country. The lustration law in place in Libya should therefore be either abolished or substantially amended. There are less destabilizing political methods by which to deal with former regime figures. One would be to develop a meticulous vetting process that operates within a legal framework and thoroughly screens the backgrounds of members of the past regime that want to maintain or obtain public office. Another would be to require deep, transparent reforms of the former ruling party before allowing it to continue participating in the country's politics. Tunisia is modeling a variation of this method by allowing former ruling party politicians that have not yet been charged with past violations to form new parties and run in elections. Yemen, on the other hand, has allowed the GPC to remain in power without undergoing even the slightest reforms, casting a dark shadow over the country's transition.

Ultimately, the early results in Libya, Yemen, and Tunisia suggest that while justice is essential to the transitions, "retributive justice" is not sufficient for building a strong foundation for national reconciliation and civil peace. The size of the public sectors in these countries are such that attempting to prosecute or even merely vet all of their members would not only be a logistical nightmare but extremely counterproductive to the reconciliation of these societies. As a result, "restorative justice" is badly needed. Helpfully, Arab societies are rich with cultural and restorative justice approaches that can soften the dependency on retributive justice as the only approach to dealing with past crimes. For example, a combination of truth seeking and forgiveness may present a substitute, in some cases, to firmly applying retribution. Although challenging, striking a balance between retributive and restorative justice could be a good approach for the transitioning Arab Spring countries. The extremes of broad prosecutions and purges or blanket amnesties should be avoided in the long and difficult quest for peace, justice, and reconciliation following the revolutions.

Another layer of politicizing accountability has been added with the outbreak of civil wars in Libya (2014) and Yemen (2015). Warring parties in both countries have reached a balance of power where neither one is able to militarily defeat the other. Military solutions in both countries have almost no chance, and this opens the door for political settlements whether through UN intervention or directly among the parties. As most wars in the region have demonstrated, with political settlements parties make concessions but also make gains in terms of escaping accountability. Negotiators on both sides usually rush to agree on eliminating accountability of warlords in order to reach settlements. Neither commanders of Libya's militias nor Houthis leaders in Yemen will accept settlements that take them to court. Ironically, agreements and political settlements usually end up rewarding militia commanders rather than holding them accountable. The political settlement of the Lebanese civil war, the 1989 Taif Agreement, for example, led to warlords replacing their military uniforms with fancy suits and ties and becoming parliamentarians representing their political parties. No accountability was ever applied in Lebanon, thus it is no wonder that the country has continued to experience fragility and political instability twenty-seven years after signing the agreement.

Whatever the exact approach each country chooses, they will be best served to arrive at that choice through an inclusive, transparent process. Ideally, how to deal with the former regime would be an agenda item for a national dialogue conference. At a minimum, it should be openly debated by a democratically elected, representative government. The major stakeholders that will have to implement and comply with the accountability and lustration policies should be involved in the debates and decisions as much as possible, to increase their ownership and commitment to the agreed-upon approaches. Making these important decisions in a collaborative way can help to lay the foundation for a broad-based reconciliation process.

NINE

Institutional Reform

Government institutions represent the skeletons of regimes, and therefore only deep institutional reform can ensure that structures and abuses of past dictatorships are not recreated under new systems. Institutional reform therefore includes changes in the security sector, political apparatus, and other arms of the state. To be successful, it must be overarching, affecting all government sectors. As explained in broad terms by Derick W. Brinkerhoff, "The design and implementation of governance reforms in post-conflict states target three areas: (1) reconstituting legitimacy, (2) re-establishing security and (3) rebuilding effectiveness." Regaining legitimacy is critical for a government to function, as respect for the administration dwindles if it is not considered to be just or appropriate. This process of legitimizing the new government involves the delivery of services, constitutional reform, and strengthening the rule of law, as well as "expanding participation and inclusiveness, reducing inequities, creating accountability, combating corruption and introducing contestability (elections)." To restore security, the disarmament, demobilization, and reintegration (DDR) of past combatants is critical to strengthening official security forces while simultaneously undermining ex-combatants and militias. Renewing government efficacy requires the restoration of full political, bureaucratic, and administrative function under the new regime. "Rebuilding effectiveness has to do, first and foremost, with the functions and capacity of the public sector. Good governance in this area means, for example, adequate and functioning municipal infrastructure, widely available health care and schooling, provision of roads and transportation networks and attention to social safety nets." Institutional reform is critical to the restoration of stability and government functioning in states transitioning from dictatorship to democracy.[1]

Certainly, as Stefan Wolff puts it, "institutions remain the core component of post-conflict state building. The reason behind much of this focus on institutions as the main tool for post-conflict state building is that formal institutions can be codified and adapted to suit specific needs and circumstances more readily than other factors that influence the risk of resurgent conflict, such as the level of economic development or the cultural and ethnic make-up of societies." States must move quickly though. El Salvador demonstrated just how fast the opportunity for serious reforms can evaporate, as all of its significant security reforms were undertaken within three years of the peace negotiations and agreements that mandated them. Furthermore, civil society organizations cannot grow in the absence of effective government institutions or until elites take a vested interest in a government that is considered to be both legitimate and effective.[2]

This chapter argues that Libya, Tunisia, and Yemen will have to engage in comprehensive institutional reform following the removal of their regimes in order to ensure a successful transition and prevent a return of repressive policies. The process of institutional reform will work to ensure that old systems which produced injustices and wrongdoings are no longer in service and will not be able to reconstitute themselves. Effective institutional reform in these countries will contribute considerably to the success of the overall transition process from dictatorship to a state of civil peace and, most importantly, ensure the sustainability of national reconciliation. Indeed, successful and sustainable national reconciliation is closely linked to rigorous structural and institutional reform, rather than merely agreements and understandings that may collapse with the changes in the political climate or the politics of interparty relations.

State institutions that hold a significant level of legitimacy, such as elected parliaments, should take the lead in reforming old regime structures. In the context of the Arab Spring, this reform includes changes in four primary areas: the security sector, which was responsible for many of the past human rights violations and violence; the bureaucratic system where rampant corruption existed; the media, which was responsible for the glorification and marketing of the repressive regime to the public; and the judiciary, which must ensure fair trials for former regime figures. Although Libya, Tunisia, and

Yemen all overthrew their repressive governments during the Arab Spring, it is striking that each country has taken a different approach to institutional reform. Libya has favored a purge approach, aiming to purify old institutions entirely of former regime elements, while Yemen has embarked on limited institutional reform to ensure the success of its power transition deal, and Tunisia has proceeded with institutional reform based primarily on laws initiated by its National Constituent Assembly and executive committees.

Libya

To move toward reconciliation and to prevent future human rights violations, most of the Libyan state's institutions will need to be structurally reformed. In a transitional context, reform is typically focused on the four key areas identified above: the security sector, the administrative apparatus, the media, and the judiciary. Each of these is important in the Libyan case, which requires truly comprehensive reform, as Muammar Qaddafi's regime completely dominated the Libyan state. In particular, reform of the judiciary has emerged as a top priority, and its reform can be taken as an example of the challenges facing efforts to reform other state institutions.

After the collapse of the Qaddafi regime, Libya's revolutionaries stressed the need to purge the judiciary as one of the pillars of the country's transition. Reform in that sector, they believed, would ensure justice and guarantee the complete elimination of the former dictatorship. These calls for a purge reflect a serious need to address past grievances inflicted by the Qaddafi dictatorship under a credible justice system. Success in this area has been elusive. For example, former Libyan Islamic Fighting Group (LIFG) leader Sami Esaadi was sentenced to death under the previous regime for charges related to "membership in a party that attempted to dismantle the Jamahiriya system." More recently, he said, "The judge who sentenced me to death during Qaddafi's reign is still a practicing judge. How can I trust this judge or the judiciary that employs him? I need to see new, honest judges who deliver justice to those who suffered and to those who committed crimes. That's when I'll feel confident that Libya is moving into a new era of justice and fairness. Then I'll be able to forgive and reconcile."[3]

The drawbacks of a judicial purge, however, are greater and potentially more destabilizing than most revolutionaries realize. One major obstacle is the question of who purges whom. Most judges served under Qaddafi; even the head of Libya's Fact-Finding and Reconciliation Commission (FRC), Hussein al-Buishi, worked as a judge under the former regime. Furthermore, the shortage of appropriately educated and experienced judges who did not work for the regime is serious. The question then becomes whether it is possible to set criteria that would ensure that some individuals are "cleaner" than others. The matter of which authority would establish such criteria raises further obstacles in the process of institutional reform of the judiciary.

Indeed, excluding all judges who worked under the former regime would lead to the collapse of Libya's judicial system. Training new judges is not an option in the short run, as this will take years. Noureddin al-Ikrimi, a Supreme Court judge and advisor to Libya's FRC, explained, "It takes almost ten years to train a judge, and Libya already has a shortage of trained judges."[4] One possible solution is to import judges from other Arab and Muslim countries to solve this problem in the short term. Yet this poses problems of implementation, particularly considering the lack of security in Libya. A functioning court system requires security and the enforcement of any judicial edicts. Libyan or not, judges will need an effective police force to produce witnesses and defendants, for whom the police will have to provide security—to say nothing of the need to protect the judges themselves. In a vicious cycle, though, a lack of judges will hamper efforts to (legally) restore order and keep law-breakers off Libya's streets, which will in turn worsen the security situation and further impede the establishment of the rule of law.

Instead of a straightforward purge as advocated by revolutionaries, Libyan authorities should engage in deep reform of the judiciary system. A good starting point would be remembering that not the entirety of the justice system was corrupted by the Qaddafi regime. Al-Ikrimi argues, "To a certain extent, the judiciary resisted the regime. For example, the infamous 1978 'house to its resident' law [Law No. 4/1978] was not supported by the justice system. The whole process of transfer of properties from landlords to tenants was done independently from the justice system. In addition, there were many prisoners held for years but never brought to trial simply because the judiciary refused to bargain with the regime on those cases."[5]

A reform-based approach to the judiciary, as opposed to a purge, would result in judges' being treated as innocent until proven guilty. Judges should be sacked only within a legal framework based on evidence of corruption or other forms of misconduct during the former regime. Judicial reforms must be enacted by the General National Congress (GNC), as the body enjoys a popular mandate. According to al-Ikrimi, the GNC should issue legislation that reforms the Supreme Judicial Council (SJC), the most suitable body to lead the implementation of judicial reform. The GNC could first investigate and confirm the integrity of the seven members of the SJC, then appoint new members to produce a council of, for example, fifteen members. A reconstituted SJC could then lead the reform of Libya's judiciary, not through political isolation laws but on the basis of individuals' records and past practices.

Tunisia

One major challenge of institutional reform is to ensure that past human rights violations are not repeated in the future. Only by transforming the old system into one that is transparent and accountable will individual rights be better protected from further abuse. Torture, for example, was a widespread problem in Tunisia's prisons under Zine El Abidine Ben Ali's regime. Souad Abderrahim, a representative in the National Constituent Assembly (NCA), explained that to prevent this from happening again, the NCA "passed a law to form a committee that specializes in the prevention of torture. It is a very neutral committee formed of, among others, lawyers and psychiatrists, and its main task is to monitor Tunisia's prisons and ensure that torture is not happening again. The committee has the mandate it needs to be able to conduct site visits and talk to prisoners to ensure no torture is taking place."[6]

A common challenge to engaging in institutional reform is determining which approach will ensure healthy reform: purging or vetting. Tunisia's transitional government was clear from the beginning about its preference for vetting. Abderrahim explained how this applies to the judiciary: "There is no purge proposed for the judiciary—as is the case in Libya for example. We're proposing a vetting process instead. The Constituent Assembly will form a completely independent committee and will have all the authority it needs to fairly and accurately perform its tasks of investigating possible violations and proposing the reforms needed to transform the old system."[7]

In May 2012, however, before this process came into effect, Justice Minister Noureddine Bhiri fired eighty-two judges, "citing the need to curb pervasive corruption."[8] Under strong pressure from civil society organizations, Bhiri agreed to restore nine of them to their former positions. The objecting organizations made a strong argument that the authority to sack judges does not reside with the executive branch of the state, and also that the dismissal of judges who served in the former regime should be done within a transitional justice framework. Indeed, "vetting" proponents argue that dismissals should be based on evidence that links them to charges of corruption or other past violations.

Several other sectors in Tunisia also require institutional reform, especially the media, which historically marketed the former regime and defended its mistakes. Shortly after being elected, the NCA established the National Authority for Reform of Information and Communications (INRIC) and tasked it with "proposing reforms for the information and communication sectors with consideration of international criteria on freedom of expression."[9]

INRIC has passed three major decrees, which jointly form its vision for reforming the media sector and the press code in Tunisia. The first, Decree 115–2011, guarantees "freedom of exchanging, publishing and receiving news and views of all kinds."[10] This decree attempts to provide media rights that were missing under the former regime, including journalists' access to information, the confidentiality of sources, and journalists' protection against physical or economic threats as a result of exercising these rights, expressing opinions, or disseminating information. The second decree, passed on May 26, 2011, "aims to regulate the disclosure of government documents for use by journalists." Its more significant reforms give journalists more rights and limit the government's control over the media's access to information.

Unlike during the Ben Ali regime, public administration bodies are now obligated to facilitate access to information by investigative journalists and the public—and can be held accountable if they refuse to do so. The third decree, from November 2011, "guarantees freedom in the broadcast sector and establishes an independent communications authority—the High Independent Authority for Audiovisual Communication or HAICA."[11]

On May 3, 2013, a new HAICA committee of nine technocrats, none of whom had served in the former regime, was formed. It is a fully independent commission whose members are nominated by several parties: one by the president, two by the judiciary, two by the president of the legislative authority, two by an association of media professionals, and one by an association representing owners of audiovisual companies.[12] Most importantly, HAICA holds executive powers. The independent body has regulatory, consultative, and judicial authority, including the adjudication of operating license applications, the establishment of regulations for public broadcasting outlets, and the preservation of plurality in output, especially in political programming.[13]

While Tunisia has engaged in robust media reform, one must distinguish between reform at the policy and legislative levels versus effective implementation of reforms on the ground. Rasheeda al-Neifer, one of the HAICA's nine members, said, "On the levels of reform, decrees, and legislation everything seems perfect. However, on the application level things are different. No serious changes have taken place on the ground so far. Yes, there are difficulties in applying legislations and we have to recognize this."[14] The experience of media reform in Tunisia reveals the complexity not only of initiating serious legislative reform but, more importantly, of applying such measures in practice. It is not enough to pass the legislation; implementing the reforms on the ground is the only way to ensure the efficacy of such changes.

Yemen

A key factor to successful transition in Yemen is deep institutional reform targeting the structure of the state, which, during the thirty-three-year reign of Ali Abdullah Saleh, failed to meet the aspirations of the Yemeni people.

Indeed, government institutions did not undergo any serious reforms over the course of the three-decade regime. Any changes that did take place remained solely cosmetic, as they were enacted within the narrow boundaries of what the former regime found acceptable. Highlighting the link between institutional reform and regime change, the Gulf Cooperation Council (GCC) initiative that removed Saleh from power emphasized reform of the military establishment as a major requirement for the transition to a post-Saleh government. Nevertheless, the institutional reform that has taken place within the framework of the GCC initiative has remained limited, focusing mostly on the military and favoring cosmetic adjustments rather than fundamental regime change. Such limited institutional reform will only have a limited ability to create sustainable state institutions to form the backbone of a successful transition to peace and stability.

Restructuring the military was a pillar of the November 2011 GCC-brokered transition agreement, as it dictates that the government must "integrate the armed forces under unified, national and professional leadership."[15] Under the Saleh regime, military and security institutions were loyal primarily to the leaders of individual units rather than to the state. The Republican Guards, for example, pledged their loyalty first and foremost to General Ahmed Saleh—one of the president's sons—rather than to the Ministry of Defense. Heads of military and security units all remained loyal to President Saleh, but after the revolution, a division emerged when General Ali Mohsen al-Ahmar defected and allied himself and his unit, the powerful First Armored Division, with the uprising. As a result, the security units became part of the problem rather than the solution during the uprising, as they became divided between different loyalties and were unable to act as a united front to stem the rising tide of violence. In fact, most security and military units concentrated their presence in Sanaa, splitting the capital into a number of territories controlled by different security units with various political loyalties while leaving the rest of the country without a state security presence.

Given this diffusion of the security and military establishments during the uprising, reforms to unite all units under government leadership became a major requirement for any future comprehensive institutional reform. Successful security reform in Yemen would first and foremost require the shift of units' loyalties from individuals to the state and its Ministry of Defense.

In fact, Yemen's transitional government under President Abd Rabbu Mansour Hadi made significant changes in security sector reform on two levels. First, the new government managed to incorporate all security units into the official structure of the state. Military and security units were re-structured to become parts of the Ministry of Defense and the Ministry of Interior; scattered loyalties were united under loyalty to the state. Second, the transitional government was able to remove the top leadership of security and military institutions, which had supported both the former regime and the uprising. Indeed, the government believed that both parties had to be removed in order to end the quarrel and assign fresh leadership to all security institutions. On April 10, 2013, President Hadi removed Saleh's relatives—who protected the former regime—as well as General Ali Mohsen al-Ahmar—who defected and supported the uprising—from top military posts and reformed the Ministry of Defense. Hadi made al-Ahmar a presidential advisor and appointed Ahmed Saleh, Saleh's son and head of the Republican Guard, "an elite army unit that was once the backbone of Saleh's rule," as ambassador to the United Arab Emirates. Two of Saleh's nephews—Ammar, who had been the deputy intelligence chief, and Tareq Yahia, head of the Presidential Guard—received postings as military atta-chés in Ethiopia and Germany, respectively.[16]

Despite these changes in the top security and military sectors, the 2014 Houthis-Saleh coup proved that the loyalties to the former autocrat were much deeper than just the removal of his relatives from their senior positions. The structure of the deep state proved to be much stronger than what Hadi thought and therefore needed substantially deeper reform in order to ensure successful rebuilding of state institutions. Saleh's loyalties within the Yemeni army allowed the Houthis to take over Sanaa without showing any serious resistance.

Efforts to reform state institutions in Yemen were not solely limited to the security sector, however. The National Dialogue Conference's (NDC) State Building Working Group, for example, issued recommendations in

September 2013 to reform the justice system. The group determined that 15 percent of the Judicial Supreme Council would be academics and 15 percent would come from the lawyers' syndicate. Meanwhile, judges would be elected and confirmed by parliament, not appointed by the executive.[17]

On the governmental level, President Hadi was "mandated to reshuffle the cabinet and restructure the consultative upper house of parliament, the Shura Council, to give greater representation to the south . . . and to Zaidi Shia in the north" by the NDC.[18] Furthermore, on June 26, 2013, Hadi issued twenty-four presidential decrees aimed at restructuring the Ministry of Interior. He appointed a general inspector who "would have broad powers to monitor the work of security forces in the ministry and security departments in various governorates in order to reduce corruption and prevent violations of human rights."[19]

NDC recommendations for national reform extended to other areas as well. The conference reached agreements to "abolish early childhood marriage; create a truly independent anti-corruption body; and advance the rights of women including 30% representation in the public office."[20]

Despite reform efforts that have been made since the signing of the power transition deal in November 2011, real progress toward comprehensive and genuine institutional reform in Yemen remains extremely limited. The security sector has experienced limited reforms in its top leadership but definitely more than other sectors. Yet, aside from military restructuring, institutional reform in Yemen exists only in terms of theory and recommendations. Institutional reform in the country is far from complete, while the transition process holds serious challenges that may restrict reform to the theoretical level.

The most serious impediment to institutional reform in Yemen is the power transition deal itself, despite the security reforms it initiated. In addition to granting immunity against prosecution to Saleh and the people who worked around him, the GCC-brokered initiative facilitated the transition of the former ruling party to the new political arrangements, including the cabinet, where Saleh's General People's Congress (GPC) retains 50 percent of the posts, and the parliament, where the GPC has a majority.

Even more serious, the transition deal retained the state's bureaucratic system, which existed under Saleh, intact. Through the GCC's power transition deal, former bureaucrats—both senior and junior—kept their positions, while the same systems and procedures for that sector were maintained in the post-Saleh era. The old regime's bureaucratic system was excessively inflated, and rampant corruption made good governance almost impossible. The oversized bureaucratic system had as many as one million people working in state institutions, which equates to approximately one-fifth of Yemen's workforce working in the public sector. Bloated bureaucracy in Yemen has been associated with low productivity and poverty. Indeed, unemployment increased from 9 percent in 1992 to 35 percent in 2010—when the uprising broke out—while the poverty rate rose from 19 to 42 percent during the same period.[21] Again, the GCC agreement in Yemen that allowed the former ruling party to transition to the new system without requiring party or public sector reform made deep institutional reform difficult, as members of the bureaucracy are resistant to reforms that could remove them from their posts. To make things worse, the corruption that prevailed in state institutions under the former regime has also managed to persist in the post-uprising bureaucracy.

The Houthis' takeover of Sanaa in September 2014 added additional layers of complexity to Yemen's institutional reform process. First of all, the recently reformed Yemeni national army, which was supposed to protect the country's sovereignty and maintain its territorial integrity, collapsed. It offered little resistance to the Houthi onslaught, allowing the rebels to capture most state institutions in less than a day. Clearly, the reforms to the military were unsuccessful. Second, having occupied the capital, the Houthis started to demand the reform of some institutions on their own terms. In particular, the Houthis sought to gain long-term control of state institutions, especially the army and other security bodies, through having them hire thousands of Houthi members and supporters. This would allow the Houthis to reward their followers for helping them to take control of Sanaa while compromising the sovereignty of these institutions by staffing them with thousands of individuals who would be more loyal to their

Houthi leaders than their governmental superiors. This would be a serious obstacle to future reform as it would disrupt command structures and effectively weaken these institutions. Reform in this case will require, first and foremost, a political agreement with the Houthis before Yemen's security apparatus will be able to exercise its national duty.

Yemen's ability to hold free and fair general elections that lead to the formation of a new parliament and government could also bring about greater institutional reforms. If an elected national parliament could keep the legislative branch independent from the executive, it would give hope that through the legislature, Yemen would be able to issue new policies that may facilitate serious institutional reform.

Institutional Reform: Comparative Aspects

Analysis of Libya, Tunisia, and Yemen shows that past human rights abuses and misuse of power were part of a comprehensive system rather than sporadic incidents. Repressive regimes functioned as cohesive units to suppress their citizens and ensure the government's survival. This approach to abuses makes it necessary to reform the institutions that produced such injustices, rather than solely removing leaders from power. Indeed, it was not only Ben Ali who was involved in the abuses of Tunisia's political opposition, but most importantly, it was the system that supported him—including the security services that conducted torture, the judiciary that tried prisoners for their speech, the media that marketed the regime, the bureaucratic system that corrupted individuals, and even the education system, which glorified the dictatorship. A successful transition from a dictatorship therefore requires comprehensive reform that involves the security, judicial, media, bureaucratic, and educational systems. The escape of Ben Ali represented only the starting point—rather than the end—of the revolution.

The question of how best to reform the institutions of former regimes has proven difficult to answer. Two broad approaches have emerged as the leading ways to restructure post-dictatorship governments: purging personnel or reforming institutions. Ideally, a purge approach to bureaucracies that were compromised under old regimes is effective in engineering radical change by elevating a new crop of civil servants that will counter the practices of old regimes. However, a purge approach, as seen in the Libyan case, is often unrealistic due to limited resources and the inability to replace an entire bureaucratic system. In addition, a mass purge is likely to set the country on a track for a counter-revolution and further instability. Certainly, such radical change in a short period often leads to polarization, and so the chances of achieving comprehensive national reconciliation decline. The reform approach therefore seems more practical and suitable for fixing institutions that were compromised in the past, while also moving to end polarization and build national reconciliation. A limited or shallow approach to reform, however, as seen in the Yemeni case, is likely to preserve the old regime and could waste the opportunity to institute important changes. Transition from dictatorship to a stable civil peace should in fact take a "deep reform" approach that engages in changing systems and procedures while also building new structures that prevent future corruption and human rights violations. The approach of replacing top leaders loyal to the former regime—as in Yemen—proved to be an ineffective approach to reform. Obviously, loyalties run much deeper into the structure of the deep state than only the top level. It was ultimately the mid-level security and army officers who allowed the Houthis-Saleh alliance to succeed in taking over Sanaa with almost no resistance. Reform therefore must include systems, policies, and personnel in state institutions—not simply a limited number of the top leadership.

This chapter's country analysis shows that institutional reform in post-dictatorship periods is challenged on two levels: policy and implementation. On the policy level, political entities leading institutional reform need to possess sufficient legitimacy to allow them to issue legislation for major reform. In particular, parliaments need to take the lead in determining the shape and approach of reform, as they benefit from popular legitimacy. However, such legitimacy is linked to elections, which in turn can only be held in relatively stable environments. In Yemen, for example, the parliament leading the change in post-Saleh arrangements is still the one that was elected under Saleh's reign, as new elections have not yet been held. Such a compromised parliament lacks legitimacy, especially among the youth who led the revolution against the old regime and were excluded from post-Saleh arrangements. In contrast, the NDC, which was organized after Saleh's reign, has engaged in some reform policies, yet it was also appointed rather than directly elected by the people, which again raises the question of legitimacy.

Even more serious than policy legislation is the implementation of these policies on the ground. Indeed, implementation is generally faced with challenges like maintaining the balance of power among the various stakeholders, enforcing legislated changes, obtaining the budget—usually massive—needed to implement reforms, and securing human capital to apply these changes. In the Tunisian experience, the NCA has changed most of the former regime's policies, but these changes have mostly remained on paper. Implementation has been complicated by a lack of resources and other factors. It will take Tunisia more time and possibly a more robust electoral system that elects strong parliaments to make implementation feasible. A key to overcoming obstacles facing implementation is inclusiveness. Certainly, it is unlikely that one party will be able to implement institutional reform alone. Close collaboration among the various stakeholders and direct engagement with those who might be affected as a result of the application of these policies is the best way to ensure the efficacy of legislative changes.

Importantly, institutional reform cannot be separated from the political process. For the achievement of effective implementation, institutional reform requires the proper political framework and environment. The reason behind widespread support among Libyan revolutionaries for a purge approach to institutional reform is simply that Qaddafi and his loyalists were totally defeated and the conflict ended up being a zero-sum game. The winner in the Libyan case, therefore, had no incentive to demand less than a complete purge. In Yemen, however, where a power-sharing formula was reached through the GCC initiative, "shallow institutional reform" that ensured the survival of the former ruling party in state institutions became the dominant approach to reforming the public sector. A purge was never an option, and instead, minor institutional reform was the only formula that corresponded to the larger political framework outlined by the GCC initiative.

The political aspects of institutional reform cannot be avoided. Those who launched the revolutions and toppled former dictatorships now demand more representation and services from their government. For several decades, many of these citizens were not even allowed employment in the public sector. Now that they have successfully ousted those who deprived them of the right to run for public office, they hope to hold authority and benefit from the success of their political struggles.

Meeting the demands of victims of past injustices, navigating vigorous political struggles, and securing needed resources are all serious challenges to the process of institutional reform. A good starting point to dealing with such massive challenges would be securing elected parliaments, which provide a legitimate institutional setting for the deep institutional reforms that are critical for the success of the transition process as a whole.

PART III

Agents of Reconciliation

TEN

Civil Society Organizations

Roberto Belloni defines civil society, an often broadly used term, as "the set of voluntary organizations and groups not created by the state." This comprehensive definition allows civil society to include a wide range of organizations that are not governmental and also distinct from political parties that participate in state-sanctioned elections. The civil society sector, therefore, includes human rights groups, women and youth organizations, trade unions, and so on. It is important to note, especially when we discuss the involvement of civil society organizations (CSOs) in peacebuilding, that civil society does not have a single position regarding the peace process or transition phase. There will always be certain groups that are more active than others and more involved in peacebuilding than others, which means civil society is by no means monolithic, or even united, in the ways governments and political parties most commonly are.[1]

Why should civil society be involved in the processes of political transition, peacebuilding, and reconciliation? To what extent can CSOs be influential agents of reconciliation in societies undergoing transitions? Belloni argues that "the inclusion of civil society representatives in peacemaking negotiations can increase the legitimacy of a peace agreement and the prospects for its implementation." Desirée Nilsson agrees that civil society is often viewed as able to contribute precisely by generating legitimacy for a peace process. If this is the case, how exactly can CSOs create legitimacy for reconciliation and peacebuilding processes? Nilsson suggests three ways in which CSOs may contribute to creating legitimacy and fostering local ownership of peace processes. First, consultations with CSOs allow other groups to become acquainted with their perspectives on issues discussed by the warring parties. Second, civil society groups that have a degree of political support may also be given a seat at the negotiation table in order to influence the process through representative decision-making. Finally, the inclusion of CSOs allows direct participation by actors at the grassroots level, engaging in intercommunity meetings and other public forums.[2]

Another primary reason for involving civil society in peacebuilding and reconciliation processes is to achieve what Nathan C. Funk and Abdul Aziz Said call "localizing peace." They argue, "Ultimately, peace must be defined and constructed locally, and peacebuilding efforts become energetic and sustainable only to the extent that they tap local resources, empower local constituencies, and achieve legitimacy within particular cultural and religious contexts." Of course, no party is better equipped to empower local constituencies than CSOs that are working at the grassroots level. In Yemen, for example, non-governmental organizations (NGOs) were able to work in remote areas that are considered unsafe and unstable, like Shabwa and Mareb, while the government has failed to deliver even basic services to these districts. Peace can only be reached at the local level in these places through NGOs that are connected to local and tribal authorities. John Paul Lederach, a leading advocate for building peace on the grassroots level, further emphasizes the significance of grassroots peacebuilding: "Indigenous people should be viewed as primary resources for conflict resolution and encouraged to take up the task of building peace themselves in their own locales. . . . We have to look for the cultural resources that exist for building peace."[3]

There are both regional and international examples of CSOs making significant contributions to national reconciliation. NGOs in Lebanon engaged in wide-ranging grassroots peacebuilding and training campaigns after the country's fifteen-year civil war ended in 1990. The Permanent Peace Movement conducted training in a total of ninety villages, involving hundreds of trainees, while the "Memory for the Future" project focused on documenting the war and the Association of the Disappeared worked to uncover what happened to the seventeen thousand Lebanese citizens who disappeared during the conflict.[4] In Uruguay and Paraguay, CSOs took on the responsibility of conducting investigations, thereby representing their constituents' interests and providing some independent oversight.[5] Argentina's National Commission on the Disappearance of Persons, a human rights NGO, collaborated extensively with the government to unearth new knowledge, and demonstrated how such groups can counterbalance "the tendency of post-dictatorship regimes to limit the scope of the truth."[6] In Sierra Leone, the interfaith community had played such a meaningful role in the peace process and pursuit of reconciliation that when the country's truth and reconciliation commission was established, religious leaders chaired it and "were involved in all its activities, including truth telling and conflict resolution sessions, sensitization, statement taking and reconciliation initiatives."[7]

Significantly, Nilsson also emphasizes the link between the involvement of CSOs in the reconciliation process and the sustainability of peacebuilding outcomes: "Common for all these forms of participation is the notion that a peace process that is not merely top-down, but also contains elements of peacebuilding from below, is expected to produce more stable outcomes. Here civil society actors are key as they can contribute by creating an ownership of the peace agreement."[8] This was the case in Northern Ireland, as peace and conflict resolution organizations promoted inclusivity and provided venues where militants could transition into community activism and eventually mainstream politics, through which they had a positive impact on the peace process.[9]

In line with this theoretical framework, this chapter takes two cases—Tunisia and Libya—and studies the role of CSOs in the transitions that followed the removal of repressive regimes in these nations. The chapter argues that CSOs are effective agents of reconciliation and have earned their role as integral parts of the transition process. Specifically, it finds that CSOs have delivered results where states and political parties have failed, built peace in remote and unstable areas, intervened in crises between governments and political parties, advised and trained on the mechanics of transition, and built capacity, peace, and reconciliation in political transitions following the Arab Spring.

For each one of the "agents of reconciliation" studied in this book—civil society organizations, tribes, and women—I take only two country cases per agent. The third case may still be important, but I believe that studying the role of each agent in two cases is sufficient to demonstrate how each particular group can contribute to successful transitions and national reconciliation.

Tunisia

The remarkable contribution of CSOs to Tunisia's transition toward peace and reconciliation can be seen in three major areas: the development of a transitional justice law, the hosting of a representative national dialogue, and the defusing of a major political crisis by facilitating key agreements and compromises.

A number of CSOs played a critical role in drafting the transitional justice law in Tunisia. This process started as part of the aforementioned Tunisian General Labor Union (UGTT)–sponsored national dialogue, which established a committee to address the issue. Khaled Kchier, a member of that committee, described its work: "We met constantly. We debated all aspects of transitional justice such as truth seeking, lustration laws, compensation, etc. We brought in international experts and heard their recommendations; we met with the victims and their families in many districts in Tunisia. We all came from different organizations in Tunisia and represented over seventy civil society organizations. This is a small and successful model of a larger national dialogue."[10]

CSOs went on to provide technical support in the actual drafting process and development of the law. The Ministry of Human Rights formed a drafting committee with twelve members to support the development of the transitional justice law. Ten of those members came from CSOs, with the remaining two coming from the ministry. Among the organizations that took leading roles in developing the law were the al-Kawakibi Democracy Transition Center, the Tunisian Network for Transitional Justice, the Tunis Center for Transitional Justice and Human Rights, and the International Center for Transitional Justice. The National Constituent Assembly (NCA) nearly unanimously passed the Draft Organic Law on the Organization of Transitional Justice Foundations and Area of Competence on December 15, 2013. The law puts forward a detailed plan for dealing with past human rights violations. It establishes a "Truth and Dignity Commission and addresses reparations, accountability, institutional reform, vetting, and national reconciliation."[11]

The major contribution of the CSOs to the establishment of the transitional justice law in Tunisia was indispensable to the country's successful transition. Ten CSOs began working in a bottom-up approach to draft a transitional justice law. They divided the country into six districts, each of which was composed of four areas. The group then formed subcommittees in each area and began to meet with the victims of the former regime's abuses in many Tunisian cities and towns. In this way, CSOs were able to hear directly from victims and their families about their past suffering as well as their visions of what a fair transitional justice law would look like. CSOs then began drafting the transitional justice law, and on October 28, 2012, submitted a complete draft to the government.[12]

No other actor in Tunisia would have been suited to play this role of engaging with victims of the former regime and the general public in the development of such a controversial law. The government certainly was not in a position to do so, because the law should be fair and neutral and the government is a major stakeholder. Similarly, political parties would have likely looked to draft a law in a way that would promote their own agendas. For these reasons, only a wide-ranging and politically neutral civil society could provide the different kinds of services needed for the law's drafting and implementation. Amine Ghali of the al-Kawakibi Democracy Transition Center explained the CSOs' unique contributions to the process of drafting the law: "The secret for the success of transitional justice law in Tunisia is the fact that it came from civil society adopting a bottom-up approach, not a top-down approach as the government used to do in the past. When we began talking to the people about transitional justice, it was like we were speaking Chinese to them. Many did not even know what the term meant. We established the culture of transitional justice in Tunisia through our public awareness campaign. That helped people understand what transitional justice is and how important it is for a successful transition in Tunisia. One example is that our center delivered over twenty training workshops with over one thousand beneficiaries from the government, civil society, and other institutions."[13]

Certain Tunisian CSOs trained others involved in the management of different aspects of the transition process. Rim El-Gantri, an expert at the International Center for Transitional Justice, explained, "We provided training on subjects like 'gender, children, and transitional justice,' accountability, reparation, and constitutional drafting. We provided the ministry with South African experts in writing transitional justice laws, we organized trips for them to Peru to meet representatives of National Reconciliation committees and learn about their experience in reparations."[14]

The unique contributions of the CSOs to the development of the transitional justice law has given the judicial branch a significant boost toward sustainable stability and the promotion of neutrality and justice. The fact that representatives from CSOs met with victims and heard firsthand about their experiences and their visions for solutions helped to create a sense of local ownership of the law. Tunisians, as a result, will fight to protect the law, as they contributed to its drafting. Long-term sustainability, then, is another benefit of the CSOs' bottom-up approach, as it allows citizens to contribute to the law-making process, making them more likely to accept and promote its application.

It is important to note that the role of CSOs in Tunisia's transition to sustainable reconciliation goes far beyond drafting the transitional justice law. Intervention, mediation, and conflict resolution among Tunisia's political parties have also been aided by the intervention of Tunisia's CSOs. In July 2013, in particular, they helped to resolve perhaps the country's biggest political crisis since the fall of Zine El Abidine Ben Ali. This crisis emerged in the aftermath of the assassination of opposition leader and member of the NCA Mohamed al-Brahmi, who is believed to have been killed by a Salafi extremist. The entire opposition bloc withdrew from the NCA in protest, suspending its work for approximately six months.[15] The opposition escalated protests against the troika government, and the standoff between the two camps threatened to return the country to chaos, instability, and disorder, perhaps even to the degree seen in Egypt after the collapse of the Muhammad Morsi government. In the midst of the failure of Tunisia's political parties—those of the troika government and the opposition—to resolve their crisis, it was the UGTT that intervened. After months of debate and deliberation, the UGTT was able to deliver a resolution to the crisis. Its president, Hussein al-Abbasi, met with the two camps, transmitted messages between them, suggested compromises, and proposed arrangements and solutions. The crisis finally ended with the resignation of the troika government, the formation of a new technocratic government, and the setting of a specific date for new general elections. Undoubtedly, this solution would not have been reached without the committed intervention of the UGTT, another example of CSOs' considerable contributions to Tunisia's transition to peace and reconciliation.

Holding a wide and inclusive national dialogue is the third area where Tunisia's CSOs have had great influence, as described in the chapter on national dialogues. The UGTT-facilitated dialogue that lasted for over a year and aimed to forge agreements on key challenges facing the country, including the nature of the state, the timing and type of elections, and basic elements of the constitution. More than sixty political parties and fifty CSOs participated in this dialogue and another national dialogue run by the presidency.[16] The UGTT national dialogue led to agreements on a number of key points: a firm rejection of violence, the prioritization of the national economy, a roadmap for the political transition, and a consensus on major issues like a civil state and constitutional system, the independence of the judiciary, freedom of the press, and freedom of assembly. The national dialogue later formed a committee of seventeen political parties and four CSOs to implement these agreements.[17]

Through its contributions to national dialogue, crisis intervention, and transitional justice, Tunisia's civil society has earned its position within the structure of the country's transition process toward sustainable reconciliation. CSOs will likely continue to be important actors in post–Ben Ali Tunisia.

Libya

With the goal of solidifying the absolute control of his Jamahiriya regime, Muammar Qaddafi effectively stunted the growth of a civil society sector in Libya. Only a select few organizations were allowed to operate during his reign. In contrast, within a year of the Qaddafi regime's collapse, hundreds of new CSOs were established. These organizations were formed in a variety of areas, including youth, women, charity, media, conflict resolution, and politics. While there are limits to how much these newly formed CSOs can influence the process of national reconciliation in Libya, this growing array of CSOs nonetheless has a unique role to play. Specifically, Libya's civil society can contribute to restoring stability, encouraging cooperation among groups, and defusing local conflicts.

In the absence of strong central state authority, CSOs can assume some of the state's responsibilities for promoting stability and peace. The collapse of the Qaddafi regime left a power vacuum not only in Tripoli but especially in remote areas. In many cases, CSOs have helped restore security and order in these areas outside the government's purview.

The non-authoritative nature of CSO participation helps elicit a special type of collaboration. Unlike the state, CSOs are not acting from a position of authority that allows them to impose a solution, so instead they seek to involve disputing parties in genuine dialogue. Furthermore, CSOs do not share the state's bureaucratic or political nature, but are based instead on voluntarism and individual efforts. Hussein al-Habbouni and Abdulnaser Ibrahim Obaidi of the Wisemen and Shura Council (WSC) hail from the eastern town of Tobruk. As part of their peacebuilding work, they travel hundreds of miles to Tripoli and the western Nafousa Mountains, where they stay for more than a month at a time to focus fully on mending ties among local tribes. They initially undertook this task on an entirely volunteer basis, although the Libyan authorities have now recognized the importance of their work and have begun to contribute to their travel and hotel expenses. As WSC president al-Habbouni said, "We are the unknown soldiers who are working on the ground to solve conflicts that the state has abandoned."[18]

CSOs' familiarity with cultural and tribal values can make their interventions more effective. In its intervention between the Zentan and Mashaysha tribes in the Nafousa Mountains, for example, the WSC ensured that any proposed solutions were made in line with local customs and norms. According to al-Habbouni, "The fact that solutions originate from the cultural norms of that area makes them both acceptable and sustainable."[19]

The work of the WSC demonstrates the larger role CSOs could play in national reconciliation. The WSC has worked in tense areas throughout Libya, especially in the Nafousa Mountains. In such areas, the group has focused on defusing conflict between tribes used by Qaddafi to defend his reign and neighboring tribes that worked to promote Qaddafi's overthrow. With state authority functionally absent in these areas, the WSC has been instrumental in ending deadly tribal clashes. On June 17, 2012, for example, fierce fighting erupted between the Zentan and Mashaysha tribes in the western Nafousa Mountains over disputed land and the Mashaysha's alleged alliance with the former regime. Resulting violence left an estimated three hundred dead and wounded on both sides, in addition to more than eighty-five held as prisoners. The WSC successfully negotiated an end to the violence and the release of all captives. The council also convinced the tribes to sign a "code of ethics," according to which any tribe member engaged in fighting after December 9, 2012, would represent only himself; combatants would no longer enjoy tribal protection, thus preempting further large-scale conflict. In addition, an arbitration committee was formed to address points of contention between the two tribes. To make the agreement more broadly applicable, the WSC included other Nafousa tribal branches that were accused of siding with Qaddafi, including the al-Shaqeeqah, Mazda, Fsano, and Awainiyya.[20]

For an example of how CSOs can assume government functions and compensate for state failure, we can also look to the work of activist Wafa Tayyeb al-Naas. Al-Naas established the Society of Understanding and National Reconciliation (SUNR) in Tripoli immediately after the collapse of the Qaddafi regime. SUNR targeted the poor, crowded Tripoli neighborhood of Abu Salim, which was traditionally considered a stronghold for Qaddafi loyalists. In the midst of the chaos that accompanied Qaddafi's fall, the neighborhood was in dire need of basic humanitarian aid. SUNR provided food and blankets, and after the situation became more stable, began organizing education and training programs in the area. Once it had established firm ties with the people of Abu Salim, SUNR put together sporting events involving people from tribes and towns considered enemies of Abu Salim. "We organized a soccer championship in conflict zones," said al-Naas, "and we had forty-five teams participating from different towns including ones who have historical and political rivalries such as Misrata and Warfalla. During the games, their hostile attitude against each other was replaced with collaboration to make the championship a success."[21] SUNR later extended its services to southern Libya and to Libyan refugees in Tunisia, in addition to facilitating reconciliation in the south between tribes like the Tuareg and towns like Ghadames.

The Society of Libya without Borders (SLWB) has also assumed the traditional state functions of peacebuilding and conflict resolution. The SLWB helped to end the fighting between the town of Zewara, seventy-five miles west of Tripoli, and the rival neighboring towns of Raqdaleen and Aljmayyel. Zewara had supported the revolution, while the other two had allegedly stood with the former regime. The SLWB was able to intervene, bring an end to the fighting, and even arrange a prisoner swap.

This network of CSOs has played a critical role in advancing peacebuilding and uniting Libya. Of course, there are limits to what they can accomplish on their own. International Crisis Group Libya country director Claudia Gazzini said, "The WSC were very effective in conflict resolution in the east of Libya—the Benghazi area—and were also able to stop the fighting between the Zentan and Mashaysha tribes." Gazzini pointed out, however, that the WSC has been less able to push for implementation of these agreements; the Zentan-Mashaysha prisoner release, for example, has not been completed. Furthermore, she said, "Misrata did not collaborate with the WSC fully. They accused WSC of being *azlam al-nidham* [regime cronies] and said that they were trying to defend the other party, Bani Waleed."[22]

Of course, CSOs will always face limitations in light of their restricted authority and resources. Still, this does not negate the significant role that CSOs can play in fostering peacebuilding, bridging divides, and helping transition processes overcome major obstacles.

Civil Society and the Transition to Civil Peace: Comparative Aspect

CSOs have earned their positions in the transition processes that followed the fall of former repressive regimes in Tunisia and Libya. They have succeeded where the state and political parties have failed, delivering peace to remote areas when central governments were still struggling to restore order in their capitals. CSOs forged agreements, bridged divides, and helped the progress of the overall transition processes. In Tunisia, the UGTT was able to broker a peace deal for a unity and technocratic government after the ruling coalition and opposition political parties failed to reach an agreement. In Libya, the collapse of the Qaddafi regime created a power vacuum where the transitional council had no ability even to resolve conflicts in the capital. In this environment, newly formed CSOs were able to deliver peace agreements among tribes in the remote areas of Libya, such as the Nafousa Mountains.

Nonetheless, CSOs are not and should not be substitutes for the state or political parties. The nature, structure, and role of CSOs are fundamentally different from those of governments and political parties. For that reason, their contributions complement the work of governments and political parties, rather than replacing them. The efforts of CSOs are not confined by the bureaucracy and political considerations that often hinder the function of governments, nor do they have the narrow agendas that usually characterize political parties. The flexible structures of CSOs—often supported by voluntarism—help them to be more effective in responding quickly to escalating crises. The unique role of CSOs has helped to bridge divides in Tunisia's political crisis among political parties as well as in Libya's tribal conflicts.

CSOs are therefore an integral part of transition processes, as they can help counter polarization and aid transitions to peace and justice in ways that governments are often unable to perform. As this chapter has shown, CSOs in Tunisia and Libya were able to make positive contributions in the following areas: drafting and developing a transitional justice law; facilitating a national dialogue; building peace and stabilizing remote, tribal-dominated areas; intervening in political crises; and delivering humanitarian aid at times of crisis. CSOs used different methods to deliver these services, including training and advising, especially on technical issues related to political transition, facilitating group meetings, and coordinating educational trips and site visits to countries that have undergone political transitions in the past, such as Peru and South Africa.

Analysis of both Tunisia and Libya shows that the work of CSOs has solidified the concept of citizenship among participants, eliciting a collaborative attitude and stronger commitments among people to serving their countries and ending polarization. These resulting feelings of patriotism and devotion to serving a national cause will help to move parties away from polarization and confrontation and instead toward collaboration. Both the UGTT in Tunisia and the WSC in Libya have performed most of their crisis intervention and peacebuilding on a strictly volunteer basis, with the leaders of these organizations acting firmly out of a desire to help their countries peacefully pass through the critical phase of political transition. Civil society leaders invested a great deal of their time, personally funded most of their work, and even risked their own personal security to help resolve conflicts and build peace in such a challenging period. Their crisis intervention, peacebuilding, and conflict resolution is as important as fighting the old dictatorships and toppling repressive regimes.

Finally, the experiences of CSOs in both Tunisia and Libya show that there are limits to what civil society can accomplish. The major limitation is that the work done by CSOs remains sporadic, unsystematic, and random unless placed within a larger context set by the government itself. Due to their small sizes, CSOs are not capable of composing or implementing plans for the country as a whole. To have a national impact, a broader strategy that involves other parties is necessary, in particular the state. CSOs can definitely assist in implementing a national strategy, but they have not yet demonstrated the ability to develop and lead one. Rather, a major part of their work is in reaction to crises that erupt in specific areas. They hear of tribal fighting in the Nafousa Mountains in Libya, for example, and move rapidly to secure a ceasefire. CSOs are therefore rarely proactive in their intervention, largely because they lack the capacity for nationwide planning and implementation of their goals. For the national dimension of peacebuilding and reconciliation to be achieved, the state must enhance its capabilities to complement and support the role played by CSOs, so they can work together to reach sustainable peace and political stability.

ELEVEN

Women

The impact of armed conflicts on women is enormous. This is the case in most violent struggles around the world, and the Arab Spring uprisings were certainly not an exception. Living under tyrannical regimes, Arab women, like men, were penalized directly for their involvement in opposition politics, as well as indirectly, as they were often used as a means of pressure or collateral against relatives that were active in opposition movements. Although women share a major burden of war and conflict, they are rarely represented in peacemaking, which often leads to the drafting of agreements that are not gender sensitive and consequently less able to sustain long-term peace and reconciliation. This chapter argues that the inclusion of women in post–Arab Spring transitions is necessary to ensure the credible representation of the primary concerned parties, as well as the legitimacy and sustainability of the reconciliation process. Women are undoubtedly part of the conflict and therefore must be part of the solution.

Armed conflicts affect women in a variety of ways. The use of rape, kidnapping, and trafficking as tools of war most frequently victimizes females. Furthermore, women are often left with children, parents, and extended families to support if their husbands are killed in fighting. The situation becomes even worse when such women are not employed or highly skilled and yet are expected to support dependents. Andrea Fischer-Tahir describes "the war and the enduring climate of violence and insecurity" in Iraq as causing "a proliferation of kidnapping, rape, 'honour' crimes, homicide and trafficking. At the same time, a fragile state and a weak civil society allow violence against women—justified by local, ethnic, religious, and tribal customary law—to occur, and leave women unprotected with regard to practices such as forced marriage, the 'exchange' of sisters among men, or the giving and receiving of women as gifts in order to end or prevent a conflict between tribal groups."[1]

Despite the enormous challenges that women face during violent conflicts, they are significantly underrepresented in peace agreements worldwide. Women actively participate in times of war yet are notably absent in times of peace. For example, over the past ten years, there have been approximately thirty-nine conflicts in which negotiations and subsequent peace agreements did not include female participants.[2] Furthermore, out of the 585 peace agreements drafted in the past two decades, only 16 percent contained specific reference to women.[3] According to a 2010 analysis by the UN Development Fund for Women, of 24 peace processes since 1992, women represented only 2.5 percent of signatories, 3.2 percent of mediators, and 7.6 percent of negotiators.[4] Such figures raise serious concerns about representation and the inclusiveness of such agreements. Indeed, "the importance of bringing gender into peacebuilding is not confined to redressing the violations of the human rights of women or addressing women's economic, social, or justice needs. Instead, for many, a gendered perspective represents peacebuilding as a process of inclusion."[5]

International organizations recognize this disparity between participation in the "price of conflict" and the "solution of the conflict." The UN, for example, has acknowledged this gap and called for a change. In 2000, the body's Security Council adopted Resolution 1325, which "acknowledges the disproportionate impact of violent conflict on women and recognizes the critical roles women can and should play in the processes of peacebuilding and conflict prevention. These include participating in peace talks, conflict mediation and all aspects of post-conflict reconstruction."[6] Significantly, the resolution "stresses the importance of equal participation and full involvement of women in all efforts for the maintenance and promotion of peace and security."[7]

Women are partners in conflict and should be partners in peace as well. Women's contributions to peacebuilding are invaluable. No one understands the needs of women like women themselves, and their participation in the negotiation and drafting of peace treaties will ensure real representation of the issues and the parties of the conflict. Furthermore, "because women are the central caretakers of families in many cultures, everyone suffers when women are oppressed, victimized, and excluded from peacebuilding. Their centrality to communal life makes their inclusion in peacebuilding essential."[8] The needs of women must be included in any peacebuilding process to ensure its sustainability.

Women have been active globally in contributing to peace by launching initiatives that challenge the violence they face and the formal negotiation processes that often exclude them. For example, in Liberia, a group of Catholic and Protestant mothers formed a coalition across the lines of conflict and defied the prevailing narratives in the 1990s. Christian and Muslim women also used to organize sit-ins at Liberian markets and refused to work in order to stop the violence of Charles Taylor and his militias.[9]

Women contribute not only to building peace during times of war and violence but also in post-conflict reconstruction and reconciliation. South Africa provides one example where women participated, and were greatly successful, in affecting different phases of the country's Truth and Reconciliation Commission. Dorothy Driver explains that "forgiveness was feminized: women comforters were almost invariably used to sit with the witnesses; the voices of women were often used to give judgment on whether forgiveness would be granted and humanity bestowed; and women typically functioned in the position of mourners whose ritual task had to do with the restoration of social order, not an exhortation to revenge."[10]

Women played a vital role in the Arab Spring uprisings. Yemeni and Libyan women helped to spark the uprisings against their dictators. Once the repressive regimes were toppled, women played important roles in rebuilding the transitioning nations. Women in Libya and Yemen adopted the goal of peacebuilding after having achieved the goal of liberation. The cases of Libya and Yemen, discussed below, show the importance of female involvement in creating sustainable peace after conflict. Women in Tunisia played a critical role in both the uprising and transition, but I am limiting the discussion of the role of agents of reconciliation to two cases only.

Libya

Although they face considerable challenges and constraints, women have secured a prominent place in Libya's post-conflict national reconciliation.

They played an important role from the revolution's outset. In fact, it would not be an exaggeration to argue that it was women who sparked the revolution against Muammar Qaddafi. Considering their important contributions to the revolution, they are now well positioned to serve as agents of change in the transitional phase toward civil peace.

For almost a year before Libya's February 17 Revolution, the female relatives of the victims of the Abu Salim prison massacre demonstrated in front of Benghazi's court every Saturday. These protesters demanded one thing: the truth about what had happened to their 1,270 relatives. On February 15, two days before the start of the revolution, the female protesters escalated their protest by moving it from the court to the offices of interior security. At the outset, they chanted for "reforming the regime." After a few hours, however, they started to chant for "changing the regime."[11]

The Abu Salim women's movement was the basis for a culture of resistance against the Qaddafi dictatorship at a time when the rest of the country remained silent about the government's repression. According to Rida Altubuly, president of the women's activist organization Ma'an Nabneeha (Together We Build It), "The regime offered to strike deals to settle the prisoners' cases outside the court by paying financial compensation and for the mothers not to go pursue the issue legally or take any other actions. The regime simply offered to buy off the silence of the families of the victims. Many women refused to make a deal with the dictator. They continued to protest in front of the court, which was something new for Libya. They wrote slogans, authored poetry, released statements of resistance, painted pictures, and [engaged in] several other forms of nonviolent resistance."[12] The women of Abu Salim effectively provided a model of a mini-revolution against the Qaddafi dictatorship, demonstrating how to protest against one of the region's most repressive tyrannies. Their protest was without precedent since Qaddafi's arrival in power.

Even when the Libyan revolution turned violent, women continued to play vital roles in the struggle to topple the regime. They contributed to the revolution's media effort, in addition to serving as medics, providing food supplies, and offering other forms of logistical support to fighters in the revolutionary struggle. "Smuggling weapons was an area in which women excelled during the revolution," said Altubuly. "They were less likely to be stopped at checkpoints, and they had an easier time moving around than men."[13]

Women should have a prominent role in Libya's national reconciliation process not only because of their role in the revolution but also because women suffered uniquely from crimes like rape during the revolution. Indeed, Qaddafi used rape as a means of war during the Libyan revolution, which affected women in cities and towns throughout the nation. It is difficult to know the exact number of cases given the lack of reporting of the crime; indeed, a strong social stigma is associated with rape in Libya's conservative society. Nevertheless, interviewees talked about numbers ranging from as few as two hundred to as many as seven or eight hundred cases. Misrata, Ajdabia, and the Western Mountains are cited as places where systematic rape took place during the revolution. Regardless of the numbers of cases, these crimes remain largely unresolved. If they are not handled properly, such unresolved crimes will likely obstruct efforts at reconciliation. If reconciliation is to be achieved in a case like the conflict between Misrata and Tawergha, women—the most affected by the heinous war crime of rape—will have to be part of any resolution. For the sake of a reconciled Libya, women should be among those developing the strategies to deal with these offenses.

Various parties, including Libya's civil society organizations, are actively pushing for female involvement in the reconciliation process. The Association of Supporting Women in Decision-Making, for example, is a lobbying group that formed after the fall of Qaddafi to promote women's involvement in national leadership positions. The organization's president, Nadine Nasrat, explained, "We advocate the incorporation of female voices in the process of conflict resolution and national reconciliation in Libya, in accordance with Security Council Resolution 1325."[14]

In February 2015, in response to the deteriorating security situation in Libya, the Libyan Women's Platform for Peace (LWPP) released an initiative that addresses the causes and issues of instability in the country. The LWPP was originally formed in 2011 by over thirty-five women who came from different cities and backgrounds to "ensure that women remain a vital part of post-Gaddafi Libya, with a particular emphasis on inclusive transition, [and] women's rights."[15] Their "comprehensive strategy to achieve stability in Libya" called for, among other things, the application of Security Council Resolution 2174, demanding an immediate ceasefire and inclusive political dialogue, applying the rule of law, providing international assistance in securing Libya's borders, rebuilding security infrastructure, securing safe passage for people fleeing warzones, and immediately addressing the needs of displaced communities.

The important message here is that women organizations must remain active in the post-regime transition and national reconciliation process. Taking initiative and releasing visions and strategies will help keep Libyan women a part of the debate and allow them to help with the solution to the current civil strife, transition, and national reconciliation.

Yemen

Like their Libyan counterparts, Yemeni women played a significant role in initiating and sustaining the uprising against President Ali Abdullah Saleh during the revolution. They can play a similarly significant role in supporting the reconciliation process. Yemeni women, who have long suffered from social marginalization, took on leadership roles in the early days of the uprising. In fact, their involvement gave street protests momentum by playing on deeply rooted social norms among Yemeni men, who were expected to take to the streets and protect their women. Mohammed Qahtan of the Islah Party explained, "To see those endless waves of women protesting in the streets left no option for Yemeni men but to rush to the streets as well and to do their part in supporting the uprising and demanding regime change." One prominent example of the role of women in the uprising is Tawakul Karman, the first Arab woman and at that time the youngest person to win the Nobel Peace Prize. Karman was nicknamed by some as the new Queen of Sheba in reference to the region's historic female leader.[16]

Yemeni women paid a heavy price for their participation in the uprising, with large numbers killed, wounded, imprisoned, and tortured. This suffering was in addition to past grievances. During the six wars in Saada, many women were widowed and became responsible for fully supporting their families. Fighting between the Yemeni Army and al-Qaeda in the Arhab district throughout 2011 and 2012 left an estimated thirty thousand women internally displaced. For these reasons and others, Yemeni women must be part of the national reconciliation process. Activist Sarah Ahmed reasoned, "Women made up approximately 50 percent of the participation in the revolution and must be represented with at least 30 percent in the national dialogue." She argued that a role for women could prove critical to reconciliation: "Women tend to forgive when they become part of a process."[17]

Yemeni women participated effectively in the post-Saleh transition and in particular in the National Dialogue Conference (NDC). There were 161 female representatives in the NDC out of 565 total participants, giving women 28 percent of the conference seats.[18] This is considered a very high proportion by Yemeni and regional standards. In addition, three of the nine working committees were chaired by women. The NDC recommended that the government adopt a quota system, allocating 30 percent of seats to women in all three branches of government.[19] The NDC also made significant recommendations to ensure the fair representation of women in Yemeni public life, including suggestions to establish a Supreme National Council for Maternity and Childhood, to restructure the National Committee for Women, to have 30 percent of the team writing the new constitution be female, and, finally, to have 30 percent of seats on elected legislative assemblies be drawn from women.[20]

A number of implications could be drawn from women's participation in the NDC. It has recognized the participation of Yemeni women in public life, which is something that was not fully welcomed in conservative Yemeni society prior to the uprising against Saleh. Women's active participation in political life has taken the debate over gender equality a step further toward institutionalizing women's empowerment, in particular through allocating quotas, namely a 30 percent quota system for women in the three branches of government. The NDC has also confirmed a leadership role for women, although they were historically denied this. Women's leadership is being recognized, and their leadership role could be seen clearly in their heading up working committees, for example, where powerful male tribal leaders sat, listened, and asked for permission to speak. Finally, the NDC confirmed the need for a role for women in the mechanics of a transition process and the drawing up of a roadmap to national reconciliation.

Women as Agents of Reconciliation: Comparative Aspect

The cases of both Libya and Yemen confirm the fact that women take on a significant portion of the hardships that result from war and violence. Women have been partners in the immense suffering that Yemen and Libya experienced in the past few decades. Especially in the city of Misrata, Libyan women experienced rape and various types of abuse during the revolution against Qaddafi. Yemeni women, on the other hand, endured notable oppression during times of "negative peace" and faced the hardship of caring for extended families—after losing their husbands in internal wars—without having the right sets of skills for such a challenge. In the Libyan and Yemeni experiences, women have been partners in the hardship and therefore should be partners in peace and reconciliation. Excluding women will lead to a distorted transition and unjust post-conflict arrangements.

Women are agents of change. In Yemen and Libya, it was women who began the uprisings against the dictatorships that eventually changed the prevailing status quo of repression. The mothers of Abu Salim prison massacre victims launched the uprisings against Qaddafi, and it was women in Yemen who first went to the streets to defy Saleh. Taking on leadership roles in the uprisings, women defied the prevailing social systems that hinder their participation in public life, thereby promoting change within the system itself. The political stigma against women's participation in the public sphere has "suddenly disappeared."[21] In fact, in Yemen, "Tribal men brought their wives and daughters to the squares and women gained respect for their participation."[22]

Women are of critical importance for reconciliation efforts in both Yemen and Libya. Yemeni women participated effectively—and claimed a leadership role—in one of the country's pillars of reconciliation: the NDC. They participated equally in the proceedings of the ten-month conference, chaired working committees, and inserted their views into the roadmap for the country's transition. Libyan women, despite the challenges they encountered under Qaddafi, quickly claimed their position in the transition process and successfully launched initiatives that contributed to resolving communal conflicts and reconciling social relations.[23] It is striking how quickly Libyan women became aware of their role in the transition process and were able to organize themselves into civil society groups like the Association of Supporting Women in Decision-Making.

It is noteworthy how committed women proved to be to the principles of truth seeking, justice, and reconciliation. Libyan women's steadfastness against Qaddafi in particular is remarkable. They refused his offers to settle the cases of their massacred children in Abu Salim prison and instead insisted on knowing exactly what happened and on holding the perpetrators accountable for their crimes. Over the course of one year of weekly protests, Libyan women challenged the regime and proved to have established a foundation for the larger uprising that overthrew the dictatorship.

Women have shared in the sufferings and hardships of war, conflict, and tyranny. During the revolutions, women not only participated in but led uprisings that resulted in the toppling of longstanding and brutal dictatorships. Later, during times of transition, women organized themselves quickly in civil society groups and contributed to social stabilization, communal conflict resolution, and reconciling relations among various rival groups. This leaves no doubt that women are strongly positioned to be agents of reconciliation during times of war, conflict, and the transition to civil peace.

TWELVE

Tribes

For the purposes of this chapter, the term "tribal" is used to refer to a society that organizes individuals into a system of concentric circles of social belonging. The largest concentric circle is the nation, followed by the tribe, section, clan, sub-clan, and finally individual household.[1] The tribe, in the context of Arab culture, is a powerful social force that has historically played a considerable role in political transitions both during colonial times and more recently during the uprisings of the Arab Spring. Organizationally, Arab tribes preserve a coherent social structure with a well-defined hierarchy and with members following the guidance of their leaders. Nadwa al-Dawsari, an expert on tribal conflict resolution in Arab states, defines the tribe in Yemen as "a social organization that gains its legitimacy from a set of traditional rules that constitutes a social contract among the tribe's members as well as between them and their sheikhs and other tribes. The social contract, or Customary Law, governs public affairs, protects common interests, and extends protection and economic support to tribal members."[2]

Tribes are often unfairly perceived as spoilers to reconciliation efforts. In general, academic literature treats tribes with a degree of suspicion: their role in society is considered predominantly a negative one, and their relations with the state are viewed as similarly corrosive to the central state structure. The assumption that tribes are fundamentally incompatible with modern nation-states leads to the perception that tribes exist in competition with the state. In Yemen, for example, tribes are viewed as constituting a "state within the state," as they maintain almost full autonomy from the central government in managing their own territory. Some also argue that tribes prevent the development of state institutions in such areas, and that the state is therefore weaker because of the presence and activity of tribes.[3]

Nevertheless, tribes can play a vital role in helping transition processes to overcome the serious challenges that emerge after the removal of former regimes, as happened during the Arab Spring. In tribal societies like Yemen and Libya, the involvement of tribes in transitional political arrangements is particularly vital for successful reconciliation.

Achieving stability through an improvement of the security sector is certainly one area in which tribal participation can aid the broader process of transition. This can happen in two ways. First, tribes can help to provide security in areas outside the control of the central government. Because the Arab uprisings were concentrated primarily in urban centers, regimes responded by building up security apparatuses primarily in the capitals. This centralization of security forces created a power vacuum in the rest of the country. In the words of political scientist Daniel Corstange, tribes are the "second-best substitutes for an absent or weak state."[4] The role of tribes in internal security becomes even more vital when the regime is removed and the country enters a state of transition. Tribes in this case help to keep the country together and prevent the collapse of order. Tribes in countries like Yemen and Libya are large and powerful enough to have a major impact on the transitional period. The Warfalla in Libya, for example, has approximately one million members in a country of almost six million, and is therefore well positioned to play a role in providing internal security. Because no transition or reconciliation can succeed in the absence of security, the tribal role in the security sector is particularly important.

Second, due to their non-ideological and non-political nature, tribes are strongly positioned to mediate between the regime and opposition. When clashes occur, state institutions become paralyzed and are often unable to provide solutions or reach compromises. Tribes in Yemen intervened between the state and opposition parties several times during the country's political crises, and have therefore helped to avert a serious nationwide political catastrophe.

Arab tribes abide by a rigorous and well-established customary law that is dominant in many, often rural parts of their countries. Indeed, in some areas, Arab tribes have established tribal laws that predate even Sharia law. This customary law can also help to provide order during times of crisis and transitions when formal law is not yet fully functional in all areas of the country. In fact, before the Arab Spring uprisings, tribal customary law was preferred in many areas of Yemen over the formal law "because of perceived corruption, nepotism, lack of integrity, and inefficiency, as well as the length of judicial processes and the government's inability to reinforce the law and court orders."[5] The fact that tribal customary law is well developed makes it well suited to provide solutions to most conflicts that emerge during times of crisis. For example, tribal law in Iraq stipulates the payment of *diya* (blood money) by the perpetrator of a crime to the victim's family. Once the facts are established, wrongdoing is acknowledged and diya is paid. The two parties and their families then enter into what is called *sulha*, which aims to restore peace, normalize relations, and set the parties on track for reconciliation.[6]

Tribes can help the state not only in maintaining security in the absence of a strong state apparatus but also in resolving communal and sectarian disputes using the conflict resolution aspects of tribal customary law. Katherine Blue Carroll explains that in Iraq during 2008–2009, when the state was forced to deal with large-scale sectarian violence in the absence of an active legal system, it was the *fasel* process (an Iraqi tribal approach to conflict resolution, also called *sulha*) that allowed Baghdad's sheikhs to reach some form of reconciliation. Indeed, tribal sheikhs began to use the fasel process to settle crimes of a sectarian nature, and in the process helped to create reconciliation between Sunnis and Shi'a. One of the sheikhs said, "Sectarian killing is tough, but in 2 years we have done maybe 110 such cases." Carroll found that sheikhs, but also many others, "argued that the shaykhs were the best hope for reconciliation. This was, they said, because tribalism is neither 'political' nor 'religious' nor sectarian." This politically and religiously neutral aspect of tribes refutes widespread notions of tribes existing in constant struggle and rivalry with the state. The state and opposition parties in countries like Iraq and Syria were structurally created with political and even sectarian dimensions. The fact that the tribe is both a non-religious and non-political entity immediately takes it out of direct competition with the state, thereby making it a more suitable, unbiased arbitrator of conflicts.[7]

In Arab culture, tribal involvement in communal and social conflict is in fact difficult to avoid. The tribe must become involved at some point to ensure sustainable conflict resolution. In an Arab cultural context, tribes will, to a certain extent, be involved in the de facto escalation or de-escalation of conflicts on the ground. This was particularly clear in Iraq, for example, because "Iraqi culture holds families and larger communities responsible for the good or bad behavior of their members."[8] This cultural element has significant implications for post-regime change reconciliation. National reconciliation processes must take a society-wide, communal approach to end polarization and build social cohesion within society. To do so, tribes must be involved; an individual approach to reconciliation will not be functional or enforceable.

Values of tribal conflict resolution are particularly helpful to transition processes and to the achievement of sustainable reconciliation. Following the fall of dictatorships or after civil wars, countries often undergo periods of violence, increased crime, and feuds. Contrary to the common perception that repressive regimes are generally responsible for these violations, individuals and communities are equally responsible for a major portion of violations against one another. Attempting to settle these communal and individual conflicts through a formal legal system would overwhelm the state, even during times of peace and stability. Such an approach would jeopardize the transition process and risk diverting its attention toward further civil conflicts, as notions of vengeance and retaliation would become more widespread in the absence of legal settlements. Tribal conflict resolution systems offer important counter-values to revenge by emphasizing instead the acknowledgment of wrongdoing, apologies, and forgiveness. Furthermore, tribal conflict resolution provides coping mechanisms for both victims and perpetrators to come to terms with the past and move toward reconciliation. For example, "the *fasel* process, among Iraqi tribes, is designed to allow individuals to move forward after crime with the support of the community, and this is exactly what reconciliation requires. For many Iraqis, the *fasel* process makes reconciliation culturally acceptable, and participation in the process is also a way that many Iraqis can again find a much needed common ground in their own heritage."[9]

This chapter argues that tribes can potentially become spoilers to reconciliation or agents of reconciliation in Yemen's and Libya's political transitions, depending on how the authorities engage with them, in addition to how the state's interests are perceived. Authorities can manipulate tribes to serve their own interests and thus hinder reconciliation efforts. As agents of reconciliation, however, tribes can help to advance transition processes by strengthening stability and security, and by resolving conflicts using tribal customary laws and conflict resolution systems.

To examine this argument, the cases of Yemen and Libya are the focus, as tribes have a strong presence in these two nations. Tunisia has been excluded since tribes do not have a notable impact on public life there.

Yemen

Yemen's tribes have been described as "fiercely independent" entities, competing with the state and focusing primarily on their own narrow interests.[10] This perception was reinforced by the tribes' relationship with the former regime, which outsourced security in large portions of the country to local tribes. The state intervened directly only when the regime's interests were at stake. Tribal leader Sheikh Mifreh al-Bahabeih, however, rejects this perception of Yemeni tribes' existing in competition with the state, arguing that tribes in fact suffer the most in the unstable security situation that the central government has failed to address. He explains, "Tribes are tired of fighting and doing the state's job of security. They find themselves in a vicious arms race with each other, and all that comes at the expense of their children's food and education. We want the state to come maintain security so we can take care of our own matters."[11]

National reconciliation in Yemen can benefit from the tribes' involvement in four important ways. First, the weakness of the central government and its inability to guarantee security outside Sanaa make it necessary for the state to involve politically independent actors, like the tribes, as security to begin to sustain a national reconciliation process.

Second, tribes possess robust conflict resolution, mediation, and reconciliation systems that can technically support a larger national reconciliation process.[12] Studies conducted by local organizations in Yemen indicate
that 90 percent of conflicts in certain areas are prevented and resolved using the tribes' customary law system. Tribes have succeeded several times
where the state has failed in resolving political standoffs. In January 2012,
for example, an estimated two hundred al-Qaeda militants seized control of
the town of Rada'a in Yemen's Hajja district, leading the army to withdraw
from the area. Only through successful mediation conducted by a group
of tribal leaders were the al-Qaeda militants persuaded to withdraw. In another instance, a different group of tribal leaders was able to negotiate the
release of seventy-three members of the Yemeni military in Abyan province
in April 2012.[13]

Third, Yemeni society remains largely tribal, and therefore tribes cannot be ignored if national reconciliation is to have popular support. In this
regard, tribal leaders can use their legitimacy and power to validate agreements with other parties and create public momentum among their own
tribes to support those agreements.

Lastly, the tribal value system includes not only vengeance but also,
according to al-Bahabeih, "justice and forgiveness."[14] The tribal code ultimately revolves around maintaining the honor and reputation of the tribe.
It therefore requires fairness in the tribe's external and internal affairs. The
same ideals of justice and forgiveness promoted by tribal codes are central
to a national reconciliation process, which is meant to facilitate the resolution of previously intractable conflicts. To be successful, the reconciliation
process must foster a new culture of forgiveness, which can be promoted by
Yemen's tribal value system.

On the other hand, tribes played an important role in the civil war in
Yemen as many of them took a position against the Houthis-Saleh alliance.
Especially in the provinces of Mareb and Shabwa, tribes fought vigorously
against the Houthis-Saleh forces and protected their provinces from falling
into the hands of the alliance. Depending on the way one looks at it, this
participation could be seen as a negative role with the tribes making the
civil war worse, but it can also be seen as a positive role in which tribes

protected their provinces and filled the security gap created by the collapse of the central state in Sanaa.

It is worth noting that tribal leaders have participated in the process of national dialogue and reconciliation not as tribal representatives but through various political parties. For example, the leader of Yemen's most powerful tribe, Hashid, participated as part of the Islah Party, while the sheikh of the Bakeel tribe has contributed as a member of the Justice and Development Party. Still, the inclusion of more tribal leaders—not as tribal leaders *per se*, but in their capacity as political or social leaders—could provide a significant boost to the process and its legitimacy.[15]

Libya

From the outset of the uprising against him, Muammar Qaddafi threatened to "arm the tribes." His warning reflected the former leader's understanding of Libyan society's primarily tribal structure, as well as his ability to manipulate it. Qaddafi hoped to transform the conflict from a popular uprising against his own authoritarian regime into a civil war in which Libya's tribes played a central role. He succeeded in securing the support of some tribes, and to this day, tribes like Warfalla, which fought alongside him three years ago, are marginalized in a society fractured by tribal antagonism.[16]

Libyan tribes by and large realized that they had been deceived and manipulated by the Qaddafi regime. Such sentiments were explained by Sheikh Khalifa al-Rayayneh, a tribal leader from the Nafousa Mountains. "Some tribes weren't able to accurately read the protests when the revolution began," he said. "They didn't have Facebook or Twitter to know what exactly was happening. Their representatives in the Qaddafi regime told them Qaddafi had everything under control, and they just listened and refused to join the revolution. Obviously, they paid a heavy price for that later."[17]

Qaddafi's abuse of tribalism exacerbated pre-existing rivalries in a divide-and-conquer approach to rule. Certainly, inter-tribal relationships are complex, and past conflicts can easily be reignited to stir disagreement among them. The Zentan tribe in the Nafousa Mountains, for example, considers their tribal neighbors and historical rivals, the Western Rayayneh, to be former allies not only of Qaddafi but also of Italian colonialism in the 1940s. At the outset of the February 17 Revolution, Western Rayayneh allied with Qaddafi, while the Zentan joined the revolution, bringing the long-latent antagonism between the two tribes to new levels of violence. After Qaddafi's downfall, the Zentan insisted that the Western Rayayneh pay the price for their alliance with him. The conflict between the two tribes resulted in, among other things, the displacement of 470 families from the town of Western Rayayneh.

Notably, the tribes in Libya contributed significantly to the 2014 civil war. Some joined Operation Dignity, especially in the east, and others joined Libya Dawn in the west of Libya. In June 2015, a large number of tribes from the east, center, and south of Libya attended a tribal conference in Cairo and declared their support for Operation Dignity. Furthermore, a former Qaddafi regime figure, General Omar Tantoush, led what was called a "Tribal Army" of approximately one thousand fighters in support of General Khalifa Haftar and the Zentan Brigades in the western part of Libya. The Tribal Army clashed with Libya Dawn in the town of Warshefana and in the fight over Libya's international airport. There is no doubt that tribal participation in the civil war contributed to its brutality and deepened divisions within Libyan society.

Despite its role in fueling conflict in Libya, tribalism also has the potential to aid post-Qaddafi conflict resolution. In fact, it is such an important factor that it cannot be ignored by any national reconciliation project which hopes to be successful. Tribes that fought with Qaddafi—including portions of the Warfalla, Maqarha, Qathathfa, and Tarhouna—represent a significant portion of Libyan society. Together, they number around two million people, or one-third of Libya's total population. "There is no national reconciliation without these tribes," says al-Rayayneh. "They definitely can't be excluded."[18]

Tribes can contribute to reconciliation through their unique role in maintaining security in the country. The tribal role in security is particularly important because post-Qaddafi Libya has more or less witnessed a collapse of the central state, with government authority not even extending throughout the capital, let alone into most Libyan cities and towns. Among Libya's social forces, the tribes are the best positioned to fill this vacuum. Furthermore, the tribal role in security has an historical precedent: the Libyan state has traditionally relied on the tribal component of society to sustain its power and control over the country. However, despite the tribes' ability to play a role in improving security in Libya, there is also potential for this role to backfire, mainly because many tribes were politicized under Qaddafi. Indeed, the former leader privileged some tribes over others, leading to rivalries and antagonism. Carving out a security role for some tribes in the post-Qaddafi era may trigger a bitter response by their rivals.

Finally, tribal leaders can play a part in breaking the cycle of revenge, thus improving conditions for peace and reconciliation. Tribal leaders have substantial power to compel their tribes' members to refrain from revenge killings and to forge ceasefire agreements with other tribal leaders. As Hussein al-Buishi, head of Libya's Truth and Reconciliation Commission, explained, "Generally, youth start problems and the tribes hurry to resolve them."[19] Indeed, it was local tribes that were able to stop the fighting in Bani Walid, and there is no reason that they cannot play the same peacekeeping role elsewhere.

Tribes and Reconciliation: Comparative Aspect

Tribes are powerful actors in any peace and reconciliation process; their role cannot and should not be ignored. While they have the capacity to sabotage a reconciliation process, they also have the potential to enhance its successes. Tribes' roles in a transition process depend primarily on the way their sheikhs use such opportunities either to support or hinder peace. There seems to be grounds for long-held suspicions about the role of tribes in transition and reconciliation processes. However, it is neither fair nor accurate to view them only as a liability to a national reconciliation process.

The experiences of Yemen and Libya in particular illustrate the ways in which repressive regimes have manipulated tribes to serve their political agendas. In Yemen, President Ali Abdullah Saleh outsourced security tasks in large areas of the country when he redeployed his own security units to the capital with the hope of preserving the regime's power. Tribes in Yemen also played a political role when tribal leaders received direct funding from Saudi Arabia in return for their support of Saleh's regime. Meanwhile, in Libya, Qaddafi delegated a military role to the tribes by arming and engaging them in the fight against the revolution. These experiences demonstrate that the relationship between tribes and repressive regimes were not unidirectional, as regimes not only used the tribes to suit their own ends, but the tribes also entered these relationships to serve their own agendas.

In both Libya and Yemen, tribes participated in civil wars in 2014 and 2015, taking positions on both sides depending on a number of variables including geographic location, their own interests, and their understanding of the political process. Tribes in southern Yemen, for example, fought vigorously against the Houthis coming from the North. Likewise, many of Libya's tribes in the east supported Operation Dignity and General Haftar, who was based in the eastern city of Tubruk. In both countries, however, tribes filled security vacuums in their own territories created as a result of the collapse of the central state in both capitals, Sanaa and Tripoli.

Analysis of Yemen and Libya shows that tribes' contributions to stabilization, transition, peacebuilding, and reconciliation are quite significant. Particularly in Yemen, when the regime forces withdrew from remote areas of the country, it was the tribal forces that maintained order and prevented the country from sliding into chaos, instability, and even civil war. Similarly, when the central government in Tripoli collapsed after the killing of Qaddafi, the maintenance of order and security in the remote areas in Libya became the primary task of the tribes. This was the situation especially in the south of Libya and in the Nafousa Mountains in the west.

Tribal customary law and tribes' expertise in resolving internal conflicts can aid the central legal system by contributing to the resolution of local disputes in both countries. In Yemen in particular, we have seen more organized tribal interventions resolving local conflicts using tribal customary law. In addition, tribal presence and effective participation in Yemen's national dialogue confirms the significant role of tribes as agents of reconciliation in that country. It should also be mentioned that tribal engagement in transition processes produced similar results in other countries in the region beyond Libya and Yemen. Iraqi tribes got extensively involved and made noticeable progress in sectarian peacebuilding, bringing Sunni and Shi'ite communities closer to each other in a number of areas of the country.

A major contribution of tribes to reconciliation is their ability to legitimize the political process that should lead the political transition. Tribes are powerful political players, so their participation seriously affects the perceived legitimacy of any political settlement. Especially in tribal societies like Yemen and Libya, the involvement of powerful sheikhs in any process sends a clear message to their members that they will accept the outcomes of such a political process. Particularly when the outcomes lay the groundwork for a national reconciliation process, the participation of the tribal sheikhs could not be more necessary. This was demonstrated during Yemen's national dialogue, which aimed to set a roadmap for the political transition toward peace, development, and reconciliation. Likewise, a major factor that allowed Saleh to come to power in Yemen in 1978 was the support he received from Sheikh Abdullah al-Ahmar, the leader of the Hashid tribe, who was also the parliament president and described as one of the most powerful men in Yemen's recent history. The approval of such influential leaders has historically granted significant legitimacy to political transitions and can do the same in the present era.

Conclusion

N early four years after the uprisings of the Arab Spring broke out, the societies affected remain deeply polarized, as transitions from dictatorships to civil peace and stable governance have thus far failed. This increasing polarization has formed primarily along lines of sectarianism, tribalism, regionalism, political parties, former and new regimes, and even within revolutionary groups that fought together against the former dictators. Such divisions are likely to intensify in the coming years since efforts to end them remain lackluster. This situation threatens the entire transition process and future stability of Arab Spring countries, and if it is not sufficiently addressed, these countries may experience civil wars—as is the case in Libya and Yemen in 2014 and 2015—or protracted chaos and violence. Arab Spring countries do, however, have an alternative to polarization: the immediate engagement in inclusive national reconciliation processes. Such processes must reveal the truth about the past, deliver reparations to victims of earlier crimes, hold perpetrators accountable, and reform state institutions to prevent the recurrence of past crimes. Only through wide-ranging and genuine national reconciliation can any of the Arab Spring societies make a successful transition from dictatorship to sustainable peace and political stability.

The matter of selecting the appropriate participants for a national reconciliation process is quite challenging. Successful reconciliation must be first and foremost inclusive of all primary parties to the conflict. Anyone engaged in reconciliation will inevitably encounter resistance to inclusivity of all parties, however. Indeed, statements like "we are not willing to reconcile with those responsible for the killing of our children" are common, often signaling an objection to inviting some of the primary parties to the past conflict. Such attitudes hinder a successful reconciliation process; certainly, reconciliation is made with enemies, not friends, and is therefore necessarily difficult and oftentimes contentious. As challenging as it is for victims and their families to sit with former regime elements, they must realize that no better future can be forged without sitting and talking to all primary stakeholders of the conflict. An inclusive reconciliation process is the only substitute for the polarization, divisions, and marginalization that otherwise will cause continued conflict and suffering. Consequently, the political isolation laws that were introduced in Tunisia and Egypt and adopted in Libya are counterproductive, and, if applied firmly, they will lead to greater divisions, establishing a foundation for counter-revolutions and pushing these countries into new cycles of violence and chaos. This does not mean that former regimes are blameless and will not be punished, but a vetting process that individually targets those who were directly responsible for human rights abuses and that functions within a transitional justice framework—and under the rule of law—serves as a credible alternative to such exclusionary measures.

Determining the appropriate timing for pursuing national reconciliation is equally challenging. Should it be held early, immediately after the end of fighting, or at a later stage? How can we be certain that a reconciliation effort is not undertaken too early or too late? After regimes fall or civil wars end, deciding the proper timing for reconciliation among rival parties becomes a challenge and affects the entire transition process. Pursuing reconciliation too early will most likely be counterproductive, as the parties have not yet overcome their suffering and still harbor feelings of hatred and desire for revenge. Indeed, not all women who lost their children in Libya's Abu Salim prison massacre, for example, would have been open to engaging with former regime figures immediately after the fall of Muammar Qaddafi's regime. Pursuing reconciliation too late, however, will be difficult as well, as the parties will have moved on and will be less likely to be interested in returning to the conflict, engaging with their former enemies, and making changes to their newly stable lives.

Qaddafi regime figures in exile, for example, would have been interested in reconciliation at an early stage, since this would have facilitated their return to their homes and communities. However, participating in a reconciliation effort at a later stage is less enticing, as they have set up new lives abroad. It seems that the best timing for reconciliation, then, is determined primarily by the presence of the right set of conditions that make it possible and realistic. Most Libyans interviewed for this project were equally opposed to engaging in reconciliation, whether shortly after the removal of Qaddafi or at a later stage. They were concerned primarily with what should be achieved before engaging in a dialogue with former regime figures. Most importantly, they wanted to see the application of impartial justice and accountability, receive some reparations as victims of past crimes, and know exactly what had happened during the conflict. When people are assured that some of these goals will be addressed, and a proper foundation is established for civil peace, they will be more willing to collaborate and seriously engage in a substantive national reconciliation process which can contribute to ending polarization and moving the nation beyond conflict.

National reconciliation processes are, by their nature, nonlinear and complicated. Although the ingredients of national reconciliation (truth, reparations, accountability, institutional reform, and national dialogue) are known, the process itself rarely follows a direct path on its way to achieving reconciled relations among former foes. National reconciliation can undertake all of these components at the same time or only some of them, depending on the circumstances of the individual case. National reconciliation can also make progress on some tracks while encountering serious setbacks on others. Tunisia, for example, made remarkable progress in the first three years of its transition on national dialogue, accountability of former regime figures, and even institutional reform. At the same time, it struggled seriously in providing reparations for victims of past crimes, especially victims of torture, which led many to protest for over five months at government offices, demanding fair solutions to what they considered to be legitimate demands.

Furthermore, national reconciliation can make progress on developing policies and laws while failing to implement the newly adopted regulations. Yemen was remarkably successful in its ten-month-long National Dialogue Conference (NDC) in proposing solutions and roadmaps for addressing most of the challenges to the country's political transition and reconcilia-tion, yet made very little progress toward implementation in the first year after the conference. Even worse, this lack of progress provided a pretense for the Houthis to launch a territorial conquest, culminating in the Sep-tember 2014 takeover of the capital and most state institutions. In January 2015, they, in alliance with Ali Abdullah Saleh, forced President Abd Rabbu Mansour Hadi to resign, prevented peaceful protests, and pushed the coun-try to civil war. Tribes, popular resistance groups, youth, and other political parties started to push back and clash with the Houthis-Saleh forces and their control of most of Yemen. The Yemeni civil war spilled over to Saudi Arabia, which also became involved and started to inflect heavy airstrikes in March 2015 against the Houthis, who the Saudi perceived to be proxies of Iran in Yemen. In the most acute crisis since the beginning of Yemen's uprising in 2011, the Houthis have risen up against not only the state but also all other actors who had contributed to the national dialogue and reconcili-ation process. By signing off on the NDC's recommendations, the Houthis raised hopes for successful implementation, but instead, they dealt Yemen's transition its most serious setback. That violence broke out before the re-sults of the dialogue could be implemented demonstrates the non-linearity and unpredictability of the reconciliation process.

Transitions and reconciliation should not be viewed completely inde-pendently from their regional context. It is not purely a domestic process that involves only the militias and their rivals. The civil war in Libya, for ex-ample, is largely seen as being supported by regional forces, with the United Arab Emirates (UAE), Egypt, and Saudi Arabia supporting General Khalifa Haftar and his Operation Dignity, while Turkey and Qatar support Libya Dawn and February 17 revolutionaries. In August 2014, a U.S. official told the *New York Times* that Egypt and the UAE were behind several airstrikes against Islamist-allied militias battling for control of Tripoli in what was a further escalation of a regional power struggle between Islamists and the governments that oppose them across the Middle East.[1] Similarly, Yemen's crisis also has a regional aspect. The Houthis are known to have ties to Iran, while Saudi Arabia and the other Gulf states have expressed support for Hadi and Yemen's transitional process, according to the 2011 Gulf Cooperation Council initiative. Many analysts saw the Yemeni civil war as a proxy conflict between Saudi Arabia and Iran. In fact, the major motive for Saudi Arabia's military intervention in Yemen was to prevent Iranian influence on the Saudi's southern border. While a military solution is not possible to resolve Yemen's problems, such an approach tends to redirect transitions from moving toward sustainable peace and reconciliation to moving toward protracted conflict and civil war.

Domestic as well as external forces often drive national reconciliation in countries undergoing political transitions. Arab countries have experienced models where external actors led national reconciliation, as seen with the role of the UN in Yemen and the United States in Iraq, while internal players drove the entire process in Tunisia. To maximize success, national reconciliation must be homegrown. It should capitalize on domestic resources like civil society, women, and political parties, allowing them to take leading roles in the national reconciliation process. Major advantages of homegrown reconciliations are sustainability and ownership. Externally led processes will risk the primary parties losing ownership. Of course, if parties fail to take ownership of the process, its sustainability will be at risk. Homegrown reconciliation in Tunisia has motivated all parties, both within the government and opposition, to work hard to protect their country's accomplishments and ensure the success of its dialogue.

The uprisings of the Arab Spring were leaderless, motivated at the grassroots level, and lacked a theoretical framework to guide their progress. National dialogue is therefore an indispensable tool to guide members of these revolts toward developing newly defined objectives in the post-dictatorship era. Spontaneous, uncoordinated, and leaderless Arab uprisings broke out in response to the stern repression that had lasted for over four decades in the region. Certainly, the protesters in Tahrir Square in Cairo did not discuss the structure of the state they wanted to create after Hosni Mubarak; instead, they focused on demolishing the autocratic regime. There was no specific ideology to inform the protesters; certainly, they did not know whether the new state would take on the form of a Western democracy, Turkish-style Islamist democracy, an Arab version of democracy, or even an Islamic Caliphate. Now that a number of Arab dictators have been toppled, the question of the nature of these new states can no longer be ignored. In order to resolve this question and prevent Islamists, Socialists, Ba'athists, and Nationalists, all of whom participated in the uprisings, from becoming polarized opponents, national dialogue must occur.

A successful homegrown national dialogue in Tunisia gave a significant boost to the entire transition process, enabling political parties to solve political crises and draft a new social contract in the form of a new constitution. A marginally successful national dialogue in Yemen, despite subsequent failures in implementation and civil war, helped the transitional government and political parties to develop a vision for the resolution of the challenges to the nation's unity, security, and development. The national dialogue in Yemen produced a roadmap that, despite the violence that broke out in 2015, will remain a point of reference for any resumption of the transition process in the future. The recommendations of the NDC will remain the solution for the parties to implement in order to move forward, simply because all parties, including the Houthis and Saleh's party, the General People's Congress, signed off on its final recommendations. The absence of a national dialogue in Libya, however, has allowed the gaps among the country's different parties to widen, mistrust to be reinforced, and a disastrous security situation to be exacerbated, all of which led to a civil war breaking out in 2014. Libya faces the possibility of prolonged instability or even fragmentation; national dialogue can be the first step toward preventing continued instability. The UN-led peace talks in Libya in 2015 provide a starting point for what could become in the future an inclusive national dialogue. The peace talks focused on ending the fighting among the various revolutionaries but never included parties from or issues pertaining to the former Qaddafi regime, so reconciliation with Libya's forty-two years under Qaddafi has not even started.

Public uprisings produced a culture of division, which has become apparent in the language and narratives used after the revolutions by members of the uprisings and of the former regimes. Such rhetoric must be replaced with unifying language in order for transition and reconciliation to succeed. The polarizing language is reflected in the popular terminology of *thuwar* (revolutionaries) versus *azlam* (Qaddafi cronies) in Libya, and *tagheer* (change) versus *fulool* (remnants of the old regime) in Egypt. In Libya, new narratives later emerged reflecting the conflict among the revolutionaries themselves. The camp of General Haftar started calling revolutionary Islamists "terrorists," while the latter began calling the former "militias of the retired general." Such terms reinforce divisions, making polarization more vicious and unity more elusive. This dynamic also runs counter to the spirit of the uprisings, which aimed to replace authoritarian practices of repression, exclusion, subjugation, and despotism with values of freedom, justice, inclusion, and equality. If this culture of division prevails, Arab Spring societies risk replacing the former regimes with new ones that similarly privilege certain groups at the expense of others.

Reconciliation cannot take place in the context of insecure environments; rather, power diffusion must end, and the state must establish a monopoly on the legitimate use of force. The lack of security, especially in Libya and Yemen, has significantly derailed the national reconciliation process. The behavior of revolutionaries in post-Qaddafi Libya, for example, created—immediately after the fall of Qaddafi—two parallel states: the official state and the revolutionary state. The revolutionaries and their militias established secret prisons, practiced torture against former regime elements on a large scale, assassinated public figures, and clashed with each other, taking the security situation to low levels and leading to civil war. The lack of security coupled with the behavior of revolutionaries led first to two states running in parallel, but later to multiple miniature states functioning in different parts of Libya, with each militia having its own authority structure and applying its own rules. Revolutionaries must be aware that they risk transforming from victims to tyrants, and may spur a return to widespread civil conflict if they refuse to integrate into the new state. Likewise, the Houthis and Saleh's forces disrupted Yemen's transition process and set the country on a track of violence and civil war that will have a long-term impact on the country's national reconciliation process. To give dialogue and reconciliation a chance, Libya's revolutionaries must join state institutions or NGO-run disarmament, demobilization, and reintegration (DDR) programs. Houthis in Yemen too will have to disarm and become a political party that practices politics equally like all other Yemeni political parties.

Although there is no consensus on the issue, dealing with the past is critical to achieving sustainable national reconciliation in Arab Spring societies. Uncovering the truth about the past is highly politicized, with major political parties often objecting because they stand to lose credibility and popularity due to such a process. Others raise concerns about the truth leading to social conflicts, especially in tribal societies where violence is often considered a means of resolving disputes. However, avoiding the past because it is painful or controversial will only complicate the process of reconciliation and lead to future instability. Similarly, obscuring the past will only serve as a source for renewed conflict in the future and make the victims' mourning process more complicated. Furthermore, ignoring the past will aid the political parties that were part of that painful past in preserving their political gains and likely exacerbate the suffering of their victims. Such an outcome will widen chasms in society, setting it up structurally for future conflicts and making national reconciliation unattainable. The truth, instead, will help victims come to terms with the past and heal their wounds.

Victims of past crimes deserve not only the truth but also suitable financial and moral reparations for their past suffering. This will no doubt be challenging, especially in terms of providing financially for the large number of victims in an environment of constrained fiscal resources. Nevertheless, leaving a significant group in the society—the victims, who made significant sacrifices in the struggles against the dictators—without proper compensation will likely lead to a distorted reconciliation process that may reward the politically powerful while further marginalizing victims of the former regime. Moral reparation is equally important and is necessary to heal the traumas of past crimes and violations. Victims of past crimes need not only money to make livings but also recognition of their past suffering. The state owes them acknowledgment and apology for what they went through. Acknowledgment is a powerful tool to help the victims overcome their traumas and must be granted for those whose rights were violated under the former dictatorships. Paying them money only will be buying off their silence and will not be a healthy track for genuine reconciliation. During my conversation with the families of the Abu Salim prison massacre in

Tripoli in 2012, some of them confirmed to me that they received attractive financial offers from Qaddafi before the uprising to settle their cases. The response of the mothers of the victims, however, was to insist on knowing the truth about what had happened to their children and on receiving an acknowledgment of the wrongs done before any negotiations could happen. For genuine reconciliation to take place, one needs first to apologize to the victims and their families.

Sustainable national reconciliation requires the dismantling of old systems and embracing deep institutional reforms. To ensure that past human rights violations are not repeated, Arab Spring countries must rigorously inspect their state institutions and conduct in-depth reforms. Given the totalitarian nature of the former regimes, these reforms must be comprehensive. While all state institutions should be subject to reform, particular attention should be paid to the following sectors: the security services, given their responsibility for torture and human rights violations; the administrative apparatus and its bureaucracy, given their endemic corruption; the media, long responsible for the glorification of the dictatorships; and the judiciary, which must be trusted to faithfully and honestly implement transitional justice. Superficial reforms, like removing the top leadership of the security sector in Yemen, are not the types of reforms that successful transitions need. Institutional reform must be deep enough to address the resilience of the deep state and to ensure that the old regime will not wage a counterrevolution in the future.

Successful national reconciliation processes in the post–Arab Spring Middle East must engage, among others, their societies' powerful agents of reconciliation: women, civil society, and tribes. Together, these elements play a unique role during political transitions as they often succeed where the state has failed. Complementing, rather than replacing, the state, Arab agents of reconciliation often deliver services in security, mediation, conflict resolution, and reconciliation. Women effectively contributed to launching the uprisings as well as beginning reconciliation efforts after the former regimes collapsed. Civil society groups have mediated political crises and resolved communal disputes. Tribes in particular have contributed to maintaining security during times of transition. Particular attention should therefore be given to tribes, as their powerful position is often exploited by the ruling strata.

As the success of transitions to peace and stability in the Arab Spring countries is of interest to domestic and international actors, outside players in particular can contribute to making this success a reality. A credible, transparent, and well-defined role for the international community will be pivotal in helping Arab Spring countries' national reconciliation processes. Arab countries in transition require technical assistance on developing and applying transitional justice laws, investigating past crimes, holding transparent and fair trials of corrupt figures, repairing injury done to victims and their families, and engaging in deep institutional reforms to prevent the repetition of past human rights violations. The support that the international community can provide in these areas is invaluable and will save Arab Spring countries from re-inventing the wheel, as experiences from other countries can be instructive. Of course, any approach must be adapted to fit the Arab cultural context. Direct financial support—especially for countries that are unable to finance national reconciliation processes—is desperately needed to satisfy the grievances of the victims of past crimes, heal their wounds, and help them come to terms with the past and be able to move forward to build a better future.

The international community will benefit from successful national reconciliation in the Arab Spring countries in at least two ways. First, their success will provide a significant contribution to the evolving body of knowledge about the process of transitioning from a state of conflict, civil war, or dictatorship to sustainable peace and reconciliation. Second, successful Arab transitions will help to improve security in the region, which is also of critical interest to the international community. The international community should provide political, financial, and technical support, but it should also respect the independence of these countries. The process of national reconciliation should always be homegrown and locally led. Domestic ownership of the process is necessary for its sustainability, while external leadership is likely to develop a sense of dependency and a tendency to import often-inappropriate solutions to local challenges, which in turn may harm the reconciliation process down the road. Only local ownership will provide the impetus for the process to overcome the enormous challenges that face a transitioning state.

Unfortunately, all Arab Spring countries—with the exception of Tunisia—lag seriously behind in their efforts to end polarization and proceed toward building good governance and sustainable peace. Yemen made some progress on the theoretical and planning level, yet has struggled with implementation and counter-revolution. Libya has not even begun its reconciliation process and instead is drifting toward total chaos and instability. Egypt has experienced serious setbacks—especially with the overthrow of elected president Muhammad Morsi and the military's seizure of power. This second political transition created profound divisions within society that are unlikely to heal in the foreseeable future. Violence in Syria must end, after which that country will be forced to implement all the elements of national reconciliation discussed in this book. In other words, the Arab region, in its search for peace, stability, and development, will continue to deal with aspects of national reconciliation for decades to come. I am therefore hopeful that this book will benefit the countries that are going through the experience of national reconciliation, and those that will join at some point in the future, both in terms of policy advice as well as recommendations on the mechanics of transition and reconciliation.

I also hope that this book provides a foundation for future research on transitions and national reconciliation in the post–Arab Spring Middle East. This book is only the first step in what could become a milestone in research on transitions, reconciliation processes, and sustainable peace in the region. Many unanswered questions remain, and future study can help provide answers. Some issues of particular interest include the following: First, due to a variety of reasons, there seems to be a tendency for Arab Spring societies to avoid dealing with their pasts. How will this affect the future prospects of peace and stability in these countries? Second, there seems to be a huge gap between expectations of victims of past human rights violations and the states' ability to accommodate these expectations. What type of impact will this have on the victims' willingness to alter their expectations, be part of peace efforts, or simply become spoilers to peace processes? Third, how do victims of past crimes become victimizers? There is serious research needed in the area of DDR of ex-combatants and why these programs have failed miserably in places like Libya. This failure is certainly alarming, and peace research should try to uncover the reasons behind such breakdowns in security. Fourth, institutional reform has in some cases succeeded in terms of developing plans and policies. Implementation, however, has proven to be challenging in a number of areas. Future research could focus on developing mechanisms of implementation that can aid the success of institutional reform. Finally, future research might focus on how national reconciliation would differ in countries that are likely to embark on such processes in the future, such as Syria, and what that means for peace research in general.

The Gulf Cooperation Council Initiative for Yemen

UN Translation

The signatories to this Agreement, desirous of achieving a political settlement of the crisis in Yemen, acting in accordance with the terms of the initiative proposed by the Gulf Cooperation Council on 21 April 2011 and pursuant to the following basic principles:

- That the solution resulting from this Agreement shall preserve the unity, security and stability of Yemen;
- That the Agreement shall fulfil the aspirations of the Yemeni people for change and reform;
- That the transfer of power shall be smooth, secure and based on national consensus in order to avoid a descent into anarchy and violence;
- That all parties are committed to removing the sources of tension in political and security terms;
- That all parties are committed to ending all forms of reprisals, pursuit and prosecution by extending guarantees and pledges towards that end;

Have agreed on the following implementation steps;

1. On the first day of the Agreement, the President of the Republic shall request the opposition to form a government of national

unity with 50 per cent representation from either side. That government shall be formed no later than seven days after his request.

2. The newly formed government shall create the appropriate atmosphere in order to achieve national consensus and put an end to the sources of tension in political and security terms.

3. On the 29th day after the Agreement enters into force, Parliament, including the opposition, shall adopt laws granting immunity from legal and judicial prosecution to the President and those who worked with him during his time in office.

4. On the 30th day after the Agreement enters into force, once Parliament, including the opposition, has adopted the law on safeguards, the President of the Republic shall tender his resignation to Parliament. When Parliament has accepted his resignation, the Vice President shall become the legitimate President by appointment.

5. The President by appointment shall call for presidential elections within 60 days in accordance with the Constitution.

6. The new President shall establish a constitutional committee to oversee the preparation of a new constitution.

7. When complete, the new constitution shall be submitted to a popular referendum.

8. If the constitution is approved by referendum, a time frame for parliamentary elections shall be determined in accordance with the new constitution.

9. After the elections, the President shall request the Chair of the party that has gained the greatest number of votes to form a government.

10. The States members of the Gulf Cooperation Council, the United States of America, the European Union and the Russian Federation shall be witnesses to the implementation of this Agreement.

11. This Agreement has been prepared in four original copies in the Arabic language.

It shall enter into force on the date when all parties have signed it.

The Socialist Party Lays out a Set of Determinants and Outcomes for Dialogue and the Resolution of the Southern Issue

April 29, 2012, Sanaa

The Secretariat-General of the Yemeni Socialist Party has, in its recent regular meetings, taken up a number of internal organizational issues, as well as the national political developments that the country is undergoing. These developments are linked to the facts and results of the implementation of the GCC initiative and its operational mechanism. This is in addition to the ongoing preparations for the national dialogue stipulated by both the initiative and its operational mechanism and the positions taken by the country's various parties on that dialogue.

The Secretariat-General has been following all administrative, political, and military developments [in Yemen], especially after early presidential elections were held and the new president, Abd Rabbu Mansour Hadi, secured popular legitimacy. It was that legitimacy that enabled him to make a number of crucial decisions to meet the aspirations of the people for change; for the liberation of the country from the yoke of rule by a single family; and for the preparation of the appropriate conditions for a comprehensive national dialogue in which the country's parties will participate without exceptions and without preconditions. That dialogue aims to arrive at serious solutions for all the issues facing the country, with the Southern issue at their forefront.

In this regard, the Secretariat-General of the Yemeni Socialist Party has saluted the masses involved in the popular resistance in Abyan province and their heroic response, alongside the security forces, to armed groups affili-ated with the terrorist organization al-Qaeda. That organization has pushed a number of cities and regions in Abyan into a vortex of uncontrollable vio-lence. This is in addition to what it represents in terms of a threat to political and social stability and the dragging of the entire country into a pit of total chaos, collapse, and disintegration.

The Secretariat-General believes that the fight against terrorism and the elimination of the armed remnants of al-Qaeda require concerted popular and official efforts. It requires a comprehensive confrontation at all levels to eliminate this dangerous epidemic and eradicate it once and for all.

As the party prepares to participate in the comprehensive national dia-logue, the Secretariat-General emphasized the extraordinary importance the party gives to this dialogue. It is an opportunity to save the country from the crises under which it is being crushed, to prepare the means for a peaceful transition from its current situation, and to address the worsening issues with which it has been burdened. It should aim for practical and fundamental solutions that create appropriate conditions for Yemen's future resurgence, insofar as that helps realize the political and socioeconomic aspirations of its people. From this vantage point, the Secretariat-General urged the party's team, made up of several of the Secretariat-General's members, to prepare the party's positions on all issues to be raised during the dialogue.

The Secretariat-General believes it necessary to produce a constructive atmosphere that will help the comprehensive national dialogue make real progress in reaching effective solutions for the issues to be raised. Especially regarding the Southern issue, a number of political and administrative steps must be taken by President Abd Rabbu Mansour Hadi and the national unity government led by Muhammad Salim Basindwa. These steps would eliminate all doubt over the state's seriousness about the dialogue and the results that can be achieved. They would likewise confirm that the country, in its new state, cannot accept the evasions long practiced by the former regime, a regime that the revolution of February 11, 2011, came to eradicate and do away with its destructive methods and policies.

In this regard, the party's Secretariat-General highlighted the impor-tance of the new president and the national unity government undertak-ing a number of decisions and preparatory measures aimed at building an atmosphere of confidence and ensuring [the dialogue's] seriousness. The decisions and steps that would pave the way for a serious dialogue to address the Southern issue include the following:

1. The immediate restoration of civilian and military employees who were displaced, arrested, sent to forced retirement, or migrated abroad due to the war of summer 1994 to their jobs, as well as the payment of anything legally entitled to them.
2. The payment of salaries and amounts due to those who lost their sources of income due to the theft or privatization of public institutions and companies in which they had been working.
3. The formation of a national body for reconciliation and justice whose members would be representatives of those detained, injured, or otherwise concerned. This body would resolve the complaints and grievances of detainees and deportees, and its decisions and actions would be binding for related government agencies.
4. The return of properties and money seized after the 1994 war, whether they belonged to individuals, parties, unions, or the state; a halt to the seizure of lands; and the return of lands disposed of without right, with priority given to the people of the South's provinces in making use of these lands.
5. The prosecution of corrupt figures involved in the manipulation of the state's lands, properties, and resources, as well as any public money and cooperative properties. The prosecution should begin with those most responsible for plundering the South and should return everything stolen.
6. The restoration of the *falaheen* (peasants) who were driven from the lands of which they were making use and who lost possession of their lands in the South due to the war and its subsequent repercussions to their homes and lands.
7. The treatment of all victims of the 1994 war as martyrs and the treatment of the injured and their families and the families of martyrs equally in terms of rights and care.

8. Communication with the parties of the Southern Movement's peaceful struggle, as well as with its leadership abroad, and inviting them to take part in the national dialogue.

9. The abolition of a culture of glorifying civil wars and calling for retaliation and political revenge in educational curricula and in media and cultural outlets; the removal of any manifestations of injustice, degradation, and exclusion directed against the cultural, artistic, and social heritage of the South; and the restoration of the South's political history, which has been subjected to obliteration and abolition since the 1994 war.

10. A formal apology to the people of the South for injuries to them as a result of the 1994 war and for oppression and pains inflicted upon them by the regime's destructive post-war policies.

11. The immediate release of all political prisoners arrested for their participation in the revolution and the peaceful Southern Movement, and a halt to the suppression of peaceful political and popular activities.

12. Permission for *al-Ayyam* newspaper to resume publication, compensation for damages to it and its editorial board, and a lifting of the ban imposed on Southern websites irrespective of their orientation.

Legislation No.13 of 2013 of the Political and Administrative Isolation (translation by the Libya Herald)

The General National Congress, Tripoli, May 5, 2013

Article 1

The standard requirements for holding any public positions, refers to the restrictions that must be applied in the cases of those assuming any of the public positions stipulated in these legislations from the 1st Sept 1969 to the Liberation date of 23rd Oct 2011 and includes the following;

The First Category: Anyone held one of the following positions during the period, from 1st September 1969 and the country's liberation announcement date of 23 October 2011;

1) Members of what used to be known as the "Revolution Command Council" of the 1969 Coup, members of used to be known as the "Liberated Officers" and all members of used to be known as "Gaddafi's Comrades Association."

2) Organizers of social people's masses on municipality or national levels.

3) Chairman, Deputy Chairman and members of the Generals People's Congress or held the position of a chairman of any municipality or province.

4) Chairpersons and heads of sectors, institutions, organizations, companies or councils affiliated with the Prime Ministry, the

Revolution Command Council or what used to be known
as the General Peoples' Committee or the General People's
Congress.

5) Anyone held the position of a Prime Minister or Chairman
of the General Peoples' Congress, deputy chairman of such
position, minister or the secretary or the deputy of the General
People's Committee for any specific sector, the public notary
of the General Peoples' Congress or any particular General
People's Committee, or held the position of a Secretary of any
Popular Committee of a municipality or province or a secretary
of any Sector's Popular Committee within the province.

6) Anyone served as an ambassador, secretary at any Public Office, held the position of a permanent representative of Libya
at any International or Regional organization of any types, held
the position of charge de affairs or consul.

7) Anyone who held the position of a chancellor or deputy
chancellor at a University or was a chairman of a People's
Committee of a university or served as the general registrar of a
university.

8) Anyone who served as the head of the interior and exterior
security agencies, military intelligence, security brigades, or
served as the head of department of any of these institutions,
or served as the head of any of the quarter security offices or
the head of any political office at one of the military or security
institutes.

9) Heads of student unions in and outside the country affiliated
with the General Union of Libyan Students.

10) Anyone who held a leading position of any institute connected
with any of Gaddafi's family members or was a partner with
them in any type of business.

11) Members and employees of the Revolutionary Committee Liaison Office, Coordinator of any Revolutionary Office, a member
of any Revolutionary work team or Revolutionary Convoys or a
member of the Special Courts or prosecution offices, members

of the so called "Revolutionary Nuns," Heads and members of the Revolutionary Guards, Heads and members of the Eliminating/Assassins Committees, Public Guard leaders of main headquarters and branches and anyone who participated in the revolution administration forums.

12) Anyone who held the position of a director, general manager or researcher at any of what used to be known as "the Green Book Research and Study Centers," Green Stadium lecturers or held a leading role in one of the media institutes.

13) Anyone that held a command position at an army base, or was a commander of a defensive zone, or held the position of a president or a commander of a military establishment, body, or institute.

14) Anyone who belonged to an international organization that posed a threat to the territorial integrity of Libya and adopted violence as a strategy.

The Second Category: Relates to the Political and Administrative isolation for this category and the behavior that led to the corruption of political, economic and administrative life in the country during the period referred to in the previous article as stated in the following behavior patterns:

1) Civilians who collaborated with Gaddafi's security agencies and their collaboration proven to have led to human right violations.

2) Anyone known for his/her constant praise and glorification of Gaddafi, his regime and his green book, whether through media or through the delivering public talks.

3) Anyone who took a hostile position towards the 17 February revolution by action, incitement, collaboration or provision of any kind of support.

4) Anyone who committed or helped in any way to kill, imprison or torture Libyan citizens, home or abroad, on behalf of the previous regime.

5) Anyone who unlawfully seized or caused damage to any public or private property during the previous regime for political reasons.

6) Anyone involved in stealing the Libyan people's wealth or became rich on Libyan people's account or gained wealth, funds, benefits unlawfully inside or outside of Libya.

7) Anyone involved in scientific, artistic, intellectual, religious, cultural or social activity which aimed at glorifying Gaddafi, his regime or propagated the so called reform project known as, "Libya Alghad" Tomorrow's Libya.

8) Anyone who used religion to support or give credibility to Gaddafi's regime or Gaddafi's actions, or considered openly, the 17February revolution as being in disobedience to an official ruler.

Article 2

Persons included in Article 1 of these legislations are not allowed to hold the following positions and employment:

1) Leadership and membership of legislative, regulatory or foundation bodies on any national or international levels.

2) Leading state positions.

3) Executive positions ranging between the head of state or the head of government and including the position of a general director on national and international level.

4) Chairmanship and membership of boards of directors, executive, administrative and regulatory functions, such as, the position of Director and above in management bodies, institutions, banks and public and investment companies, that are solely or partly owned by the Libyan state or by one of its institutions, inside or outside the country.

5) Membership of any judicial bodies.

6) Leading positions at security and military establishments.

7) Ambassadors, consulates, delegates to international and regional organisations as well as other diplomatic functions and technical attachés.
8) Chairmanship and membership of governing bodies of political parties, entities, institutions and Commissions of a political nature.
9) Presidency of universities, academies, colleges and higher education institutions.
10) Finance Auditor.
11) Leadership positions in various media and publishing institutes.

Article 3

A committee should be formed under the provisions of these legislations under the name, 'the supreme commission of applying the required standards for holding public positions.' The commission shall be independent and shall be independently financed and will be based in Tripoli. The commission may open branches or offices in other cities.

Article 4

The chairman and members of the commission are those whose names were mentioned in the NTC decision, No. 16 of 2012 relating to the naming of the chairman and members of such commission. The Supreme Judiciary Council must undertake the task of applying the standards stipulated in article one and article five of these legislations, the Supreme Judiciary Council must also nominate those whose membership had expired and which must first get the approval by of the GNC.

Article 5

Persons chosen for the membership of this commission must meet the following conditions:

1) Must be a Libyan national.
2) Must be known for integrity.

3) Must not be under 35 years of age.

4) Must not be convicted in any criminal offence or felony relating to honour.

5) Must not have been dismissed from any position except for political reasons.

6) Must not be affiliated with any political entity or party.

7) Must have an academic Degree in Law and above.

Article 6

The chairman and members of the commission must make the oath before the GNC prior to resuming their duties in a manner determined by the GNC.

Article 7

Commission members shall appoint, from among them, during their first convened meeting a Chairman and a deputy Chairman for the commission as well as official spokesman from among themselves, the commission shall issue the decisions and regulations of the administrative and financial system, the commission shall also prepare a budget which then needs to be approved by the GNC on recommendation of the commission's chairman.

Article 8

Should the commission's chairman position become vacant, the commission's deputy replaces him and assumes all his duties according to provisions of the law until such time when a new chairman is appointed.

Article 9

The chairman and members of the commission must abide by the same laws governing members of the judicial authorities in accordance with law No. 6 of 2006 relating to the judicial system and its amendments, in respect of disciplinary, investigation and the filing of criminal law suits. They will also have the same immunity similar to that given to the judicial members hence it is not permissible to file a criminal suit or interrogate any of them, accept by a GNC decision, giving authority of that effect, in case of any commission member having a final decree or judgment made against him/ her or vacated his position, the Supreme Judiciary Council then nominates a replacement who then gets a final approval of the GNC.

Article 10

The commission is entitled to investigate any candidate applying for a position, and to seek information on that person as it deems necessary. The commission has the right to summon the relevant individual/s in question and hear their testimony. They can also cross-examine his verbal or written submitted report. The commission has the right to use all necessary means and methods to verify the authenticity of the given information and testimonies referred to in Article 10 and has the right also to use the help of whom ever the commission deems appropriate to help it accomplish its duties.

Article 11

The commission referred to in Article 3, is under obligation to implement the standards stipulated in Article 1 against those assuming or nominated for positions in accordance with these legislations, the commission decisions may be issued by half of its members plus one, indicating the applicability or non-applicability of standards within a maximum period of 21 days from the date the commission receives the financial testimony clearance and the person's Curriculum Vita, making sure all needed documents and information are provided.

Article 12

Those concerned may lodge an appeal against the decisions made by the Commission at the Administrative Justice Department of the Appeal Court, where the position or employment, the decision's subject matter, is located within ten days from the date of announcement by the entity they belong to.

The Administrative judiciary circle must make a final decision on the lodged appeal within 21 days from the date of lodging the appeal without the need to go through the preparation procedures. The administrative judiciary circle must collect all information and evidence on which the first decision was based before making a final decision of the appeal. The defendants have the right to appeal the decision made by the Administrative judiciary circle in front of a high court within 10 days of the judiciary decision. The high court is under obligation to make a decision of the appeal within 1 month of the date of first lodging the appeal, defendants must provide their statements within the time period allocated above.

Article 13

The commission must make its decisions relating to the applications of standards of assuming public positions in accordance with the rules and regulations provided within its adopted work charter and which should be approved by the GNC.

Article 14

It is forbidden for the commission's chairman, members and workers to disclose any classified information or data received by them or their commission as part of their duties; however the commission is under an obligation to make all its decisions and reasons for making such decisions public without disclosing classified information and he who violates that will be sacked.

Article 15

The candidate or institute making a nomination for a position must fill in the special application prepared by the commission. The nomination must be submitted along with the candidate's personal data as well as the candidate's financial clarification and an undertaking to accept full legal responsibilities for the authenticity of the supplied information sealed with his signature and finger prints.

Article 16

With exception to what is stipulated in article three, the Supreme Judiciary Council undertakes the task of applying the standards provided for in Article one in respect of Judicial members.

Article 17

Without prejudice to any other severe penalty provided by law, anyone who declines, neglects or give incorrect information in the submitted questionnaire requested by the commission shall be imprisoned for a period of no less than one year. The same penalty shall be applied in the case of any employee or person who declines to provide the commission or refuses access to any evidence or documents under his disposal or refuses to provide help in that matter or destroys evidence.

The same punishment shall also be applicable to those who carry on in their position after a decision of a non-compatibility of standards was issued against them as stipulated in the provisions of this law.

Article 18

This legislation will be in force for ten years from the date of issue.

Article 19

Legislation No.20 of 2012 relating to the Supreme Integrity Commission and its amendments shall herewith be rendered null and void from the date these legislations take effect.

Article 20

This legislation shall come into effect, thirty days from the date of issue and all other legislation contrary to this shall be made void. This legislation should be published in the official gazette.

This is not a legal translation of the law. Readers should seek a legal translation for total accuracy.

NOTES

Introduction

1. Tunisian official, interview with the author, June 2013, Tunis, Tunisia.
2. Rasmussen, "Negotiating a Revolution," 121; Lederach, "Civil Society and Reconciliation," 847.
3. Nadine Nasrat, Association of Supporting Women in Decision Making, interview with the author, January 2013, Tripoli, Libya; Sharqieh, *Reconstructing Libya*.

Chapter 1. Libya

1. The First and Second Theories were, according to Qaddafi, capitalism and Marxism. He regarded both as imperialist.
2. United Nations Support Mission in Libya, "Transitional Justice"; C. J., "International Commission on Missing Persons"; United Nations Support Mission in Libya, "Conference on Truth and Reconciliation"; Salah, "Libya's Justice Pandemonium."
3. Salem al-Ahmar, interview with the author, January 2013, Tripoli, Libya. Al-Ahmar was disbarred by the Integrity Commission.
4. Al-Sadeq al-Shuwaihdi was a student leader active in the Libya Salvation Bloc. He and some of his fellow students were caught by regime forces and executed in a public place, a school, in Benghazi in 1984.
5. Al-Ahmar, interview.
6. Rania Swadek, interview with the author, January 2013, Tripoli, Libya.
7. Peou, "Implementing Cambodia's Peace Agreement," 524; Castillo, "Post-Conflict Reconstruction," 1980.
8. At the same time, we should not assume that disarmament must precede a national reconciliation process. National reconciliation is not linear, and given the chaotic

nature of a post-conflict environment, parties will sometimes need to balance competing priorities. That is, issues of reconciliation and disarmament may have to be addressed simultaneously and in parallel.

9. Salomons, "Security: An Absolute Prerequisite."
10. Haidar Hasan, Misrata Brigades leader, interview with the author, January 2013, Tripoli, Libya.
11. Transitional Libyan Government: Prime Minister's Office, "Takhrij al-duf'ah al-ula"; Transitional Libyan Government: Prime Minister's Office, "Tadabir amaniya tutakhath"; Al Tommy, "Militia Men Join Army."
12. Salem and Kadlec, *Libya's Troubled Transition*.
13. Lamloum, "Libya Leader's Car Shot Up"; Al Jazeera, "Libyan Parliament Sessions Shelved"; Shennib and Donati, "Gunmen Surround Libyan Ministry"; Laessing and al-Warhalli, "Libyan PM Says Kidnapping."
14. Said Ferjani, interview with the author, May 2013, Tunis, Tunisia.
15. Hasan, interview.
16. Abedajo, "Liberia: A Warlord's Peace," 620; Boduszynski and Fabbe, "Libya's Militia Problem."
17. Sufyan Omeish, filmmaker and civil society activist primarily in reconciliation and peacebuilding, interview with the author, January 2013, Tripoli, Libya.
18. Sharqieh, "Beware Libya's Fair Dictator."
19. Eljarh, "The Supreme Court Decision."
20. United Nations High Commissioner for Refugees, "Global Appeal 2012–2013," 132–136; Internal Displacement Monitoring Centre, *Global Overview 2014*, 61; Chonghaile, "Libyans Displaced by Civil Conflict."
21. Chonghaile, "Libyans Displaced by Civil Conflict."
22. Internal Displacement Monitoring Centre, *Libya: State Collapse*, 7–9. See also Bradley, Fraihat, and Mzioudet, *Libya's Displacement Crisis*.
23. Abrahams, "Why Have We Forgotten?"
24. Ali al-Tawerghi, interview with the author, January 2013, Tripoli, Libya.
25. Salah al-Marghani, interview with the author, January 2013, Tripoli, Libya.
26. Hasan, interview.
27. Bawabat al-Wasat, "Itifaq bayna Misrata wa Tawergha'."
28. Khalifa al-Rayayni, head of the reconciliation committee between Rayayneh and Zentan, interview with the author, January 2013, Tripoli, Libya.

Chapter 2. Yemen

1. "Gulf Cooperation Council Initiative," in International Crisis Group, *Yemen: Enduring Conflicts, Threatened Transition*. See appendix A for text.
2. Ghobari, "Yemeni Government Apologises"; Agence France-Press, "Yemen Parties Agree on Federalism."

3. Southern activists, discussion with the author, May 2012, Sanaa, Yemen.
4. *Al-Eshteraki*, "al-Hizb al-'Ishtiraki yad'a jumla." See appendix B for translation.
5. Al-Hirak, which literally means "mobilization," is a coalition demanding greater independence for South Yemen, either through increased autonomy or secession.
6. Ali Nasir Muhammad twice served as president of South Yemen before being ousted after 1986's bloody infighting in Aden. Haidar Abu Bakr al-Attas succeeded Muhammad as president prior to unification in 1990. He also served as prime minister of South Yemen before unification, of unified Yemen afterward, and of the secessionist Democratic Republic of Yemen in 1994.
7. BBC News, "'Iqrar al-'aml bil-nitham al-fidirali."
8. As minority Zaidi, or "Fiver" Shia, Houthis are distinct from the much more prevalent "Twelver" Shia found predominantly in Iran, Iraq, and Lebanon. Zaidis have different beliefs about who can be imam and how the imamate should be established, and have traditionally been more accommodating of Sunnis, from whom their practices differ little. See Salmoni, Loidolt, and Wells, *Regime and Periphery in Northern Yemen*.
9. Houthi representatives in al-Sumoud Tent (the Houthis' information center), interview with the author, May 2012, Sanaa, Yemen. Al-Ghadeer is a festival day observed by Shi'ite Muslims on the 18th of the month of Dhu al-Hijja in the Islamic calendar. It commemorates what Zaidi Shia see as Prophet Muhammad's appointment of his cousin Ali ibn Abi Talib as his immediate successor.
10. *Barakish.net*, "al-Huthayun yu'alinun 'an 'ashira shurut."
11. Houthi representatives, interview.
12. Alabassi, "Yemen Leak."
13. Ghobari, "Houthi Rebels Sign Deal."
14. Mohammed Qahtan, interview with the author, May 2012, Sanaa, Yemen.
15. Abdulkarim al-Iriani, formerly Yemen's prime minister (1998–2001), advisor to the president, and head of Yemen's Technical Preparatory Committee for the NDC, interview with the author, May 2012, Sanaa, Yemen.
16. Al-Haj, "Yemen's Shi'ite Rebels Reject Agreed Federal Plan."
17. Al-Haj, "Yemen Arrests 2 Frenchmen"; Baroumy and Ghobari, "Clashes Hit Yemen Capital Again"; Ghobari, "Yemen's Houthis Dissolve Parliament."
18. Agence France-Presse, "Shiite Militia Tightens Grip on Yemen"; Agence France-Presse, "Gulf Neighbors Denounce Houthis"; Agence France-Presse, "Arab League Condemns Houthi 'Coup.'"
19. Ghobari and Mukhashaf, "Yemen's Hadi Flees to Aden."
20. Agence France-Presse, "UN Security Council Affirms Support for Yemen President."
21. http://www.un.org/en/sc/documents/resolutions/2015.shtml.
22. Tolba and El Dahan, "Saudi Arabia Says Talks to End Yemen Crisis"; Hasad al-Youm, "al-Houthiyyun yarfudun hiwar al-Doha."

23. Agence France-Presse, "First Iran Flight Lands."
24. al-Kamali, "al-Yemen: al-Houthiyyun yuwaqi'aun itfaqiyyat."
25. Agence France-Presse, "Yemen Militia Sends Forces South."
26. Mazzetti and Kirkpatrick, "Saudi Arabia Leads Air Assault in Yemen."
27. Abdallah and Aboudi, "Yemeni Leader Hadi Leaves Country."
28. Browning and Charbonneau, "UN Envoy to Yemen Resigns."
29. Sharqieh, "Yemen Can't Do It Alone."
30. Baron, "What We Get Wrong about Yemen."
31. Interview with Mohammed Azzan, https://www.youtube.com/watch?v=QjtQHVzoTHU, accessed June 11, 2015.
32. Riedel, "Yemen Falls Apart."
33. Greenfield, "Yemen Crisis: A Coup in All but Name."

Chapter 3. Tunisia

1. Faten Smat, professor of Futuristic Studies at Manouba University, interview with the author, May 2013, Tunis, Tunisia.
2. The opposition party Nedaa Tunis threatened to try Prime Minister Ali al-Araidi, Ennahda President Rachid Ghannouchi, and President of PRCs Mohammed Mualej at the International Criminal Court for the death of Nageth. Rashid Khashana, prominent Tunisian journalist, interview with the author, April 2013, Doha, Qatar.
3. Said Ferjani, interview with the author, May 2013, Tunis, Tunisia.
4. Ibid.
5. In Tunisia, two types of Salafis have emerged: "scientific Salafism," which distances itself from violence and extremism, and "jihadi Salafism," which resorts to extreme measures and has adopted violence as a legitimate means to advance its doctrine.
6. Saidani, "A Gathering Storm."
7. Sharqieh, "Tunisia's Lessons"; Rafik Abdul Salam, interview with the author, May 2013, Tunis, Tunisia.
8. Al Jazeera Center for Studies, "Tunisia: National Dialogue"; Agence France-Press, "Suspected Assassin Killed."
9. Ferjani, interview.
10. Ibid. Maleki is one of the schools of Fiqh (Islamic jurisprudence) and was founded by Malek Ibn Anas. Malekism historically focused on knowledge, science, and enlightenment (in opposition to conservatism and extremism). Traditionally, it was said, "no one is to issue a fatwa when Malek (Ibn Anas) is in the Madiena," referencing Malek's being the most knowledgeable and thus best able to issue a fatwa.
11. Alia Alani, interview with the author, May 2013, Tunis, Tunisia.

Chapter 5. National Dialogue

1. Jessop and Milofsky, "Dialogue: Calming Hot Spots"; Papagianni, *National Dialogue Processes*, 1; International Institute for Democracy and Electoral Assistance and the World Bank, "Experiences with National Dialogue," 3.

2. Papagianni, *National Dialogue Processes*, 1; United Nations Development Programme, "Why Dialogue Matters," 2; Mirimanova, *Mediation and Dialogue*, 19.

3. International Institute for Democracy and Electoral Assistance and the World Bank, *Experiences with National Dialogue*, 4.

4. United Nations Development Programme, "Why Dialogue Matters," 2; Mirimanova, *Mediation and Dialogue*, 19; International Institute for Democracy and Electoral Assistance and the World Bank, *Experiences with National Dialogue*, 4.

5. United Nations Development Programme, "Why Dialogue Matters," 3.

6. Jessop and Milofsky, "Dialogue: Calming Hot Spots."

7. Papagianni, *National Dialogue Processes*, 2.

8. International Institute for Democracy and Electoral Assistance and the World Bank, *Experiences with National Dialogue*, 4.

9. Papagianni, *National Dialogue Processes*, 11; United Nations Development Programme, "Why Dialogue Matters," 3.

10. Pruitt and Käufer, *Dialogue as a Tool*, 23; Mirimanova, *Mediation and Dialogue*, 10; Ropers, *From Resolution to Transformation*, 2; United Nations Development Programme, "Why Dialogue Matters," 3.

11. Traboulsi, "Yemen's National Dialogue."

12. National Dialogue Conference, "NDC Member Selection Mechanism"; Bafana, "National Dialogue: Panacea or Pain"; Agence France-Presse, "Yemen Begins New National Talks."

13. National Dialogue Conference, "Conference Topics"; al-Hassani, "Political Parties in the NDC."

14. Greenfield, "Yemen Faces Fresh Challenges"; al-Hassani, "Yemeni Will Have Six Regions."

15. Greenfield, "Yemen Faces Fresh Challenges"; Ghobari, "Yemeni Government Apologises"; Agence France-Press, "Yemen Parties Agree on Federalism."

16. Al-Jubari, "Working Group Reforms Judiciary"; Greenfield, "Yemen Faces Fresh Challenges."

17. Greenfield, "Yemen Faces Fresh Challenges."

18. Day, "'Non-Conclusion' of Yemen's National Dialogue"; Reuters, "South Yemen Leader Pulls Out."

19. Alwazir, "Myth of the 'Yemen Model.'"

20. Houda Cherif, interview with the author, May 2013, Tunis, Tunisia.

21. Sami Tahri, spokesman of the UGTT, interview with the author, May 2013, Tunis, Tunisia.
22. Marwan Hubaita, interview with the author, May 2013, Tunis, Tunisia.
23. Said Ferjani, interview with the author, May 2013, Tunis, Tunisia.
24. Sami Esaadi, interview with the author, January 2013, Tripoli, Libya; *Nasharat Akhbar*, "Libya: al-'A'lan al-dasturi kamila."
25. Libyan observers, interview with the author, January 2013, Tripoli, Libya; Sharqieh, *Reconstructing Libya*.
26. For more on the relationship between state and revolutionary councils, see Sharqieh, "Libyan Revolution at Two."
27. Guma El-Gamaty, interview with the author, January 2013, Tripoli, Libya.
28. Esaadi, interview.
29. Agence France-Presse, "Libya Launches National Dialogue"; *Tripoli Post*, "National Dialogue Initiative Criticised."
30. Fatima Hamroush, coordinator of the Libyan National Group for Civil Democracy, interview with the author, July 2014, Dublin, Ireland.
31. Shabbi, "Algeria Pushes for National Dialogue."
32. Maghur, "The UNSMIL Draft Agreement."
33. United Nations Support Mission in Libya, "Libyan Municipalities, Local Councils Reps Meet"; United Nations Support Mission in Libya, "Meeting of Libyan Political Parties."
34. Eljarh, "Libya's Geneva Talks."
35. Kadlec, "Libya's Peace Talks."
36. *Middle East Eye*, "Tripoli Parties Reject Draft"; *al-Araby al-Jadeed*, "Libya Talks in Jeopardy."
37. *Xinhua*, "Militias Refuse UN Call"; *Xinhua*, "Militias Demand UN to Withdraw."
38. *Libya Herald*, "Dignity Rejects UNSMIL Invitation"; *Al Jazeera*, "Tobruk-Based Government Attacks Tripoli."
39. Kadlec, "Libya's Peace Talks."
40. See Zartman, *Ripe for Resolution*.
41. International Crisis Group, *Libya: Getting Geneva Right*, ii; Eljarh, "Scenarios for Libya Going Forward."
42. "Partially boycotted" refers to the refusal of one party in the South—al-Hirak—to participate in the national dialogue or accept its agreements.
43. For more on this, see Justice and Development Party, "Pillars of National Dialogue."
44. A number of Yemeni interviewees supported involving Ansar al-Sharia in national dialogue if the group disarms and becomes part of the formal political process. Proponents of their involvement argued that Ansar al-Sharia members are Yemeni citizens and should therefore be included in the dialogue if they accept the rules

of participation, most importantly the disarming. Ansar al-Sharia has been linked to al-Qaeda in the Arabian Peninsula. See Raghavan, "Al-Qaeda Emboldened in Yemen."

45. See appendix B for the Socialist Party's conditions.

Chapter 6. Truth Seeking and Grappling with the Past

1. Elmaazi, "Urgent Need for Reconciliation."
2. Mazzei, "Finding Shame in Truth," 434.
3. Kaye, "Role of Truth Commissions," 715; Popkin and Roht-Arriza, "Truth as Justice," 115.
4. Mendeloff, "Truth-Seeking, Truth-Telling, and Postconflict Peacebuilding," 358–361; Minow, *Between Vengeance and Forgiveness*, 61–87; Hayner, *Unspeakable Truths*, 133–153; Goldstone, "Justice as a Tool," 491; Hayner, "Fifteen Truth Commissions," 607–609.
5. Brahm, "Uncovering the Truth," 20–21; Republic of South Africa, Office of the President, "National Unity and Reconciliation Act"; Popkin and Roht-Arriaza, "Truth as Justice," 113–114; Crenzel, "Argentina's National Commission," 190.
6. Popkin and Roht-Arriaza, "Truth as Justice," 115; Ignatieff quoted in Tepperman, "Truth and Consequences," 145.
7. Mazzei, "Finding Shame in Truth," 435.
8. Volkan, *Blood Lines*, 48.
9. According to Volkan, chosen glories are "reactivated again and again to summon support for a group's self-esteem." Volkan, "On 'Chosen Trauma.'"
10. Omar al-Mukhtar organized and led Libyan resistance against the Italians for nearly twenty years until he was captured and executed by Italian forces in 1931. In fact, al-Mukhtar is perceived to be a chosen glory not only for the Libyans but also for many other Arab peoples inspired by his resistance to colonialism.
11. Al Jazeera, "al-Ra'is al-Tshadi yattahimu Libya"; *al-Sharq al-Awsat*, "Tarablus wa Beirut 'azimatan."
12. Human Rights Watch, "Libya: June 1996 Killings"; author's attendance at the annual meeting of the Association of Families of the Martyrs of the Abu Salim Massacre, January 5, 2013, Tripoli, Libya.
13. United Nations High Commissioner for Refugees, "Housing, Land and Property Issues," 32; Libyans, interview with the author, January 2013, Tripoli, Libya.
14. Sufyan Omeish, filmmaker and civil society activist primarily in reconciliation and peacebuilding, interview with the author, January 2013, Tripoli, Libya.
15. Hussein al-Buishi, interview with the author, December 2012, Tripoli, Libya; Sadeq al-Gheryani, interview with the author, January 2013, Tripoli, Libya; Sharqieh, *Reconstructing Libya*.

16. Cook, "Lockerbie Bombing."
17. *Mareb Press*, "al-Nasseriyyun yutalibun bil-kashf."
18. Yemeni activists, interview with the author, May 2012, Sanaa, Yemen; Hammond, "Yemenis Paint Disappeared Activists."
19. Tutu, *No Future without Forgiveness*, 10–36.
20. Yasin Saeed Noman, interview and subsequent correspondence with the author, May 2012, Sanaa, Yemen.
21. Yaser al-Awadi, interview with the author, May 2012, Sanaa, Yemen.
22. Abdulhakim Helal, interview with the author, May 2012, Sanaa, Yemen; Mahmoud Nasher, interview with the author, May 2012, Sanaa, Yemen.
23. Rafik Abdul Salam, interview with the author, May 2013, Tunis, Tunisia.
24. Al Jazeera, "al-Hud al-manjami 2008."
25. Former prisoners, interview with the author, May 2013, Tunis, Tunisia. On the day of the interview, the prisoners had been protesting for over 130 consecutive days.
26. Ibid.
27. International Center for Transitional Justice, "Tunisia's Truth and Dignity Commission."
28. Oula Ben Nejma, interview with the author, May 2013, Tunis, Tunisia.
29. Said Ferjani, interview with the author, May 2013, Tunis, Tunisia.

Chapter 7. Reparations

1. Roht-Arriaza, "Reparations Decisions and Dilemmas," 157; Wessells and Monteiro, "Reconstruction in Angola," 22.
2. Ajetunmobi, "Victims' Responses after Mass Atrocities," 46–47.
3. Lambourne, "Transitional Justice and Peacebuilding," 41.
4. Laplante and Theidon, "Truth with Consequences," 249–250.
5. Keller, "Seeking Justice," 217.
6. Bloomfield, Barnes, and Huyse, *Reconciliation after Violent Conflict*, 148.
7. Oula Ben Nejma, interview with the author, May 2013, Tunis, Tunisia.
8. Amine Ghali, al-Kawakibi Democracy Transition Center, interview with the author, May 2013, Tunis, Tunisia.
9. Ibid.
10. Ben Nejma, interview.
11. Protesters in front of government offices in Tunis, Tunisia, conversation with the author, May 2013. The protesters displayed pictures of a former prisoner serving in a public school's garden.
12. Tunisian Network for Transitional Justice, public presentation at Novotel Hotel, May 2013, Tunis, Tunisia.

13. Sharqieh, "International Intervention, Justice, and Accountability"; Human Rights Watch, "Yemen Needs Accountability."
14. Sharqieh, "Yemen Can't Do It Alone"; Sharqieh, *A Lasting Peace?*
15. This number came up in several conversations the author had with Libyans, some of whom received treatment in Jordan.
16. Annual meeting of the Conference of the Families of the Martyrs of the Abu Salim Massacre, January 5, 2013, Tripoli, Libya.
17. Former prisoners of Qaddafi, conversation with the author, February 2013, Tripoli, Libya.
18. United Nations High Commissioner for Refugees Libya, "External Update—May 2014."
19. There are hundreds of pictures in the information office of the Tawergha IDP camp near Tripoli documenting severe torture. The torture was reportedly carried out by revolutionaries in the secret prisons of neighboring Misrata. The author could not verify the source of the pictures.
20. Ali al-Tawerghi, interview with the author, January 2013, Tripoli, Libya.

Chapter 8. Dealing with the Former Regime

1. Mendez, "Accountability for Past Abuses," 261.
2. David and Mzioudet, *Personnel Change or Personal Change?* 5. A variety of lustration laws have been implemented following political transitions, particularly in post-Communist Eastern Europe; see David, "Lustration Laws in Action."
3. Lambourne, "Transitional Justice and Peacebuilding," 38–39.
4. Bloomfield, Barnes, and Huyse, *Reconciliation after Violent Conflict.*
5. Ibid., 98.
6. Kaye, "Role of Truth Commissions," 715–716.
7. Bloomfield, Barnes, and Huyse, *Reconciliation after Violent Conflict*, 98.
8. Huyse, "Justice after Transition," 58.
9. Ibid., 62.
10. Cohen, "State Crimes of Previous Regimes," 21.
11. Offe, "Coming to Terms with Past Injustices," 197.
12. Shawqi Benyoub, a Moroccan lawyer and expert on transitional justice, public lecture, June 2013, Tunis, Tunisia.
13. Horne, "Vetting, Lustration, and Trust Building," 16–17.
14. Letki, "Lustration and Democratisation," 541–542.
15. Horne, "Vetting, Lustration, and Trust Building," 18–20.
16. Letki, "Lustration and Democratisation," 535.
17. Waters, "Libya's Home Court Advantage."
18. Human Rights Watch, "Rwanda: Justice after Genocide."

19. For more on retributive and restorative justice, see Sharqieh, "Vengeance Has No Place."

20. Sami Esaadi, interview with the author, January 2013, Tripoli, Libya.

21. The Political Isolation Law's Arabic name, *qanoun al-azl al-siyasi*, is also sometimes translated as Political Exclusion Law. BBC News, "Libya Parliament Bans Officials"; *Libya Herald*, "Legislation No. 13 of 2013."

22. Libyans, discussions with the author, January 2013, Tripoli, Libya.

23. Muhammad Suwan, interview with the author, January 2013, Tripoli, Libya.

24. Sharqieh, "Ill-Advised Purge in Libya."

25. Stephen, "Law May Affect 500,000"; *Libya Herald*, "National Forces Alliance Sweeps Party Lists."

26. Some members of the Muslim Brotherhood opposed the PIL, as it penalizes individuals not necessarily linked to corruption or past crimes. They argue that this should not be the case in Islam, which emphasizes that every individual is responsible for his or her own actions. The Brotherhood's leadership, on the other hand, supported the PIL as a preemptive act that does not deprive individuals of their rights but rather is a necessary measure to protect the revolution. Suwan, interview.

27. Nichols, "Exclusion Law Likely Violates Rights"; al-Hadi Bu Hamra, of Tripoli University, interview with the author, January 2013, Tripoli, Libya.

28. Mohammed Toumi, correspondence with the author, January 2015.

29. A tribal figure, interview with the author, January 2013, Tripoli, Libya.

30. Stephen, "Law May Affect 500,000"; Menas Associates, "Judicial Committees on Strike"; BBC News, "Libya GNC Chairman Resigns."

31. Saad al-Deen, interview with the author, January 2013, Tripoli, Libya; Galtier, "Commission for Integrity and Patriotism."

32. Rifai, "Timeline: Tunisia's Uprising"; Reuters, "Tunisia Says Will Track."

33. *Middle East Eye*, "Tunisia Court Annuls Confiscation of Ben Ali's Assets."

34. Salim Ben Hamidane, interview with the author, May 2013, Tunis, Tunisia.

35. International Center for Transitional Justice, "Tunisia's Historic Transitional Justice Law."

36. United Nations Development Programme, "Tunisia: Draft Organic Law."

37. Mohamed Ben Aisa, interview with the author, May 2013, Tunis, Tunisia.

38. Ameera Marzouk, interview with the author, May 2013, Tunis, Tunisia.

39. Said Ferjani, interview with the author, May 2013, Tunis, Tunisia; Souad Abderrahim, interview with the author, May 2013, Tunis, Tunisia.

40. Khaled Kchier, participant in the National Dialogue Committee on Transitional Justice, interview with the author, May 2013, Tunis, Tunisia.

41. Szakal, "Circumventing Political Exclusion"; Smadhi, "Clash over Exclusion."

42. Ferjani quoted in Benoit-Lavelle, "The Future of Tunisian Democracy."

43. Sharqieh, "Tunisia's Elections Seal Transition"; Essebsi, "My Three Goals"; Sharqieh, "Essebsi Must Work with Islamists."

44. Reuters, "Muwajiha qawiyya."
45. Sharqieh, "Tunisia's Elections Seal Transition."
46. These units were commanded by Saleh's relatives: Saleh's son Ahmed led the Republican Guards, his nephew Yahya Saleh led Central Security, and his half-brother Muhammad Saleh al-Ahmar commanded the Air Force.
47. The youth protesting in Change Square were not part of the agreement; rather, they publicly opposed it. While the youth are not a distinct political party, they are to some extent represented through official political parties, including Islah and the Socialist Party.
48. Sharqieh, "Yemen Can't Do it Alone."
49. An explosion in the mosque on June 3, 2011, wounded Saleh and a half-dozen other government officials. Saleh blamed the attack on the powerful Ahmar tribe, which had been fighting his troops for two weeks prior. See Worth and Kasinof, "Yemeni President Wounded."
50. Amnesty International, "Immunity Law Deals Blow."
51. Sarah Ahmed, interview with the author, May 2012, Sanaa, Yemen.
52. Galtung, *Theories of Peace*, 12.
53. Mahmoud Nasher, interview with the author, May 2012, Sanaa, Yemen.
54. Yaser al-Awadi, interview with the author, May 2012, Sanaa, Yemen.
55. Nadia al-Sakkaf, interview with the author, May 2012, Sanaa, Yemen.

Chapter 9. Institutional Reform

1. Brinkerhoff, "Rebuilding Governance," 5–6.
2. Wolff, "Post-Conflict State Building," 1779; Call, "Democratisation, War and State-Building," 860; Marquette and Beswick, "State Building, Security and Development," 1707.
3. Sami Esaadi, interview with the author, January 2013, Tripoli, Libya.
4. Noureddin al-Ikrimi, interview with the author, January 2013, Tripoli, Libya.
5. Ibid.
6. Souad Abderrahim, interview with the author, May 2013, Tunis, Tunisia.
7. Ibid.
8. Human Rights Watch, "Tunisia: Mass Firings a Blow."
9. Decree 10 of 2011, as cited in el-Issawi, *Tunisian Media in Transition*, 8.
10. Decree 115 of 2011, as cited in ibid., 9.
11. Ibid., 8–10.
12. For more on this, see *al-Sharq al-Awsat*, "al-'A'alan 'an 'ada' al-hi'a al-'aliya al-mustaqila." The process used for the selection of the ninth member is unclear.
13. El-Issawi, *Tunisian Media in Transition*, 8–9.
14. Rasheeda al-Neifer, interview with the author, May 2013, Tunis, Tunisia.
15. Gordon, "Yemen's Military Shake-Up."

16. Al-Haj, "President Orders Military Shakeup."
17. Al-Jubari, "Working Group Reforms Judiciary."
18. BBC News, "Yemen's National Dialogue Conference Concludes."
19. Al-Hassani, "General Inspector to Monitor."
20. Greenfield, "Yemen Faces Fresh Challenges."
21. Al-Maytami, "Tadakhum hajm al-dawla," 2, 4.

Chapter 10. Civil Society Organizations

1. Belloni, "Civil Society in War-to-Democracy Transitions," 182.
2. Ibid., 199; Nilsson, "Anchoring the Peace," 247. See also Barnes, *Owning the Process*; Bell and O'Rourke, "The People's Peace?"; Koppell, "Who Belongs at Darfur Talks?"; and McKeon, "Participating in Peace Processes."
3. Funk and Said, "Localizing Peace"; Sharqieh, *A Lasting Peace?*; Lederach, *Building Peace*. See also Kelleher and Johnson, "Religious Communities as Peacemakers."
4. Safa, *Conflict Resolution and Reconciliation*.
5. Backer, "Civil Society and Transitional Justice," 310–311.
6. Crenzel, "Argentina's National Commission," 190.
7. Penfold, "Sierra Leone's Bloody Conflict," 556.
8. Nilsson, "Anchoring the Peace," 247–248. See also Lederach, *Building Peace*, and Prendergast and Plumb, "Building Local Capacity."
9. Cochrane, "Unsung Heroes?" 152–153.
10. Khaled Kchier, participant in the National Dialogue Committee on Transitional Justice, interview with the author, May 2013, Tunis, Tunisia.
11. International Center for Transitional Justice, "Tunisia's Historic Transitional Justice Law."
12. Mohamed al-Ghraibi, head of the Tunisian Network for Transitional Justice, interview with the author, May 2013, Tunis, Tunisia.
13. Amine Ghali, interview with the author, May 2013, Tunis, Tunisia.
14. Rim El-Gantri, interview with the author, May 2013, Tunis, Tunisia.
15. For more on this, see Sharqieh, "Tunisia: A Successful Revolution."
16. UGTT secretariat, interview with the author, June 2013, Tunis, Tunisia.
17. Kazdaghli, "Tunisia's National Dialogue." See also Sharqieh, "Tunisia: A Successful Revolution."
18. Hussein al-Habbouni, president of the WSC's National Reconciliation Committee, and Abdulnaser Ibrahim Obaidi, member of the WSC's National Reconciliation Committee, interview with the author, January 2013, Tripoli, Libya.
19. Ibid.
20. Ibid.
21. Wafa Tayyeb al-Naas, interview with the author, January 2013, Tripoli, Libya.

22. Claudia Gazzini, interview with the author, January 2013, Tripoli, Libya. The fighting between the Zentan, who took a leadership role in the Libyan revolution, and the Mashaysha tribes, who allegedly supported the Qaddafi regime, lasted for months and resulted in hundreds of casualties and prisoners from both sides. See *al-Watan al-Libya*, "Lajnat al-Hukama tanjah."

Chapter 11. Women

1. Fischer-Tahir, "Competition, Cooperation and Resistance," 1386.
2. Kuehnast, "Women's Involvement in Peacebuilding," 18.
3. Ibid.
4. United States Institute of Peace, "Gender, War, and Peacebuilding," 4.
5. Ibid.
6. Kuehnast, "Women's Involvement in Peacebuilding," 18.
7. United Nations Security Council, "Women, Peace and Security."
8. Schirch, *Women in Peacebuilding*, 41.
9. Kuehnast, "Women's Involvement in Peacebuilding," 18.
10. Driver, "Truth, Reconciliation, Gender," 220.
11. Nadine Nasrat, interview with the author, January 2013, Tripoli, Libya.
12. Rida Altubuly, president of Ma'an Nabneeha and member of the Libyan Women's Association, interview with the author, January 2013, Tripoli, Libya.
13. Ibid.
14. Nasrat, interview.
15. https://libyanwomensplatformforpeace.wordpress.com.
16. Mohammed Qahtan, interview with the author, May 2012, Sanaa, Yemen; al-Hamdani, "Yemen's Quota."
17. Sarah Ahmed, interview with the author, May 2012, Sanaa, Yemen.
18. Semlali, "Yemeni Women."
19. Al Hamdani, "Yemen's Quota."
20. Arab Center for Research and Policy Studies, "Yemen's National Dialogue Conference."
21. Al-Sakkaf, "Yemen's Women."
22. Raja, *Yemeni Women in Transition*, 5.
23. See chapter 10 on CSOs for a discussion of the remarkable conflict resolution work that women initiated and led through the SUNR.

Chapter 12. Tribes

1. Sultan, "Quest for Peace in Chechnya," 441.
2. Al-Dawsari, *Tribal Governance and Stability*, 5.

3. Corstange, "Tribes and the Rule of Law," 13.

4. Ibid.

5. Al-Dawsari, *Tribal Governance and Stability*, 8.

6. Carroll, "Tribal Law and Reconciliation," 11.

7. Ibid., 22, 28.

8. Ibid., 28.

9. Ibid., 29.

10. Corstange, "Tribes and the Rule of Law," 13; al-Dawsari, *Tribal Governance and Stability*, 4.

11. Mifreh al-Bahabeih, interview with the author, May 2012, Sanaa, Yemen. Al-Bahabeih used the term "tribal arms race" to describe how fighting among tribes begins with pistols and then escalates to the use of automatic rifles, RPGs, and even missiles. This type of escalation compels Yemen's tribes to engage in the arms race in order to combat other tribes if necessary and to protect their own interests.

12. Ibid. Al-Bahabeih described a tribal conflict resolution system as follows: "Whenever a conflict erupts, each tribe chooses someone from the other tribe—with whom they have a conflict—called an arbitrator, who serves as negotiator on behalf of his tribe. Both arbitrators ensure they have bonds and guarantees (e.g., cars, cows, weapons) to ensure implementation of any agreements reached. If the two arbitrators do not reach an agreement, then they resort to a third arbitrator from a neutral tribe that can contribute to the negotiation. They keep coming up with new ways until they reach an agreement, after which they ensure full implementation."

13. "Conflict Resolution in Yemen," as cited in al-Dawsari, *Tribal Governance and Stability*, 4; Haidari, "Qaeda Gunmen Quit Town"; Saeed, "Captured Soldiers in Abyan Released."

14. Al-Bahabeih, interview.

15. See also chapter 5 on national dialogue.

16. Warfalla is Libya's largest tribe and has approximately one million members. While Qaddafi did not enjoy the backing of the entire tribe, his support from the tribe was significant.

17. Khalifa al-Rayayneh, interview with the author, January 2013, Nafousa Mountains, Libya.

18. Al-Rayayneh, interview.

19. Hussein al-Buishi, interview with the author, December 2012, Tripoli, Libya.

Conclusion

1. Kingsley, Stephen, and Roberts, "UAE and Egypt behind Bombing"; Kirkpatrick and Schmitt, "Arab Nations Strike in Libya."

BIBLIOGRAPHY

Abdallah, Khaled, and Sami Aboudi. "Yemeni Leader Hadi Leaves Country as Saudi Arabia Keeps up Air Strikes." Reuters. March 26, 2015. http://www.reuters.com/article/2015/03/26/us-yemen-security-idUSKBN0ML0YC20150326.

Abedajo, Adekeye. "Liberia: A Warlord's Peace." In *Ending Civil Wars: The Implementation of Peace Agreements*, edited by Stephen John Stedman, Donald Rothchild, and Elizabeth M. Cousens, 599–630. Boulder: Lynne Rienner, 2002.

Abrahams, Fred. "Why Have We Forgotten about Libya?" CNN. March 25, 2013. http://globalpublicsquare.blogs.cnn.com/2013/03/25/why-have-we-forgotten-about-libya.

Agence France-Presse. "Arab League Denounces Houthi 'Coup' in Yemen." *Daily Star*. February 8, 2015. http://www.dailystar.com.lb/News/Middle-East/2015/Feb-08/286801-arab-league-condemns-houthi-coup-in-yemen.ashx.

Agence France-Presse. "First Iran Flight Lands in Shiite-Held Yemen Capital." Naharnet. March 1, 2015. http://www.naharnet.com/stories/en/169568-first-iran-flight-lands-in-shiite-held-yemen-capital.

Agence France-Presse. "Gulf Neighbors Denounce Houthis 'Coup' in Yemen." Naharnet. February 7, 2015. http://www.naharnet.com/stories/en/166572-gulf-neighbors-denounce-huthis-coup-in-yemen.

Agence France-Presse. "Libya Launches National Dialogue Initiative." *Gulf News*. August 25, 2013. http://gulfnews.com/news/region/libya/libya-launches-national-dialogue-initiative-1.1224018.

Agence France-Presse. "Shiite Militia Tightens Grip on Yemen after 'Coup'." Naharnet. February 7, 2015. http://www.naharnet.com/stories/en/166518-shiite-militia-tightens-grip-on-yemen-after-coup.

Agence France-Presse. "Suspected Assassin of Tunisia's Belaid Killed: Minister." *Daily Star*. February 4, 2014. http://www.dailystar.com.lb/News/Middle-East/2014/Feb-04/246350-suspected-assassin-of-tunisias-belaid-killed-minister.ashx#axzz39KT3buiG.

Agence France-Presse. "UN Security Council Affirms Support for Yemen President, Unity." Naharnet. March 22, 2015. http://www.naharnet.com/stories/en/172652-u-n -security-council-affirms-support-for-yemen-president-unity.

Agence France-Presse. "Yemen Begins New National Talks as Hadi Hails Progress." Ma'an News Agency. June 8, 2013. http://www.maannews.net/eng/ViewDetails .aspx?ID=603140.

Agence France-Presse. "Yemen Militia Sends Forces South as U.N. Warns of Civil War." Naharnet. March 23, 2015. http://www.naharnet.com/stories/en/172693-yemen -militia-sends-forces-south-as-u-n-warns-of-civil-war.

Agence France-Presse. "Yemen Parties Agree on Federalism." Al Arabiya News. September 11, 2013. http://english.alarabiya.net/en/News/middle-east/2013/09/11/Yemen -parties-agree-on-federalism-minister-.html.

Ajetunmobi, Abdulsalam. "Victims' Responses after Mass Atrocities: A Note on Empirical Findings." Contemporary Justice Review 15, no. 1 (2012): 39–56.

Alabassi, Mamoon. "Yemen Leak: Collusion between Houthis and Ex-President Saleh." Middle East Eye. January 22, 2015. http://www.middleeasteye.net/news/yemen-leak -collusion-between-houthis-and-ex-president-saleh-1125273454.

Al Hamdani, Samaa. "Yemen's Quota: Success for International Community or Yemeni Women?" Fikra Forum. September 27, 2013. http://fikraforum.org/?p=3850.

Al Tommy, Mohammad. "Some 5,000 Militia Men Join New Libyan Army." Reuters. February 15, 2012. http://www.reuters.com/article/2012/02/15/us-libya-militias -idUSTRE81E23H20120215.

Alwazir, Ataif Zaid. "The Myth of the 'Yemen Model.'" The World Post. May 29, 2013. http://www.huffingtonpost.com/atiaf-zaid-alwazir/the-myth-of-the-yemen-mod_b _3352795.html.

Amnesty International. "Yemen: Immunity Law Deals Blow to Victims of Abuses." January 24, 2012. http://www.amnesty.org.au/news/comments/27686/.

Arab Center for Research and Policy Studies. "Outcomes of Yemen's National Dialogue Conference: A Step toward Conflict Resolution and State Building?" Policy Analysis Unit. February 2014. http://english.dohainstitute.org/release/c5b3a33b-644d -47f8-9e03-85fcb852c899.

al-Araby al-Jadeed. "Libya Talks in Jeopardy as Islamists Reject UN Proposal." April 30, 2015. http://www.alaraby.co.uk/english/politics/2015/4/30/libya-talks-in-jeopardy-as -islamists-reject-un-proposal.

Backer, David. "Civil Society and Transitional Justice: Possibilities, Patterns and Prospects." Journal of Human Rights 2, no. 3 (2003): 297–313.

Bafana, Haykal. "National Dialogue: Panacea or Pain." blog|haykal bafana (blog). December 1, 2012. http://blog.haykal.sg/the-yemen/18-lp/14-national-dialogue-in -yemen-panacea-or-pain.

Barakish.net. "al-Huthayun yu'alinun 'an 'ashira shurut lil-musharika fi al-huwar" [The Houthis announce ten conditions for participation in the dialogue]. May 10, 2012. http://barakish.net/news.aspx?cat=12&sub=12&id=30061.

Barnes, Catherine. *Owning the Process: Mechanisms for Political Participation of the Public in Peacemaking*. London: Conciliation Resources, 2002.

Baron, Adam. "What We Get Wrong about Yemen." Politico. March 25, 2015. http://www.politico.com/magazine/story/2015/03/yemen-intervention-116396.html#.VXaxkc-qpBc.

Baroumy, Yara, and Mohammed Ghobari. "Clashes Hit Yemen Capital Again as Houthis Pursue Political Gains." Reuters. January 20, 2015. http://www.reuters.com/article/2015/01/20/us-yemen-security-idUSKBN0KT1JK20150120.

Bawabat al-Wasat. "Itifaq bayna Misrata wa Tawergha' bi-Janif li'i'adat al-nazihin" [Agreement between Misrata and Tawergha with Geneva for the return of the displaced]. January 29, 2015. http://www.alwasat.ly/ar/news/libya/58918/.

BBC News. "'Iqrar al-'aml bil-nitham al-fidirali fi al-Yemen" [Adopting the federal system in Yemen]. February 10, 2014. http://www.bbc.co.uk/arabic/middleeast/2014/02/140210_yemen_federation.shtml.

BBC News. "Libya GNC Chairman Muhammad al-Magarief Resigns." May 28, 2013. http://www.bbc.co.uk/news/world-africa-22693963.

BBC News. "Libya Parliament Bans Gaddafi Era Officials." May 5, 2013. http://www.bbc.co.uk/news/world-africa-22423238.

BBC News. "Yemen's National Dialogue Conference Concludes with Agreement." January 21, 2014. http://www.bbc.co.uk/news/world-middle-east-25835721.

Bell, Christine, and Catherine O'Rourke. "The People's Peace? Peace Agreements, Civil Society, and Participatory Democracy." *International Political Science Review* 28, no. 3 (2007): 293–324.

Belloni, Roberto. "Civil Society in War-to-Democracy Transitions." In *From War to Democracy: Dilemmas of Peacebuilding*, edited by Anna K. Jarstad and Timothy D. Sisk, 182–212. Cambridge: Cambridge University Press, 2008.

Benoit-Lavelle, Mischa. "The Future of Tunisian Democracy." *The New Yorker*. November 1, 2014. http://www.newyorker.com/news/news-desk/future-tunisian-democracy.

Bloomfield, David, Teresa Barnes, and Luc Huyse, eds. *Reconciliation after Violent Conflict: A Handbook*. Stockholm: International Institute for Democracy and Electoral Assistance, 2003.

Boduszynski, Mieczyslaw P., and Kristin Fabbe. "What Libya's Militia Problem Means for the Middle East, and the U.S." *Los Angeles Times*. September 23, 2014. http://www.latimes.com/opinion/op-ed/la-oe-0923-boduszynski-libya-lessons-20140924-story.html.

Bradley, Megan, Ibrahim Fraihat, and Houda Mzioudet. *Uprooted by Revolution and Civil War*. Washington, DC: Georgetown University Press, 2015.

Brahm, Eric. "Uncovering the Truth: Examining Truth Commission Success and Impact." *International Studies Perspectives* 8, no. 1 (2007): 16–35.

Brinkerhoff, Derick W. "Rebuilding Governance in Failed States and Post-Conflict Societies: Core Concepts and Cross-Cutting Themes." *Public Administration and Development* 25, no. 1 (2005): 3–14.

Browning, Noah, and Louis Charbonneau. "UN Envoy to Yemen Resigns." Reuters. April 16, 2015. http://www.reuters.com/article/2015/04/16/us-yemen-security-un -idUSKBN0N62O020150416.

Call, Charles T. "Democratisation, War and State-Building: Constructing the Rule of Law in El Salvador." *Journal of Latin American Studies* 35 (2003): 827–862.

Carroll, Katherine Blue. "Tribal Law and Reconciliation in the New Iraq." *Middle East Journal* 65, no. 1 (Winter 2011): 11–29.

Castillo, Graciana del. "Post-Conflict Reconstruction and the Challenge to International Organizations: The Case of El Salvador." *World Development* 29, no. 12 (2001): 1967–1985.

Chonghaile, Clar Ni. "Libyans Displaced by Civil Conflict Face Cruel Winter as Donor Funding Falls Short." *Guardian.* December 8, 2014. http://www.theguardian.com/ global-development/2014/dec/08/libya-displacement-civil-war-cruel-winter-donor -funding-falls-short.

C. J. "The International Commission on Missing Persons." *The Economist.* November 9, 2012. http://www.economist.com/blogs/easternapproaches/2012/11/bosnia.

Cochrane, Feargal. "Unsung Heroes? The Role of Peace and Conflict Resolution Organizations in the Northern Ireland Conflict." In *Northern Ireland and the Divided World: Post-Agreement Northern Ireland in Comparative Perspective*, edited by John McGarry, 137–155. Oxford: Oxford University Press, 2001.

Cohen, Stanley. "State Crimes of Previous Regimes: Knowledge, Accountability, and the Policing of the Past." *Law and Social Inquiry* 20, no. 1 (Winter 1995): 7–50.

Cook, James. "Lockerbie Bombing: Al Jazeera Documentary Makes Iran Link Claims." BBC News. March 11, 2014. http://www.bbc.com/news/uk-scotland-south-scotland -26528745.

Corstange, Daniel. "Tribes and the Rule of Law in Yemen." *al-Masar* 10, no. 1 (Winter 2009): 3–54.

Crenzel, Emilio. "Argentina's National Commission on the Disappearance of Persons: Contributions to Transitional Justice." *International Journal of Transitional Justice* 2, no. 2 (2008): 173–191.

David, Roman. "Lustration Laws in Action: The Motives and Evaluation of Lustration Policy in the Czech Republic and Poland (1998–2001)." *Law and Social Inquiry* 28, no. 2 (2003): 387–439.

David, Roman, and Houda Mzioudet. *Personnel Change or Personal Change? Rethinking Libya's Political Isolation Law.* Doha: Brookings Doha Center–Stanford Project on Arab Transitions, 2014. http://www.brookings.edu/~/media/research/files/ papers/2014/03/17-libya-lustration-david-mzioudet/lustration-in-libya-english.pdf.

al-Dawsari, Nadwa. *Tribal Governance and Stability in Yemen.* Washington, DC: Carnegie Endowment for International Peace, 2012. http://carnegieendowment .org/2012/04/24/tribal-governance-and-stability-in-yemen.

Day, Stephen W. "The 'Non-Conclusion' of Yemen's National Dialogue." *Foreign Policy*. January 27, 2014. http://mideastafrica.foreignpolicy.com/posts/2014/01/27/the_non_conclusion_of_yemen_s_national_dialogue_0.

Driver, Dorothy. "Truth, Reconciliation, Gender: The South African Truth and Reconciliation Commission and Black Women's Intellectual History." *Australian Feminist Studies* 20, no. 47 (2005): 219–229.

el-Issawi, Fatima. *Tunisian Media in Transition*. Washington, DC: Carnegie Endowment for International Peace, 2012. http://carnegieendowment.org/2012/07/10/tunisian-media-in-transition.

Eljarh, Mohamed. "Libya's Geneva Talks and the Search for Peace." *MENASource* (blog). February 6, 2015. http://www.atlanticcouncil.org/blogs/menasource/libya-s-geneva-talks-and-the-search-for-peace.

Eljarh, Mohamed. "Scenarios for Libya Going Forward." *MENASource* (blog). March 10, 2015. http://www.atlanticcouncil.org/blogs/menasource/scenarios-for-libya-going-forward.

Eljarh, Mohamed. "The Supreme Court Decision That's Ripping Libya Apart." *Foreign Policy*. November 6, 2014. http://foreignpolicy.com/2014/11/06/the-supreme-court-decision-thats-ripping-libya-apart/.

Elmaazi, Abdullah. "Urgent Need for Reconciliation in Libya." *Middle East Online*. December 8, 2012. http://www.middle-east-online.com/english/?id=55977.

al-Eshteraki. "al-Hizb al-'Ishtiraki yad'a jumla min al-muhadidat wa al-mukharij lil-huwar wa hul al-qadiya al-janubiya" [The Socialist Party lays out a set of determinants and outcomes for the dialogue and resolution of the southern issue]. May 3, 2012. http://www.aleshteraky.com/archive/news_details.php?lng=arabic&sid=12741.

Essebsi, Beji Caid. "My Three Goals as Tunisia's President." *Washington Post*. December 26, 2014. http://www.washingtonpost.com/opinions/beji-caid-essebsi-my-three-goals-as-tunisias-president/2014/12/26/46a4dad6–8b8d-11e4-a085–34e9b9f09a58_story.html.

Fischer-Tahir, Andrea. "Competition, Cooperation and Resistance: Women in the Political Field in Iraq." *International Affairs* 86, no. 6 (2010): 1381–1394.

Funk, Nathan C., and Abdul Aziz Said. "Localizing Peace: An Agenda for Sustainable Peacebuilding." *Peace and Conflict Studies* 17, no. 1 (2010): 101–143.

Galtier, Mathieu. "Inside the Commission for Integrity and Patriotism." *Libya Herald*. April 11, 2013. http://www.libyaherald.com/2013/04/11/inside-the-commission-for-integrity-and-patriotism/.

Galtung, Johan. *Theories of Peace: A Synthetic Approach to Peace Thinking*. Oslo: International Peace Research Institute, 1967.

Ghobari, Mohammed. "Houthi Rebels Sign Deal with Yemen Parties to Form New Government." Reuters. September 21, 2013. http://www.reuters.com/article/2014/09/21/us-yemen-security-idUSKBN0HG04T20140921.

Ghobari, Mohammed. "Yemeni Government Apologises for Wars Waged by Former President." Reuters. August 21, 2013. http://uk.reuters.com/article/2013/08/21/uk-yemen-south-apology-idUKBRE97K0TS20130821.

Ghobari, Mohammed. "Yemen's Houthis Dissolve Parliament, Assume Power: Televised Statement." Reuters. February 6, 2015. http://www.reuters.com/article/2015/02/06/us-yemen-crisis-idUSKBN0LA1NT20150206.

Ghobari, Mohammed, and Mohammed Mukhashaf. "Yemen's Hadi Flees to Aden and Says He Is Still President." Reuters. February 21, 2015. http://www.reuters.com/article/2015/02/21/us-yemen-security-idUSKBN0LP08F20150221.

Goldstone, Richard J. "Justice as a Tool for Peacemaking: Truth Commissions and International Criminal Tribunals." *New York University Journal of International Law and Politics* 28 (1996): 485–503.

Gordon, Sasha. "Yemen's Military Shake-Up: Weakening Ousted Saleh's Network." American Enterprise Institute Critical Threats Project. April 12, 2012. http://www.criticalthreats.org/yemen/gordon-military-command-graphic-april-12–2012.

Greenfield, Danya. "Analysis: Yemen Faces Fresh Challenges as National Dialogue Ends." BBC News. January 28, 2014. http://www.bbc.co.uk/news/world-middle-east-25928579.

Greenfield, Danya. "Yemen Crisis: A Coup in All but Name." BBC News. January 22, 2015. http://www.bbc.com/news/world-middle-east-30941514.

al-Haidari, Fawaz. "Qaeda Gunmen Quit Yemen Town under Tribal Pressure." Agence France-Presse. January 25, 2012. http://www.dawn.com/news/690863/al-qaeda-gunmen-quit-yemen-town-under-tribal-pressure.

al-Haj, Ahmed. "Yemen Arrests 2 Frenchmen over Suspected al-Qaida Links." Associated Press. January 17, 2015. http://bigstory.ap.org/article/02a49818fabe4318b0431249 75abead8/officials-say-gunmen-abduct-head-yemen-presidents-office.

al-Haj, Ahmed. "Yemen President Orders Military Shakeup." Associated Press. April 10, 2013. http://news.yahoo.com/yemen-president-orders-military-shakeup-192231286.html.

al-Haj, Ahmed. "Yemen's Shi'ite Rebels Reject Agreed Federal Plan." Associated Press. January 3, 2015. http://news.yahoo.com/yemen-arrests-2-european-1-somali-al-qaida-132157504.html.

Hammond, Andrew. "Yemenis Paint Disappeared Activists on Sanaa Streets." Reuters. September 25, 2012. http://www.reuters.com/article/2012/09/25/us-yemen-disappeared-idUSBRE88O0YG20120925.

Hasad al-Youm. "al-Houthiyyun yarfudun hiwar al-Doha wa yurahinun 'ala al-hasm al-'askari" [Houthis reject Doha dialogue and bet on military solution]. Hasadalyoum.com. March 24, 2015. http://www.hasadalyoum.com/news5616.html.

al-Hassani, Mohammed. "Federal Region Defining Committee: Yemeni Will Have Six Regions." *Yemen Times*. February 4, 2014. http://yementimes.com/en/1752/news/3426/Federal-region-defining-committee-Yemen-will-have-six-regions.htm.

al-Hassani, Mohammed. "General Inspector to Monitor Ministry of Interior." *Yemen Times*. July 1, 2013. http://www.yementimes.com/en/1690/news/2561/General -inspector-to-monitor-Ministry-of-Interior.htm.

al-Hassani, Mohammed. "Political Parties in the NDC Must Decide What It Means to Be Yemeni." *Yemen Times*. May 13, 2013. http://www.yementimes.com/en/1676/ news/2334/Political-parties-in-the-NDC-must-decide-what-it-means-to-be-Yemeni .htm.

Hayner, Priscilla. "Fifteen Truth Commissions, 1974 to 1994: A Comparative Perspective." *Human Rights Quarterly* 16 (1994): 595–655.

Hayner, Priscilla. *Unspeakable Truths: Facing the Challenge of Truth Commissions*. New York: Routledge, 2001.

Horne, Cynthia. "Vetting, Lustration, and Trust Building: Does Retroactive Justice Increase the Trustworthiness of Public Institutions?" Paper presented at the annual meeting of the American Political Science Association, Washington, DC, September 1–4, 2005.

Human Rights Watch. "Libya: June 1996 Killings at Abu Salim Prison." June 27, 2006. http://www.hrw.org/en/news/2006/06/27/libya-june-1996-killings-abu-salim-prison.

Human Rights Watch. "Rwanda: Justice after Genocide–20 Years On." March 28, 2014. http://www.hrw.org/news/2014/03/28/rwanda-justice-after-genocide-20-years.

Human Rights Watch. "Tunisia: Mass Firings a Blow to Judicial Independence." October 29, 2012. http://www.hrw.org/news/2012/10/29/tunisia-mass-firings-blow-judicial -independence.

Human Rights Watch. "Yemen Needs Accountability, Security Reform." April 6, 2012. http://www.hrw.org/news/2012/04/06/yemen-transition-needs-accountability -security-reform.

Huyse, Luc. "Justice after Transition: On the Choices Successor Elites Make in Dealing with the Past." *Law and Social Inquiry* 20, no. 1 (Winter 1995): 51–78.

Internal Displacement Monitoring Centre. *Global Overview 2014: People Internally Displaced by Conflict and Violence*. Geneva: Internal Displacement Monitoring Centre and Norwegian Refugee Council, 2014. http://www.internal-displacement. org/publications/2014/global-overview-2014-people-internally-displaced-by-conflict -and-violence.

Internal Displacement Monitoring Centre. *Libya: State Collapse Triggers Mass Displacement*. Geneva: Norwegian Refugee Council, 2015.

International Center for Transitional Justice. "ICTJ Welcomes Launch of Tunisia's Truth and Dignity Commission." June 6, 2014. http://www.ictj.org/news/ictj-welcomes -launch-tunisia%E2%80%99s-truth-and-dignity-commission.

International Center for Transitional Justice. "ICTJ Welcomes Tunisia's Historic Transitional Justice Law." December 16, 2013. http://www.ictj.org/news/ictj-welcomes -tunisia%E2%80%99s-historic-transitional-justice-law.

International Crisis Group. *Libya: Getting Geneva Right.* Brussels: International Crisis Group, 2015. http://www.crisisgroup.org/en/regions/middle-east-north-africa/north -africa/libya/157-libya-getting-geneva-right.aspx.

International Crisis Group. *Yemen: Enduring Conflicts, Threatened Transition.* Brussels: International Crisis Group, 2012. http://www.crisisgroup.org/~/media/Files/ Middle%20East%20North%20Africa/Iran%20Gulf/Yemen/125-yemen-enduring -conflicts-threatened-transition.pdf.

International Institute for Democracy and Electoral Assistance and the World Bank. *Experiences with National Dialogue in Latin America: Main Lessons from a Round-table Discussion.* Washington, DC: The World Bank, 2001. http://web.worldbank .org/archive/website01013/WEB/IMAGES/ELSALVAE.PDF.

Al Jazeera. "al-Hud al-manjami 2008" [The mining basin 2008]. ArabSciences.com. July 2011. http://tinyurl.com/b36ef2w.

Al Jazeera. "Libyan Parliament Sessions Shelved." Last modified March 10, 2013. http:// www.aljazeera.com/news/africa/2013/03/20133101443670794.html.

Al Jazeera. "Libya's Tobruk-Based Government Attacks Tripoli Airport." April 15, 2015. http://www.aljazeera.com/news/2015/04/libya-tobruk-based-government-attacks -tripoli-airport-150415130719497.html.

Al Jazeera. "al-Ra'is al-Tshadi yattahimu Libya bi-tadrib mu'aridihi" [Chad's president accuses Libya of training his opponents]. April 27, 2013. http://www.aljazeera.net/ news/pages/2be47e91–60f2–4aa8-b39c-9b48e772d0e0.

Al Jazeera Center for Studies. "Tunisia: National Dialogue in the Context of Political and Security Challenges." Position Paper. Last modified November 10, 2013. http:// studies.aljazeera.net/en/positionpapers/2013/11/2013110123327549569.htm.

Jessop, Maria, and Alison Milofsky. "Dialogue: Calming Hot Spots Calls for Structure and Skill." United States Institute of Peace. May 1, 2014. http://www.usip.org/ olivebranch/dialogue-calming-hot-spots-calls-structure-and-skill.

al-Jubari, Rammah. "NDC Working Group Reforms Judiciary." *Yemen Times.* September 25, 2013. http://yementimes.com/en/1715/news/2933/NDC-Working-Group -reforms-judiciary.htm.

Justice and Development Party. "Pillars of National Dialogue, the Vision of the Justice and Development Party." February 13, 2012. Leaflet in the author's possession.

Kadlec, Amanda. "The Problem with Libya's Peace Talks." *Foreign Policy.* January 16, 2015. http://foreignpolicy.com/2015/01/16/the-problem-with-libyas-peace-talks/.

al-Kamali, Farouq. "al-Yemen: al-Houthiyyun yuwaqi'aun itfaqiyyat iqtisadiyya ma' Iran" [Yemen: The Houthis sign economic agreements with Iran]. *al-Araby al-Jadeed.* March 11, 2015. www.alaraby.co.uk/economy/2015/3/11/ اليمن-الحوثيون-يوقعون-اتفاقيات-اقتصادية-مع-إيران.

Kaye, Mike. "The Role of Truth Commissions in the Search for Justice, Reconciliation, and Democratization: The Salvadorean and Honduran Cases." *Journal of Latin American Studies* 29, no. 3 (1997): 693–716.

Kazdaghli, Habib. "Tunisia's National Dialogue Is the Last Hope for Solving Political Crisis." *Fikra Forum*. October 24, 2013. http://fikraforum.org/?p=3986.

Kelleher, Ann, and Meggan Johnson. "Religious Communities as Peacemakers: A Comparison of Grassroots Peace Processes in Sudan and Northern Ireland." *Civil Wars* 10, no. 2 (2008): 148–172.

Keller, Linda M. "Seeking Justice at the International Criminal Court: Victims' Reparations." *Thomas Jefferson Law Review* 29, no. 2 (2007): 189–217.

Kingsley, Patrick, Chris Stephen, and Dan Roberts. "UAE and Egypt behind Bombing Raids against Libyan Militias, Say US Officials." *Guardian*. http://www.theguardian.com/world/2014/aug/26/united-arab-emirates-bombing-raids-libyan-militias.

Kirkpatrick, David D., and Eric Schmitt. "Arab Nations Strike in Libya, Surprising U.S." *New York Times*. August 25, 2014. http://www.nytimes.com/2014/08/26/world/africa/egypt-and-united-arab-emirates-said-to-have-secretly-carried-out-libya-airstrikes.html?_r=1.

Koppell, Carla. "Who Belongs at Darfur Talks?" *Christian Science Monitor*. October 22, 2007. http://www.csmonitor.com/2007/1022/p09s01-coop.html.

Kuehnast, Kathleen. "Why Women's Involvement in Peacebuilding Matters." *Foreign Service Journal* 88, no. 4 (April 2011): 17–20.

Laessing, Ulf, and Ayman al-Warhalli. "Libyan PM Says Kidnapping Was Bid to Topple Government." Reuters. October 11, 2013. http://www.reuters.com/article/2013/10/11/us-libya-security-idUSBRE99A08F20131011.

Lambourne, Wendy. "Transitional Justice and Peacebuilding after Mass Violence." *International Journal of Transitional Justice* 3, no. 1 (2009): 28–48.

Lamloum, Imed. "Libya Leader's Car Shot up as Political Tension Soars." *Daily Star*. Last modified March 6, 2013. http://www.dailystar.com.lb/News/Middle-East/2013/Mar-06/209082-libya-interim-heads-car-comes-under-fire-minister.ashx#axzz2TMhQmJFS.

Laplante, Lisa J., and Kimberly Theidon. "Truth with Consequences: Justice and Reparations in Post-Truth Commission Peru." *Human Rights Quarterly* 29, no. 1 (2007): 228–250.

Lederach, John Paul. *Building Peace: Sustainable Reconciliation in Divided Societies*. Washington, DC: United States Institute of Peace Press, 1997.

Lederach, John Paul. "Civil Society and Reconciliation." In *Turbulent Peace: The Challenges of Managing International Conflict*, edited by Chester A. Crocker, Fen Osler Hampson, and Pamela Aall, 841–854. Washington, DC: United States Institute of Peace Press, 2001.

Letki, Natalia. "Lustration and Democratisation in East-Central Europe." *Europe-Asia Studies* 54, no. 4 (June 2002): 529–552.

Libya Herald. "Dignity Rejects UNSMIL Invitation to dialogue, Calls on Leon to Tell UN to Lift Embargo." April 29, 2015. http://www.libyaherald.com/2015/04/29/

dignity-rejects-unsmil-invitation-to-dialogue-calls-on-leon-to-tell-un-to-lift
-embargo/#axzz3cM2NsASC.

Libya Herald. "Legislation No. 13 of 2013 of the Political and Administrative Isolation." May 14, 2013. http://www.libyaherald.com/2013/05/14/political-isolation-law-the-full -text/#axzz2hJkoc7Z9.

Libya Herald. "National Forces Alliance Sweeps Party Lists as Election Results Finally Announced." July 17, 2012. http://www.libyaherald.com/2012/07/17/national-forces -alliance-sweeps-party-lists-as-election-results-finally-announced/#axzz3ApiEMyUV.

Maghur, Azza K. "The UNSMIL Draft Agreement and International Engagement with Libya." MENASource (blog). April 14, 2015. http://www.atlanticcouncil.org/blogs/ menasource/the-unsmil-draft-agreement-and-international-engagement-with-libya.

Mareb Press. "al-Nasseriyyun yutalibun bil-kashf 'an jithamin manfathi muhawila al- 'inqilab dad al-Ra'is Saleh" [Nasserists demand disclosure of bodies of those who attempted the coup against President Saleh]. October 16, 2009. http://marebpress .net/news_details.php?sid=19416.

Marquette, Heather, and Danielle Beswick. "State Building, Security and Develop- ment: State Building as a New Development Paradigm?" *Third World Quarterly* 32, no. 10 (2011): 1703–1714.

al-Maytami, Mohamed. "Tadakhum hajm al-dawla fi al-Yemen . . . al-takhalus min al- 'ahrash al-dara ki tanmu al-'ashjar al-muthmira" [Inflation of the size of the state in Yemen . . . get rid of the harmful forest to grow fruitful trees]. Center for Interna- tional Private Enterprise. Accessed August 17, 2014. http://www.cipe-arabia.org/files/ pdf/Feature_Service/Re-evaluation_of_the_Yemeni_State.pdf.

Mazzei, Julie M. "Finding Shame in Truth: The Importance of Public Engagement in Truth Commissions." *Human Rights Quarterly* 33, no. 2 (May 2011): 431–452.

Mazzetti, Mark, and David Kirkpatrick. "Saudi Arabia Leads Air Assault in Yemen." *New York Times*. March 25, 2015. http://www.nytimes.com/2015/03/26/world/middleeast/ al-anad-air-base-houthis-yemen.html?_r=0.

McKeon, Celia. "Civil Society: Participating in Peace Processes." In *People Building Peace II: Successful Stories of Civil Society*, edited by Paul van Tongeren et al., 567–575. Boulder: Lynne Rienner, 2005.

Menas Associates. "Judicial Committees on Strike." June 18, 2013. http://www.menas.co.uk/ politics_and_security/libya/news/article/3080/Judicial_committees_on_strike/.

Mendeloff, David. "Truth-Seeking, Truth-Telling, and Postconflict Peacebuilding: Curb the Enthusiasm?" *International Studies Review* 6, no. 3 (September 2004): 355–380.

Mendez, Juan E. "Accountability for Past Abuses." *Human Rights Quarterly* 19, no. 2 (May 1997): 255–282.

Middle East Eye. "Libya's Tripoli Parties Reject 'Shocking' UN Peace Draft." April 29, 2015. http://www.middleeasteye.net/news/libyas-tripoli-parties-reject-shocking-un -peace-draft-1815497370.

Middle East Eye. "Tunisia Court Annuls Confiscation of Ben Ali's Assets." June 10, 2015. http://www.middleeasteye.net/news/tunisia-court-annuls-confiscation-ousted -presidents-assets-2029086602.

Minow, Martha. *Between Vengeance and Forgiveness: Facing History after Genocide and Mass Violence.* Boston: Beacon Press, 1998.

Mirimanova, Natalia. *Mediation and Dialogue: Official and Unofficial Strands.* Brussels: Initiative for Peacebuilding, 2009. http://www.initiativeforpeacebuilding.eu/ pdf/Mediation_and_Dialogue_Official_and_Unofficial_Strands.pdf.

Nasharat Akhbar (blog). "Libya: al-'A'lan al-dasturi kamila" [Libya: The full constitutional declaration]. August 13, 2011. http://almukhtar-17-2.blogspot.com/2011/08/ blog-post_9383.html.

National Dialogue Conference. "Conference Topics." 2013. http://www.ndc.ye/page .aspx?show=67.

National Dialogue Conference. "NDC Member Selection Mechanism." 2013. http:// www.ndc.ye/page.aspx?show=69.

Nichols, Michelle. "UN Says Libya Political Exclusion Law Likely Violates Rights." Reuters. June 18, 2013. http://www.reuters.com/article/2013/06/18/us-libya-un -idUSBRE95H15Y20130618.

Nilsson, Desirée. "Anchoring the Peace: Civil Society Actors in Peace Accords and Durable Peace." *International Interactions* 38, no. 2 (2012): 243–266.

Offe, Claus. "Coming to Terms with Past Injustices." *European Journal of Sociology* 33, no. 1 (June 1992): 195–201.

Papagianni, Katia. *National Dialogue Processes in Political Transitions.* Brussels: European Peacebuilding Liaison Office, n.d. Accessed August 6, 2014. http://www.hd-centre.org/uploads/tx_news/National-Dialogue-Processes-in-Political-Transitions. pdf.

Penfold, Peter. "Faith in Resolving Sierra Leone's Bloody Conflict." *The Round Table: The Commonwealth Journal of International Affairs* 94, no. 382 (2005): 549–557.

Peou, Sorpong. "Implementing Cambodia's Peace Agreement." In *Ending Civil Wars: The Implementation of Peace Agreements*, edited by Stephen John Stedman, Donald Rothchild, and Elizabeth M. Cousens, 499–530. Boulder: Lynne Rienner, 2002.

Popkin, Margaret, and Naomi Roht-Arriaza. "Truth as Justice: Investigatory Commissions in Latin America." *Law and Social Inquiry* 20, no. 1 (Winter 1995): 79–116.

Prendergast, John, and Emily Plumb. "Building Local Capacity: From Implementation to Peacebuilding." In *Ending Civil Wars: The Implementation of Peace Agreements*, edited by Stephen John Stedman, Donald Rothchild, and Elizabeth M. Cousens, 327–349. Boulder: Lynne Rienner, 2002.

Pruitt, Bettye H., and Katrin Käufer. *Dialogue as a Tool for Peaceful Conflict Transformation.* New York: United Nations Development Programme, 2004. http://www .democraticdialoguenetwork.org/app/files/documents/222/attachment/Dialogue _as_a_tool.pdf.

Raghavan, Sudarsan. "Militants Linked to al-Qaeda Emboldened in Yemen." *Washington Post*. June 13, 2011. http://www.washingtonpost.com/world/middle-east/militants-linked-to-al-qaeda-emboldened-in-yemen/2011/06/12/AG88nISH_story.html.

Raja, Jamila Ali. *Yemeni Women in Transition: Challenges and Opportunities*. Stanford, CA: Center on Democracy, Development, and the Rule of Law, 2013. http://iis-db.stanford.edu/pubs/24327/Number_140_Yemen.pdf.

Rasmussen, J. Lewis. "Negotiating a Revolution: Toward Integrating Relationship Building and Reconciliation into Official Peace Negotiations." In *Reconciliation, Justice, and Coexistence: Theory and Practice*, edited by Mohammed Abu-Nimer, 101–128. Lanham, MD: Lexington Books, 2001.

Republic of South Africa, Office of the President. "Promotion of National Unity and Reconciliation Act (Act No. 34 of 1995)." Southern African Legal Information Institute. July 26, 1995. http://www.saflii.org/za/legis/num_act/ponuara1995477/.

Reuters. "Muwajiha qawiyya bayn 'al-haras al-qadim' wa 'haras al-thawra' fi intikhabat ri'asat Tunis" [Fierce confrontation between "the old guard" and the "revolutionary guard" in Tunisia's presidential elections]. *al-Quds al-Arabi*. December 19, 2014. http://www.alquds.co.uk/?p=267365.

Reuters. "South Yemen Leader Pulls out of Reconciliation Talks." November 27, 2013. http://www.reuters.com/article/2013/11/27/us-yemen-reconciliation-idUSBRE9AQ0RZ20131127.

Reuters. "Tunisia Says Will Track Down Ben Ali Family Abroad." January 21, 2011. http://af.reuters.com/article/tunisiaNews/idAFLDE70K23K20110121.

Riedel, Bruce. "Yemen Falls Apart." *al-Monitor*. January 22, 2015. http://www.al-monitor.com/pulse/originals/2015/01/yemen-hadi-resignation-houthi-al-qaeda-us-saudi.html#.

Rifai, Ryan. "Timeline: Tunisia's Uprising." Al Jazeera English. January 23, 2011. http://www.aljazeera.com/indepth/spotlight/tunisia/2011/01/20111414222382761.html.

Roht-Arriaza, Naomi. "Reparations Decisions and Dilemmas." *Hastings International and Comparative Law Review* 27 (2003): 157–219.

Ropers, Norbert. *From Resolution to Transformation: The Role of Dialogue Projects*. Berlin: Berghof Research Center for Constructive Conflict Management, 2004. http://www.berghof-handbook.net/documents/publications/ropers_handbook.pdf.

Saeed, Ali. "Captured Soldiers in Abyan Released." *Yemen Times*. April 30, 2012. http://www.yementimes.com/en/1568/news/777/Captured-soldiers-in-Abyan-released.htm.

Safa, Oussama. *Conflict Resolution and Reconciliation in the Arab World: The Work of Civil Society Organizations in Lebanon and Morocco*. Berlin: Berghof Research Center for Constructive Conflict Management, 2007. http://www.berghof-foundation.org/fileadmin/redaktion/Publications/Handbook/Articles/safa_handbook.pdf.

Saidani, Monji. "A Gathering Storm." *al-Sharq al-Awsat*. May 28, 2013. http://www
.aawsat.net/2013/05/article55303311.

al-Sakkaf, Nadia. "Yemen's Women and the Quest for Change: Political Participation
after the Arab Revolution." Friedrich Ebert Stiftung. October 2012. http://library
.fes.de/pdf-files/iez/09434.pdf.

Salah, Hanan. "Libya's Justice Pandemonium." *Jurist*. April 14, 2014. http://www.hrw.org/
news/2014/04/14/libyas-justice-pandemonium.

Salem, Paul, and Amanda Kadlec. *Libya's Troubled Transition*. Beirut: Carnegie Middle
East Center, 2012. http://carnegie-mec.org/publications/?fa=48511.

Salmoni, Barak A., Bryce Loidolt, and Madeleine Wells. *Regime and Periphery in Northern Yemen: The Huthi Phenomenon*. Santa Monica, CA: RAND Corporation,
2010.

Salomons, Dirk. "Security: An Absolute Prerequisite." In *Post-Conflict Development:
Meeting New Challenges*, edited by Gerd Junne and Willemijn Verkoren, 19–42.
Boulder: Lynne Rienner, 2005.

Schirch, Lisa. *Women in Peacebuilding Resource and Training Manual*. Harrisonburg,
VA: Eastern Mennonite University, 2004. https://www.emu.edu/cjp/publications/
faculty-staff/lisa-schirch/women-in-peacebuilding-pt1.pdf.

Semlali, Amina. "Yemeni Women Make Their Voices Heard." Al Jazeera. May 23, 2013.
http://www.aljazeera.com/indepth/opinion/2013/05/201352165913600148.html.

Shabbi, Omar. "Algeria Pushes for National Dialogue in Libya." *al-Monitor*. September
30, 2014. http://www.al-monitor.com/pulse/originals/2014/09/algeria-reject-foreign-
intervention-libya.html#.

al-Sharq al-Awsat. "al-'A'alan 'an 'ada' al-hi'a al-'aliya al-mustaqila lil-itsal al-sam'i al-
basri fi Tunis" [Announcing the members of the Independent Supreme Committee
for Audiovisual Media in Tunisia]. May 4, 2013. http://www.aawsat.com/details.asp?
section=4&article=727247&issueno=12576#.Ul3QZ9KmhEA.

al-Sharq al-Awsat. "Tarablus wa Beirut 'azimatan 'ala tayy safhat al-Madiyy al-'aleem wa
'ala ra'siha ikhtifa' al-imam Mousa al-Sadr fi Libya" [Tripoli and Beirut are determined to turn the page on the painful past, especially the disappearance of Imam
Musa Sadr in Libya]. January 13, 2012. http://www.aawsat.com/details.asp?section=
4&issueno=12099&article=658738&feature=#.U14U7SfFWhp.

Sharqieh, Ibrahim. "Beware Libya's 'Fair Dictator.'" *New York Times*. June 23, 2014.
http://www.nytimes.com/2014/06/24/opinion/beware-libyas-fair-dictator.html.

Sharqieh, Ibrahim. "Essebsi Must Work with Islamists to Ensure Tunisia's Transition." *World Politics Review*. January 9, 2015. http://www.worldpoliticsreview.com/
articles/14816/essebsi-must-work-with-islamists-to-ensure-tunisia-s-transition.

Sharqieh, Ibrahim. "An Ill-Advised Purge in Libya." *New York Times*. February 18, 2013.
http://www.nytimes.com/2013/02/19/opinion/an-ill-advised-purge-in-libya.html?
_r=0.

Sharqieh, Ibrahim. "International Intervention, Justice, and Accountability in Yemen." European Council on Foreign Relations. November 2013. http://www.ecfr.eu/ijp/case/yemen.

Sharqieh, Ibrahim. A *Lasting Peace? Yemen's Long Journey to National Reconciliation*. Doha: Brookings Doha Center, 2013. http://www.brookings.edu/research/papers/2013/02/11-yemen-national-reconciliation-sharqieh.

Sharqieh, Ibrahim. "The Libyan Revolution at Two." *Foreign Policy*. February 22, 2013. http://mideast.foreignpolicy.com/posts/2013/02/22/the_libyan_revolution_at_two.

Sharqieh, Ibrahim. *Reconstructing Libya: Stability through National Reconciliation*. Doha: Brookings Doha Center, 2013. http://www.brookings.edu/research/papers/2013/12/03-libya-national-reconciliation-sharqieh.

Sharqieh, Ibrahim. "Tunisia: A Successful Revolution." In *African Renaissance and the Afro-Arab Spring: A Season of Rebirth?* edited by Charles Villa-Vicencio, Erik Doxtader, and Ebrahim Moosa, 63–70. Washington, DC: Georgetown University Press, 2015.

Sharqieh, Ibrahim. "Tunisia's Elections Seal Transition, Raise Fears of Old Regime." *World Politics Review*. January 8, 2015. http://www.worldpoliticsreview.com/articles/14804/tunisia-s-elections-seal-transition-raise-fears-of-old-regime.

Sharqieh, Ibrahim. "Tunisia's Lessons for the Middle East." *Foreign Affairs*. September 17, 2013. http://www.foreignaffairs.com/articles/139938/ibrahim-sharqieh/tunisias-lessons-for-the-middle-east.

Sharqieh, Ibrahim. "Vengeance Has No Place in a Libya Free of Qaddafi." *The National*. October 6, 2011. http://www.thenational.ae/thenationalconversation/comment/vengeance-has-no-place-in-a-libya-free-of-qaddafi.

Sharqieh, Ibrahim. "Yemen Can't Do It Alone." *New York Times*. June 1, 2012. http://www.nytimes.com/2012/06/02/opinion/yemen-cant-do-it-alone.html?_r=0.

Shennib, Ghaith, and Jessica Donati. "Gunmen Surround Libyan Foreign Ministry to Push Demands." Reuters. April 28, 2013. http://www.reuters.com/article/2013/04/28/us-libya-militia-idUSBRE93R03B20130428.

Smadhi, Asma. "Clash over Exclusion of Ben Ali Officials Delays Elections Law." *Tunisia Live*. May 1, 2014. http://www.tunisia-live.net/2014/05/01/clash-over-exclusion-of-ben-ali-officials-delays-elections-law/.

Stephen, Christopher. "Jibril Says Purge Law May Affect 500,000." Bloomberg. May 8, 2013. http://www.bloomberg.com/news/2013-05-08/libya-s-jibril-says-purge-law-may-affect-500-000-people.html.

Sultan, Maria. "The Quest for Peace in Chechnya: The Relevance of Pakistan's Tribal Areas Experience." *Central Asian Survey* 22, no. 4 (October 2003): 437–457.

Szakal, Vanessa. "Circumventing Political Exclusion–RCD after the Revolution and in the Coming Elections." *Nawaa*. September 14, 2014. http://nawaat.org/portail/2014/09/14/circumventing-political-exclusion-rcd-after-the-revolution-and-in-the-coming-elections/.

Tepperman, Jonathan D. "Truth and Consequences." *Foreign Affairs* 81, no. 2 (March/April 2002): 128–145.

Tolba, Ahmed, and Maha El Dahan. "Saudi Arabia Says Talks to End Yemen Crisis to Be Held in Riyadh." Reuters. March 8, 2015. http://www.reuters.com/article/2015/03/09/us-yemen-security-saudi-idUSKBN0M4oZ320150309.

Traboulsi, Fawaz. "Yemen's National Dialogue off to a Rough Start." *al-Monitor*. March 20, 2013. http://www.al-monitor.com/pulse/politics/2013/03/yemen-dialogue-rough-start.html##ixzz2sSFVItcL.

Transitional Libyan Government: Prime Minister's Office. "al-'Amid 'Ashour Shuwail: Tadabir amaniya tutakhath hathihi al-ayam" [Brigadier Ashour Shuwail: The security measures being taken these days]. January 31, 2013. http://tinyurl.com/cvxl9ly.

Transitional Libyan Government: Prime Minister's Office. "Takhrij al-duf'ah al-ula min al-thuwwar al-mundammin tahta Wizarat al-Dakhiliyah" [Graduation of the first batch of rebel recruits under the Ministry of Interior]. March 2, 2013. http://tinyurl.com/c2wzkoj.

Tripoli Post. "Libya National Dialogue Initiative Criticised." August 27, 2013. http://www.tripolipost.com/articledetail.asp?c=1&i=10588.

Tutu, Desmond. *No Future without Forgiveness*. London: Rider, 1999.

United Nations Development Programme. "Tunisia: Draft Organic Law on the Foundations and Organization of Transitional Justice." *ConstitutionNet*. December 2013. http://www.constitutionnet.org/vl/item/tunisia-draft-organic-law-foundations-and-organization-transitional-justice.

United Nations Development Programme. "Why Dialogue Matters for Conflict Prevention and Peacebuilding." February 2009. http://www.undp.org/content/dam/undp/library/crisis%20prevention/dialogue_conflict.pdf.

United Nations High Commissioner for Refugees. "Housing, Land and Property Issues and the Response to Displacement in Libya." 2013. http://terraonullius.files.wordpress.com/2013/02/unhcr-report-hlp-issues-and-displacement-in-libya-copy.pdf.

United Nations High Commissioner for Refugees. "UNHCR Global Appeal 2012–2013." December 1, 2011. http://www.unhcr.org/4ec23100b.html.

United Nations High Commissioner for Refugees Libya. "External Update–May 2014." May 2014. http://www.unhcr.org/538484ab9.html.

United Nations Security Council. "Landmark Resolution on Women, Peace and Security." October 2000. http://www.un.org/womenwatch/osagi/wps/.

United Nations Support Mission in Libya. "Conference on Truth and Reconciliation in Libya Concludes with Recommendations on the Way Forward." December 18, 2012. http://unsmil.unmissions.org/Default.aspx?ctl=Details&tabid=3543&mid=6187&ItemID=807743.

United Nations Support Mission in Libya. "Libyan Municipalities, Local Councils Reps Meet in Brussels within Political Dialogue Framework." March 24, 2015. http://

unsmil.unmissions.org/Default.aspx?tabid=3561&ctl=Details&mid=8549&ItemID=2013714&language=en-US.

United Nations Support Mission in Libya. "Meeting of Libyan Political Parties, Political Activists Convenes in Algeria." March 11, 2015. http://unsmil.unmissions.org/Default.aspx?tabid=3561&ctl=Details&mid=8549&ItemID=2011251&language=en-US.

United Nations Support Mission in Libya. "Transitional Justice–Foundation for a New Libya." September 17, 2012. http://www.unsmil.unmissions.org/LinkClick.aspx?fileticket=8XrRUO-sXBs%3d&tabid=3543&language=en-US.

United States Institute of Peace. "Gender, War, and Peacebuilding." September 2012. http://www.usip.org/sites/default/files/NPECSG12.pdf.

Volkan, Vamik D. *Blood Lines: From Ethnic Pride to Ethnic Terrorism.* New York: Farrar, Straus and Giroux, 1997.

Volkan, Vamik D. "On 'Chosen Trauma.'" 2007. http://www.vamikvolkan.com/On-%22Choosen-Trauma%22.php.

al-Watan al-Libya. "Lajnat al-Hukama tanjah fi ra'b as-sada bishaklin awwaliyin ma bayna al-Mashashiyah wa al-Zantan: Itlaq sarah al-muhtajazin wa taslim mintaqat al-Uwayniyah" [Committee of wise men succeeds initially in bridging the gap between Mashaysha and Zentan: Release of detainees and handing over of the Alawyneh area]. December 13, 2011. http://www.alwatan-libya.com/more.php?newsid=18622&catid=1.

Waters, Timothy William. "Libya's Home Court Advantage: Why the ICC Should Drop Its Qaddafi Case." *Foreign Affairs.* October 2, 2013. http://www.foreignaffairs.com/articles/139961/timothy-william-waters/libyas-home-court-advantage#.

Wessells, Michael, and Carlinda Monteiro. "Psychological Intervention and Post-War Reconstruction in Angola: Interweaving Western and Traditional Approaches." In *Peace, Conflict, and Violence: Peace Psychology for the 21st Century*, edited by Daniel J. Christie, Richard V. Wagner, and Deborah Du Nann Winter, chapter 22. Upper Saddle River, NJ: Prentice-Hall, 2001. http://u.osu.edu/christie/files/2014/10/Chapter-22-Psychosocial-Intervention-Post-War-Reconstruction-Wessells-Monteiro-nw5b1s.pdf.

Wolff, Stefan. "Post-Conflict State Building: The Debate on Institutional Choice." *Third World Quarterly* 32, no. 10 (2011): 1777–1802.

Worth, Robert F., and Laura Kasinof. "Yemeni President Wounded in Palace Attack." *New York Times.* June 3, 2011. http://www.nytimes.com/2011/06/04/world/middleeast/04yemen.html.

Xinhua. "Libya Dawn Militias Demand UN to Withdraw Its Envoy." April 30, 2015. http://news.xinhuanet.com/english/2015-04/30/c_134200697.htm.

Xinhua. "Libya Dawn Militias Refuse UN Call for Dialogue." *Punch.* April 25, 2015. http://www.punchng.com/news/libya-dawn-militias-refuse-un-call-for-dialogue/.

Zartman, I. William. *Ripe for Resolution: Conflict and Intervention in Africa.* Oxford: Oxford University Press, 1989.

INDEX

Page numbers in *italics* indicate figures

al-Abbasi, Hussein, 85, 195
Abderrahim, Souad, 158, 175, 176
Abdullah, King of Saudi Arabia, 39
Abrahams, Fred, 35
Abu Salim prison massacre, Libya, 109, 121, 135, 136, 138, 150, 204, 209, 222
Abu Salim women's movement, 204, 208, 228–229
Accountability, 11, 17, 138; defined, 141; importance of, 142–143, 166; in Libya, 146–148; limitations on, 143–144, 168; politicization of, 167, 169; and restorative justice, 141, 148, 169; and retributive justice, 142, 146, 148, 169; in Tunisia, 154–157, 167–168; in Yemen, 41, 53, 139, 161–164, 166–167, 169. *See also* Lustration
al-Ahmar, Abdullah, 220
al-Ahmar, Ali Mohsen, 47, 115, 123, 161, 178, 179
al-Ahmar, Salem, 24, 25
Ahmed, Muhammad Ali, 82
Ahmed, Sarah, 207
Ajetunmobi, Abdulsalam, 128
Alani, Alia, 64
Algeria, 91
Amnesty, 122
Angola, 128
Ansar al-Sharia, 31, 62, 63, 93, 111

Apologies for past injustice, 116, 139, 157, 164
AQAP (al-Qaeda in the Arabian Peninsula), 53
Argentina, truth-seeking process in, 105
Arms embargo, on Libya, 95
Association of the Disappeared, 190
Association of Families of the Martyrs of the Abu Salim Massacre, 109
Association of Supporting Women in Decision-Making, 205, 209
al-Ati al-Obaidi, Abd, 147
al-Attas, Haidar Abu Bakr, 43, 82
al-Awadi, Yaser, 115, 165
Ayadh, Abu, 62
Azlam (regime loyalists), Libya, 5, 24–25
Azzan, Mohammed, 51–52

Ba'ath Party, Yemen, 80, 133, 143
al-Bahabeih, Mifreh, 214, 215
Bahah, Khaled, 55
Bani Walid, Libya, 25, 110
Bardo Museum, Tunis, attack on, 5, 62–63
Baron, Adam, 51
Basendwa, Mohamed, 47
al-Beidh, Ali Salim, 42, 43, 80, 82
Belaid, Chokri, 62, 63
Belhaj, Rafik, 155